Women, Media, and Power in Indonesia

This book demonstrates the crucial link between gender and structures of power in democratic Indonesia, and the role of the online news media in regulating this relationship of power. Using critical discourse analysis (CDA) as a theoretical framework, and social actor analysis as the methodological approach, this book examines the discursive representation of three prominent female Indonesian political figures in the mainstream Indonesian online news media in a period of social-political transition. It presents newfound linguistic evidence in the form of discourse strategies that reflect the women's dynamic relationship with power. More broadly, the critical analysis of the news discourse becomes a way of uncovering and evaluating implicit barriers and opportunities affecting women's political participation in Indonesia and other Asian political contexts, Indonesia's process of democratisation, and the influential role of the online news media in shaping and reflecting political discourse.

Jane Ahlstrand is a lecturer in Indonesian Studies in the School of Humanities, Arts, and Social Sciences at the University of New England, Australia

Asian Studies Association of Australia
Women in Asia Series
Editor: Louise Edwards (University of New South Wales)

Editorial Board:
Hyaeweol Choi (University of Iowa)
Melissa Crouch (University of New South Wales)
Michele Ford (The University of Sydney)
Trude Jacobsen (Northern Illinois University)
Tanya Jakimow (University of New South Wales)
Lenore Lyons (Independent scholar)
Vera Mackie (University of Wollongong)
Anne McLaren (The University of Melbourne)
Mina Roces (University of New South Wales)
Dina Siddiqi (New York University)
Andrea Whittaker (The University of Queensland)
Founding Editors: Susan Blackburn and Lenore Manderson

49. **Marriage, Gender and Islam in Indonesia: Women Negotiating Informal Marriage, Divorce and Desire by Maria Platt 2017**

50. **Comfort Women and Post-Occupation Corporate Japan by Caroline Norma 2018**

51. **Women's Empowerment in Indonesia: A Poor Community in Jakarta by Sri Wiyanti Eddyono 2018**

52. **Hong Kong Rural Women under Chinese Rule: Gender Politics, Reunification and Globalization in Post-colonial Hong Kong by Isabella NG 2019**

53. **Gender, Violence and Power in Indonesia: Across Time and Space**
    Edited by Katharine McGregor, Ana Dragojlovic and Hannah Loney 2020

54. **Islam, Women's Sexuality and Patriarchy in Indonesia: Silent Desire**
    Irma Riyani

55. **Women, Media, and Power in Indonesia**
    Jane Ahlstrand

Series Editor's Foreword

The contributions of women to the social, political and economic transformations occurring in the Asian region are legion. Women have served as leaders of nations, communities, workplaces, activist groups and families. Asian women have joined with others to participate in fomenting change at micro and macro levels. They have been both agents and targets of national and international interventions in social policy. In the performance of these myriad roles women have forged new and modern gendered identities that are recognisably global and local. Their experiences are rich, diverse and instructive. The books in this series testify to the central role women play in creating the new Asia and re-creating Asian womanhood. Moreover, these books reveal the resilience and inventiveness of women around the Asian region in the face of entrenched and evolving patriarchal social norms.

Scholars publishing in this series demonstrate a commitment to promoting the productive conversation between Gender Studies and Asian Studies. The need to understand the diversity of experiences of femininity and womanhood around the world increases inexorably as globalisation proceeds apace. Lessons from the experiences of Asian women present us with fresh opportunities for building new possibilities for women's progress the world over.

The Asian Studies Association of Australia (ASAA) sponsors this publication series as part of its on-going commitment to promoting knowledge about women in Asia. In particular, the ASAA Women's Forum provides the intellectual vigour and enthusiasm that maintains the Women in Asia Series (WIAS). The aim of the series, since its inception in 1990, is to promote knowledge about women in Asia to both academic and general audiences. To this end, WIAS books draw on a wide range of disciplines including anthropology, sociology, political science, cultural studies, media studies, literature, and history. The series prides itself on being an outlet for cutting edge research conducted by recent PhD graduates and postdoctoral fellows from throughout the region.

iv *Series Editor's Foreword*

The Series could not function without the generous professional advice provided by many anonymous readers. Moreover, the wise counsel provided by Peter Sowden at Routledge is invaluable. WIAS, its authors and the ASAA are very grateful to these people for their expert work.

Louise Edwards (UNSW Australia)
Series Editor

Women, Media, and Power in Indonesia

Jane Ahlstrand

LONDON AND NEW YORK

First published 2022
by Routledge
2 Park Square, Milton Park, Abingdon, Oxon OX14 4RN

and by Routledge
605 Third Avenue, New York, NY 10158

Routledge is an imprint of the Taylor & Francis Group,
an informa business

© 2022 Jane Ahlstrand

The right of Jane Ahlstrand to be identified as author of this work has
been asserted in accordance with sections 77 and 78 of the Copyright,
Designs and Patents Act 1988.

All rights reserved. No part of this book may be reprinted or
reproduced or utilised in any form or by any electronic, mechanical,
or other means, now known or hereafter invented, including
photocopying and recording, or in any information storage or retrieval
system, without permission in writing from the publishers.

Trademark notice: Product or corporate names may be trademarks
or registered trademarks, and are used only for identification and
explanation without intent to infringe.

British Library Cataloguing-in-Publication Data
A catalogue record for this book is available from the British Library

Library of Congress Cataloging-in-Publication Data
A catalog record has been requested for this book

ISBN: 978-0-367-53764-7 (hbk)
ISBN: 978-0-367-53767-8 (pbk)
ISBN: 978-1-003-08325-2 (ebk)

DOI: 10.4324/9781003083252

Typeset in Times
by KnowledgeWorks Global Ltd.

Contents

List of figures and tables		viii
1	Introduction	1
2	Women and political power in Indonesia	18
3	News media and democracy in Indonesia	38
4	Niche, yet constrained, power: Navigating women's political leadership in Kompas.com	52
5	Between the individual and the institution: Augmenting power in an established hierarchy	85
6	Courting controversy: Women as icons of contestation	113
7	Gender and news media discourse: Populism, authoritarianism, and democratic transition	148
	Index	166

Figures and tables

Figures

1.1	Conceptual relationship between discursive representations, discourse strategies, and manifestation of power	11
1.2	Example of the connection between manifestation of power, a discourse strategy, and its discursive building blocks	12

Tables

4.1	Building block 1: Gendered, familiar, and novel nomination techniques	55
4.2	Building block 2: Impersonalisation in the accumulation of power	60
4.3	Building block 3: Negotiating power in interaction with the political elite	63
4.4	Building block 4: Negotiating power in interaction with the media	66
4.5	Building block 5: Negotiating power in interaction with the ordinary people	69
4.6	Building block 1: Activation in unconventional social processes	74
4.7	Building block 2: Somatisation	77
5.1	Building block 1: Individual nomination and activation	88
5.2	Building block 2: Establishing individual power in contrast to mid-range elites	96
5.3	Building block 3: Establishing individual power in contrast to the ordinary people	99
5.4	Building block 1: Consecutive activation of the individual and the institution	102
5.5	Building block 2: Impersonalisation of social actors and institutions	105

Figures and tables   ix

6.1	Building block 1: Constructing a pervasive threat group	116
6.1	Building block 1: Constructing a pervasive threat group	117
6.2	Building block 2: Constructing worthy victims	122
6.3	Building block 3: Constructing heroic leaders	124
6.4	Building block 1: Reference to thoughts and feelings	128
6.5	Building block 2: Indirect conflict	130
6.6	Building block 3: Concealing agency and construing rumours	132
6.7	Building block 1: Legitimising conjecture by reference to expert and public opinion	134
6.8	Building block 1: Defensive elite response	138
6.9	Building block 2: Proactive elite response	141

1 Introduction

In the tumultuous 24 months surrounding the 2014 Indonesian presidential election, three female political leaders captured the public imagination, embodying both the hopes and anxieties of a nation in transition. Aided by media publicity, and in particular, emergent online media platforms, the chair of the Indonesian Democratic Party of Struggle (PDI-P), Megawati Soekarnoputri (Megawati); mayor of Indonesia's second largest city, Surabaya, Tri Rismaharini (Risma); and Minister of Maritime Affairs and Fisheries, Susi Pudjiastuti (Susi), all stood out as household names. In political contexts of transition where structures of power are historically gendered, women in non-traditional positions of power can become iconic figures due to their marked difference from the male political norm (Raicheva-Stover & Ibroscheva, 2014). While their presence in the political realm "creates a powerful public imagery," it can also result in intense scrutiny (Derichs, et al., 2006, pp. 249–250), whereby women's political participation can be seen as a threat to the masculine status quo, unless they remain within the normative boundaries of acceptable conduct. As conspicuous figures operating within historically gendered structures of power, the study of women in politics therefore becomes a salient way of assessing "the quality and development of democratic politics and transition processes" (Fleschenberg & Derichs, 2011, p. 9).

Under the authoritarian New Order government led by General Suharto from 1966 to 1998, asymmetrical structures of power were anchored to a gendered hierarchy of the family, which normalised masculine political power and women's exclusion from much of political life. The idea of the nation as a family was assimilated within a model of Arche-politics, which envisioned the nation as an organically structured, homogenous social space, defined against an enemy *other* (Duile & Bens, 2017). Those who transgressed the restrictive norms of the family state faced sanctions, or the risk of being branded a "non-citizen." After the fall of Suharto in 1998, the immediate transitional period of *Reformasi* (reform) gave way to the development of a more liberal social-political environment. Changes included legislative reforms, the separation of the military from politics, the process of decentralisation, steps to combat corruption, and the rise of women's

DOI: 10.4324/9781003083252-1

2 *Introduction*

recognition in the public realm. After the initial fervour of Reformasi, however, it became clear that both residual and emergent political practices had begun to coalesce. In the realignment of power, reconstituted manifestations of authoritarianism, conservative gender norms, and populism mixed with democratic ideals. Given the historical relationship between gender and structures of power, examining women's relationship with power contributes to a deeper understanding of the complexities of Indonesia's process of social-political change.

In the transformation of Indonesia's political space, the media, and more recently, the online media have played an important role in both shaping and reflecting political engagement (Gazali, 2014; Tapsell, 2015a). Among the online news sites covering the 2014 presidential election, Kompas.com emerged as a leading source, imbued with legitimacy as the product of a long-established and highly influential media organisation known as Kompas Gramedia. Kompas.com runs parallel, but separate to Indonesia's longest running national print newspaper, *Kompas*, a well-respected news source known to represent popular, mainstream, secular interests. Kompas.com is frequented by an educated, relatively young, predominantly male, urban middle-class audience (Kompas.com, 2016; Nilan, 2008). This group generally reflects the Indonesian political landscape, where the young, urban, educated middle class play an important role in driving the new politics of the democratic era in Indonesia (van Klinken, 2014, pp. 2–3), while political participation remains invariably dominated by men.

In the shifting dimensions of political power of post-authoritarian Indonesia, key social actors occupy prominent positions in the political space and become the topic of public discourse. This phenomenon has both historical and contemporary causes. Since independence, political discussions in Indonesia have focused more often on the individual politician, rather than debating relevant policies or issues (Duile & Bens, 2017, as cited in Melissa, 2019, p. 47). Political opposition movements, the rise of populism, and the personalisation of politics in the democratic era have also seen charismatic political outsiders emerge as prominent icons, acting as shorthand for people's beliefs. The populist leader is typically defined as a breakthrough changemaker who stands in opposition to the entrenched elite, whose members are typically defined as the enemy other. Changing news media production and consumption habits in the digital era have played a role in forging this political trend. Where changing news media practices in the online environment intersect with the rise of populism, female politicians, as political outsiders, have the potential to become highly provocative figures who defy the male political norm. Such portrayals, however, reinforce politics as a male pursuit (Ross & Sreberny, 2000, p. 93), where women must negotiate a place within entrenched masculine structures of power.

Introduction 3

In Asian political contexts of social-political transformation, several female leaders have generated intense public interest because of their perceived moral standing and difference to the male norm. Take for example, Aung San Suu Kyi in Burma, Gloria Arroyo in the Philippines, Park Geun-hye in South Korea, and Wan Azizah Wan Ismail in Malaysia. Not all of these women, however, have been able to convert their moral capital into transformative political power. Some of these so-called changemakers later became integrated in the entrenched political elite or expelled from politics altogether. While a growing body of literature examines the position of women in the male dominated political realms across Asia, the discursive dimension of their relationship with power, as well as the influential role of the news media, remains under-explored. This book plays a particularly important role in exposing the way online news discourse can determine women's political participation, and the reproduction or transformation of gendered relations of power in a country haunted by an authoritarian legacy. Moreover, the analysis of the women as "outsiders" within a traditionally male-dominated domain provides a unique perspective that challenges the taken-for-granted neutrality of masculine political power, and contributes to understanding the role of women in transitional political contexts.

Recognising the salience of both women and the online news media to the process of social-political change taking place in democratic Indonesia, this book presents an analysis of Megawati, Risma, and Susi's multifaceted representations in the discourse of the popular Indonesian mainstream online media site, Kompas.com. Spanning a 24-month period encompassing the 2014 presidential election campaign, the election, and its aftermath, this book seeks to untangle the complex web of discourses of power played out in the linguistic representations of the three women through a critical discourse analysis (CDA) framework. CDA practitioner, van Dijk (1997), adopts the position that "most phenomena in politics are forms of text and talk," which, in turn, are a form of political action (p. 12). He asserts, "problems in political science can thus be studied more completely and sometimes more adequately when it is realised that the issues have an important discursive dimension" (van Dijk, 1997, p. 12). Examining the representation of these political women in online news discourse becomes a way of evaluating Indonesia's democracy through the tripartite lens of gender, media, and politics.

Whereas mainstream studies of politics tend to focus on institutions, political processes, party politics, and typically male political figures, the study of the discursive representation of political women and their relationship with power becomes a meaningful way of examining Indonesia's process of democratic transformation over the course of the 2014 presidential election. In recognition of the overarching importance of social actors to Indonesian political discourse, this book adapts van Leeuwen's (2008)

4 *Introduction*

social actor analysis as a novel approach to analysing relations of political power in the Indonesian online news media. Concentrating primarily on the written text, the analysis draws upon social actor analysis as a common discursive framework, so that close attention can be paid to the linguistic features through which Kompas.com mediates the female leaders' relationship with power. In accordance with the aims of CDA, explanatory links are drawn between the linguistic features and Indonesia's historical context in order to interpret the meaning and implications embedded in the discourse.

The 2014 presidential election: Regime change, political women, and the rise of online media

The race for the presidency in 2014 was fiercely contested by the governor of Jakarta, Joko Widodo, colloquially known as Jokowi, and Prabowo Subianto, a former military general and son-in-law of New Order president, Suharto. Both candidates promised political renewal, while employing populist campaign strategies to win the hearts of voters. They harnessed growing public concern over the influence of pervasive elite forces, democratic stagnation, money politics, weak rule of law, and enduring corruption under the Susilo Bambang Yudhoyono (SBY) government (Fealy, 2011, 2015; Mietzner, 2012). Jokowi was nominated as a presidential candidate by the PDI-P in March 2014 under the leadership of party chair, Megawati Soekarnoputri. For many Indonesians, he became a symbolic figure of hope for political reform, harnessing the widespread public disillusionment taking root throughout the country as political capital (McRae, 2013). Pairing with vice-presidential candidate, Jusuf Kalla, he promoted a discourse of change (*perubahan*) (Widodo & Kalla, 2014) imbued with a populist approach. Jokowi's campaign style emphasised his simple, non-elite demeanour to appeal to the ordinary people, and used independence era keywords, such as *kemerdekaan* (freedom) and *kedaulatan rakyat* (people's sovereignty), as a synonym for democracy (Robinson, 2014, p. 6).

The Prabowo camp also ran an election campaign based on populist values, but his approach differed to Jokowi's, promising tougher leadership, security, and a return to the indirect electoral mechanisms of the New Order (Mietzner, 2015). His populist tactics also involved an appeal to the rural and lower classes through a pro-poor message claiming "that the rich and powerful were looting Indonesia's natural resources" (Mietzner, 2015, p. 2). The 2014 election was the first to make significant use of social media, and online news reports became a common source of public information on the campaigns. Jokowi eventually won the election by a narrow margin in June 2014, claiming 53.15% of the vote against Prabowo's 46.85% (Mietzner, 2015, p. 39). The closeness of election results was indicative of the deep split that

Introduction 5

emerged in Indonesian politics and civil society at this time. When Jokowi took power in October 2014, it was nevertheless initially regarded by certain scholars, such as Mietzner (2014), as a victory for Indonesia's young democracy.

Following the election, a record number of women were appointed to eight out of the 34 cabinet positions in the new Jokowi government. These appointments served as a particularly vivid illustration of the difference between the new government and the previous Yudhoyono presidency, and generated optimism that a fresh style of politics would lead to greater democratic reform (Muhtadi, 2015). Indeed, in the lead up to the election, women's political subjectivity had become increasingly salient to the goal of democratisation, and a point of criticism of the Yudhoyono government. Under Yudhoyono, despite the presence of a mandatory 30% quota for female political candidates since 2008, women's national parliamentary representation declined (Budianta et al., 2015). Megawati, Risma, and Susi's presence in both the political realm and in the media was thus framed by heightened levels of interest in the importance of women's political participation to democratic renewal.

Susi Pudjiastuti was among the eight women appointed to a ministerial position in Jokowi's presidential cabinet, stepping into the role of Minister of Fisheries and Maritime Affairs. Her presence quickly became known across the country thanks in large part to media coverage of her rather outlandish character as a chain-smoking, straight-talking, tattooed woman in a position of political power. Her unconventional background as a high school dropout and successful businesswoman further added to her groundbreaking persona. In the era of populism, Susi easily fit the mould of the charismatic political outsider and represented a challenge to the perceived stuffy elite male norm of Indonesian politics at the national level. Risma also rode the populist wave and became known throughout the country as a pioneering local leader oriented towards grassroots social development. Like Susi, her prominence was also a partial product of media coverage on television and in the online realm, where media outlets and internet users were both drawn to her. Unlike Susi or Megawati, Risma promoted an Islamic identity through her outward appearance, wearing a plain *jilbab,* which presented her as a morally upstanding, everyday Indonesian woman. In contrast to Risma and Susi, Megawati occupied an established position in politics. As Indonesia's fifth president, the daughter of Indonesia's first president, Soekarno, and long-term leader of the PDI-P, Megawati held significant political credentials. Despite attracting criticism along the way, in her role of party chair, and as a seasoned politician, Megawati helped guide Jokowi to victory in the presidential election.

While united by a shared gender identity, the three women clearly differed in many respects. They represented three different fields of politics—a ministry, a party, and a city, with each field playing a unique

6 Introduction

role in the political discourse of the era. The three leaders also took different pathways to political power. Risma was elected on the basis of her engagement at the grassroots level, starting out in the civil service of the municipal government; Susi was appointed to her role, arguably on the basis of her perceived difference to the political norm and her extensive business background; on the other hand, Megawati's dynastic ties to her father's powerful legacy facilitated her entry to the political arena, and sustained her enduring presence. As newcomers who differed to the elite norms of politics, Risma and Susi were aligned most strongly with the populist values circulating at the time, while Megawati was invariably aligned with the elite realm.

All three women certainly played influential roles in the political landscape of the 2014 election; however, it would be naïve to assume that their prominent presence in politics and the media signalled an overhaul of Indonesia's male-dominated political culture. Indeed, Indonesia remains hampered by the political inequality of authoritarianism underpinned by gendered structures of power. The presence of oligarchic forces supporting the interests of the political and business elite (Muhtadi, 2015; Winters, 2013) continue to operate and perpetuate a masculine hierarchy of power. News media organisations, with their strong political and business links, play a highly influential role in determining access to the political domain and perpetuating an exclusive hierarchy of power.

A number of residual and emergent factors influence the editorial agenda of Kompas.com and the reporting practices of its journalists. A history of New Order censorship and the powerful links cultivated between Kompas Gramedia owners and members of the political elite urge journalists to exercise caution in their reporting and the selection of topics. In the digital era, the rise of social media and the onset of platform convergence have brought about new patterns in news production and consumption (Hatherell & Welsh, 2017; Melissa, 2019). Media content and user interest become increasingly intertwined, leading to changing perceptions of news events and the actors involved. This changing approach to journalism means that news reports now tend to feature bite-sized information, and polarising social actors and events in a bid to prompt an audience response (Ahlstrand, 2020; Lim, 2017; Tapsell, 2015b).

Reflective of global media trends, online news organisations in Indonesia, like Kompas.com operate according to a business model aimed at immediacy, audience reactivity, and spreadability. The advent of the 24-hour news cycle and constant demand for updates throughout the day place increasing pressure on journalists to conform to commercial interests and produce a continuous stream of provocative content. The constant rapid-fire production and consumption of online media has led some Indonesian internet users to enter into "algorithmic enclaves," where those engaging with online media fall into self-perpetuating ideological-based groupings as they seek to express, defend, or reinforce

Introduction 7

their personal beliefs, while denigrating the beliefs of others (Lim, 2017). A growing tendency among readers to access online news on a mobile device further contributes to reactive, superficial engagement, whereby skim reading, impulsive sharing, and rapid movement between online media platforms become the norm (Costera Meijer & Groot Kormelink, 2015; Lim, 2013).

As the relationship between news media practices and political engagement undergoes change across the globe, new conceptual tools are required to explore the multiple interpretive possibilities of political and cultural life (Baulch & Millie, 2013). In this context of change, media scholars are recommended to explore "cultural forms and symbolic repertoires that conceal power relations" (Baulch & Millie, 2013, p. 230). In this regard, the study of power relations embedded in the representation of female political leaders in online news media discourse can shed new light on the relationship between gender, media, and power. Analysing the discourse of Kompas.com becomes an important way of capturing and critically investigating the residual and emergent structures of power, as well as attitudes towards women in power during the 2014 presidential election. The focus on Kompas.com as the primary data source limits the analysis to a singular, yet highly influential ideological perspective of middle-class, urban, males—a politically active group who nevertheless have a vested interest in maintaining the status quo. While the interpretation of the discourse does not incorporate reader reception of the news or news production practices, it does integrate findings from previous studies of news media production and consumption to help interpret the causes and consequences of the discourse in focus.

Discourse, social actors, and relations of power

Using CDA as a theoretical and methodological framework, this book examines the female political leaders' multifaceted relationship with power expressed in Kompas.com discourse. As a key tenet of CDA, the concept of discourse is defined as a representation of a social practice, which in this case relates to the practice of positioning the female leaders in an interactive social power network. While the act of representation can take place through a range of semiotic elements, this book focuses primarily on language in the news texts. The concept of discourse "implies a dialectical relationship between a particular discursive event and the situation(s), institution(s) and social structure(s) that frame it" (Fairclough & Wodak, 1997, p. 258). In other words, discourse is both socially constituted as well as socially constitutive, meaning that it is not only shaped by, but can also help to sustain, reproduce, and transform the social order (Fairclough & Wodak, 1997, p. 258). In order to make the interconnection between language and the social order visible, the linguistic data should therefore be analysed within a social context. Accordingly, this book incorporates

8   *Introduction*

knowledge of both the immediate and broader historical context of Indonesia, its politics, and in particular, the relationship between gender and power.

The analysis adopts a definition of power as an asymmetric relationship among social actors in an interactive social power network, who assume different social positions or belong to different social groups (Reisigl & Wodak, 2009, p. 89). Within this framework, power is understood as a form of control, which is exercised by an individual, group, or organisation over the actions and/or the minds of others. The way discourse represents and positions participants, their actions and interactions can lead to the overt or subtle reproduction of dominant and subordinate subject positions in this hierarchy of power (Fairclough & Wodak, 1997, p. 258; Wodak, 2004). Strategic representational choices can help construe the desired meaning of the text producer in accordance with their political, social, or commercial interests. The social power network is a dynamic hierarchy, where the dichotomy between dominant and subordinate social actors is continuously negotiated. Ultimately, however, discursive practices can conceal latent power relations, and over time limit "the freedom of action of the others, or influence their knowledge, attitudes or ideologies" (van Dijk, 1996, p. 84). The CDA researcher thus seeks to uncover these latent representations of power and draw explanatory links between the structures of discourse and broader social-political context.

Expanding upon the definition of power as a form of control, this book draws an explicit connection between power and agency. While agency is essentially defined as "the socio-culturally mediated capacity to act" (Ahearn, 2001, p. 112), this book refines the concept by anchoring it to social power and the ability to exert influence over others. According to this approach, power and agency are understood as a dual force in discourse constructed within a defined social-political context. The analysis therefore takes into account the social status of the participants in discourse, how they are represented, and how their actions are conveyed according to relevant social-political factors that define social status as well as social action. In accordance with the principles of CDA, relations of power are located at the macro-institutional level of the social order, while discourse and social interaction belong to the micro-level (van Dijk, 2015, p. 468). There are several ways to bridge the gap between the macro- and the micro-level, revealing the dialectal relationship between language and power, including the study of members and groups (van Dijk, 2015, p. 468). The identification of a suitable approach requires the development and application of a set of tailor-made "conceptual tools relevant to the research problem and context" (Weiss & Wodak, 2003, p. 7).

The study of social actors proves particularly salient to examining relations of power expressed in Indonesian news discourse over the 24-months surrounding the 2014 election. Dominated by the rise of popular individual leaders, this period saw an increasing fascination with prominent political

Introduction 9

figures as multivalent symbols among a politically engaged public. The growing influence of individual leaders upon Indonesian political discourse creates the necessity to move beyond the study of the formal structures of party politics towards the study of social actors (Sugiarto, 2006). The rise of personalised political leadership and populist political communication spread in online media, not only in Indonesia but worldwide, further underlines the salience of the study of social actors. For women operating in this context, their visibility as traditional outsiders in the political realm heightens their significance to understanding Indonesian political life and changing relations of power. Some researchers such as Brenner (2011) and Heryanto (2008) have emphasised the role of women as "sites" of public discourse and contested definitions of identity and power in post-authoritarian Indonesia. In this book, however, the examination of the representation of women and their agency in an interactive social power network not only highlights the dynamics and precarity of their relationship with power, but also, their potential political influence.

In recognition of the relevance of social actors to Indonesia's political landscape, this book engages CDA practitioner, van Leeuwen's (2008) social actor analysis as a way of identifying and critically analysing the power relations embedded in the news discourse, expressed through the multifaceted representations of Megawati, Risma, and Susi. Van Leeuwen's approach provides a taxonomy of social actor representations that span linguistic and sociological categories, acknowledging the interconnection between the two areas. The analysis encompasses the ways social actors are discursively portrayed as individuals and as members of groups, as well as how their social actions and interactions with other social actors and institutions are represented in the discourse.

Following van Leeuwen's approach, the women may be clearly identified, named by their formal title, or given an alternative name as a marker of their uniqueness or incongruity with the political realm. On the other hand, their identity may be subsumed within the city, nation, or institution they represent. Other social actors may be represented as individuals or as a collective. In discourse social actors' identity, social function, and autonomy is determined by their group membership. The study of agency in the discourse incorporates transitivity structures, which van Leeuwen adapted from Halliday's systemic functional grammar. By focusing on different types of social processes, and the activation or passivation of social actors in the discourse, the analysis can not only reveal who is acting upon whom, but also the type of actions involved. In accordance with the principles of CDA, the social, cultural, and political consequences of the representations of the social actors, their actions, and interactions depend on the historical context, and thereby the broader impact on the social-political order.

When approaching the study of power relations, it is important to acknowledge that the social power network is never static, but highly mobile.

10   *Introduction*

Influenced by changing social relations and circumstances in discourse (Foucault, 1991), relations of power are continually reshaped through constant interactions and struggles among social actors with diverse articulatory practices (Masaki, 2007, p. 34). In contexts of social-political change, where multiple social groups attempt to redefine or defend existing relations of power based on their interests, certain texts and events "accentuate difference, conflict, polemic, a struggle over meaning, norms, [and thereby] power" (Fairclough, 2003, p. 42). As the social-political context shifts, texts can thus become sites of struggle, contradictions, and ambiguity (Wodak, 2013).

The heterogeneity and at times contradictory nature of discourse are understood as a "synchronic reflex" of the process of social-political change (Fairclough, 1992, p. 36). In recognition of the multifaceted nature of power relations, amplified by Indonesia's dynamic social-political transformation, the analysis abides by a tripartite interpretation of relations of power, namely, mitigating, augmenting, and contesting power. The practice of mitigation lowers the women's perceived position in a hierarchy of power, while negotiating a range of contextually embedded political barriers and opportunities. Augmenting power highlights the women's position in a top-down, ubiquitous role of power, as individuals and as members of institutions. The power of the female leaders and institutions are constructed in a circular pattern of mutual reinforcement. Contestation involves the construal of conflict, transgression, and threat, with mixed implications for the women's relationship with power and broader structures of power. Rather than eroding existing hierarchical power arrangements, contestation can in fact reinforce them. Overall, by placing the women at the centre of these dynamic expressions of power, the analysis explores the multiple aspects of their political persona conveyed in Kompas.com discourse, while foregrounding the dialectical relationship between the discourse and the broader social-political context.

The mitigation, augmentation, and contestation of the women's position within a social network of power in Kompas.com discourse are evidenced by discourse strategies in the news discourse identified through the application of social actor analysis. Discourse strategies are defined as "the planned discursive activities, the political aims and functions of these activities, and the linguistic means designed to help realise these aims" (Wodak et al., 2009, p. 34). In this case, the discursive activities and political aims refer to the indexation of Megawati, Risma, and Susi's relationship with power, interpreted through the lens of the tripartite categories described above.

The strategies function as *stepping stones* between the micro-linguistic features of the news texts, and the contextually-located manifestations of power in the discourse. Sets of co-occurring social actor representations identified in the data, that work together to index the women's relationship with power form the *building blocks* of discourse strategies. These strategies are tied to one of the three major manifestations of power.

The strategies are most commonly gleaned from the headline and lead, as news reports are known to follow a hierarchical order of relevance, meaning that journalists tend to position the information considered most salient in the headline and lead (van Dijk, 1988). Headlines in particular attract attention, shape readers' perceptions of the news events, and influence subsequent text interpretation (van Dijk, 1988, p. 141). The emergence of cursory reading habits in the era of digital media (Costera Meijer & Groot Kormelink, 2015; Gazali, 2014) further reinforces the impact of the headline and lead. Given the importance of the upper structures of news reports, focusing on this section therefore captures the most influential aspects of the news discourse. The conceptual relationship between the expression of relations of power, discourse strategies, and clusters of social representations is presented in Figure 1.1. A more specific example derived from the analysis of Kompas.com discourse is then presented in Figure 1.2. Note that the number of building blocks is not limited to three in a discourse strategy, and the examples below function to illustrate the construction of a strategy.

The selection of data from a widely-consumed newspaper over an extended period of time, covering three different social actors and a range of events, expands the scope of this book. Adapting social actor analysis to the study of women in a fluid hierarchy of power transcends a dichotomy of power abuse or resistance, or exclusion and inclusion. This approach instead creates the possibility of uncovering the three female leaders in a range of subject positions in an interactive social power network, and revealing more subtle manifestations of power. Even discourse produced with ostensibly democratic intentions may in fact result in undemocratic outcomes by representing participants within a hierarchy marked by dominant and subordinate roles (Wodak, 1996). The analysis of heterogeneous

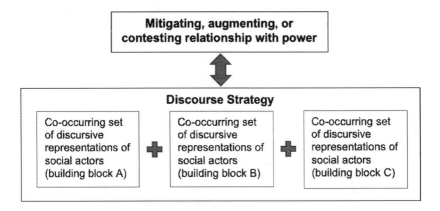

Figure 1.1 Conceptual relationship between discursive representations, discourse strategies, and manifestation of power.

12 Introduction

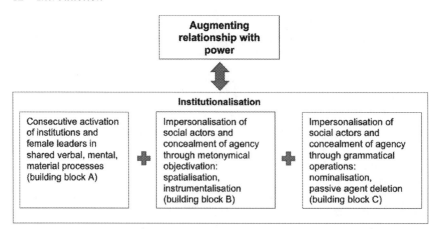

Figure 1.2 Example of the connection between manifestation of power, a discourse strategy, and its discursive building blocks.

discourse practices therefore provides greater opportunities for understanding shifting power relations among social actors, and how people are enabled and constrained by these power arrangements (Chouliaraki & Fairclough, 1999).

Chapter outline

In recognition of the salient relationship between gender and structures of power, Chapter 2 sets up a framework for understanding women's political subjectivity in Indonesia, from the New Order to the present. It outlines both the historical constraints and opportunities that have influenced women's political participation in Indonesia, and integrates knowledge of women's agency beyond Indonesia, supported by examples from existing research. The chapter then provides a description of Megawati, Risma, and Susi, including their personal backgrounds and their political careers, while drawing comparative links to other women in politics in Asia. The description of the gendered structures of power and the women and their political identity sets up a comprehensive framework to support the interpretation of the social consequentiality of the discourse.

Chapter 3 describes the role of the news media in politics from the New Order to the democratic era, including the influence of digital media upon political engagement in Indonesia and across the globe. It highlights studies of the Indonesian media industry that demonstrate key journalistic practices that flow on from the New Order to the democratic era. It outlines the evolving business model, and the boundaries in which journalists operate in a post-authoritarian era, and the relationship between business, politics,

Introduction 13

and news media production and consumption in the digital era. The chapter also provides a detailed description of the data source, Kompas.com, as a key player in the Indonesian mediasphere. The role of women in the post-authoritarian media is discussed, and to finish, the chapter outlines a chronology of the major events in which Megawati, Risma, and Susi were covered in Kompas.com reports.

The results of the analysis of the Kompas.com discourse are presented in Chapters 4, 5, and 6. These chapters illustrate how the varied representations of the women's relationship with power are realised through specific sets of discourse strategies, built upon components of social actor representations. The chapters explain the functions of the strategies in the news reports through selected excerpts that reflect the dominant features of each strategy, and explain how meaning is produced in the co-text, context, and in relation to the individual factors affecting each social actor.

Chapter 4 demonstrates how certain discourse strategies negotiate the women's position in a traditionally male realm of political power within the dynamics of a populist political climate. It shows how the discourse portrays the women's actions, interactions, and appearance through a gendered lens, which emphasises their difference, which simultaneously enables and constrains their political participation.

While Chapter 4 bears the hallmarks of a typically gendered representation of women in power, Chapter 5 examines how Kompas.com discursively positions Megawati, Risma, and Susi in a top-down role of power. It does so through the discursive portrayal of their dominant interactions with other social actors, as well as through their collaborative relationship with institutions. This form of representation simultaneously reflects an emergent fascination with strong individual leaders in the era of populism, and Indonesia's legacy of authoritarianism, including its residual trappings of a vertical hierarchy of political power.

Having demonstrated how the discourse establishes the women in a solid and stable leadership role, conversely Chapter 6 highlights the precarity of their position in the political realm, whereby Kompas.com positions them at the centre of contestation. This pattern of representation portrays the women as individual actors and in interaction with other social actors and groups in situations of alleged transgression, conflict, and criticism. Evaluating the causes and consequences of such representations, the chapter not only highlights the dynamic, yet enduring nature of hierarchical power relations, but also women's contentious position in the political realm, and the influence of commercially-driven journalistic practices.

Chapter 7 discusses the implications of the diverse discursive representations of the female leaders and their relationship with power in Kompas.com discourse. Specifically, it examines the implications of findings for women's participation in the political realm, Indonesia's process of democratisation, and the role of news media discourse in the democratic era. In these frames,

14 *Introduction*

the chapter revisits the key issues discovered in the analysis and links them to existing literature. It concludes with a discussion of the relevance of the research and directions for future research. It also updates readers on the trajectory of Megawati, Risma, and Susi's political careers beyond the period covered in this book.

This book presents a novel way of examining Indonesia's process of democratic change, by breaking away from the male political norm, and focusing on provocative, high profile female leaders in online news discourse. The use of social actor analysis reflects the salience of women, as well as the rise of the individual charismatic leader in an era of social-political change and growing populism. The analysis of Megawati, Risma, and Susi's multifaceted representations become a way of capturing and critically examining the dynamic discourses of power embedded in online news discourse. The analysis, however, does not simply focus on the linguistic elements, but also incorporates knowledge of Indonesia's historical gendered, authoritarian structures of power, intersecting with democratic, and emergent populist values.

The digital revolution taking place in Indonesia, and the onset of platform convergence, underlines the significance of the focus on online news media discourse. Located in an Asian context, the examination of female Indonesian political leaders in the online news media contributes new knowledge to studies of women, along with media and politics in the region. With a population of almost 270 million, Indonesia is the world's fourth largest nation, and the third largest democracy. This book gives due attention to the country as a serious political contender on the world stage, with an established media culture and an online savvy audience. Overall, this book provides an in-depth, nuanced evaluation of Indonesia's democracy refracted through the lens of gender and media.

References

Ahearn, L. M. (2001). Language and agency. *Annual Review of Anthropology, 30*, 109–137.

Ahlstrand, J. (2020). Strategies of ideological polarisation in the online news media: A social actor analysis of Megawati Soekarnoputri. *Discourse & Society*, October 2020.

Baulch, E., & Millie, J. (2013). Introduction: Studying Indonesian media worlds at the intersections of area and cultural studies. *International Journal of Cultural Studies, 16*(3), 227–240.

Brenner, S. (2011). Private moralities in the public sphere: Democratization, Islam, and gender in Indonesia. *American Anthropologist, 113*(3), 478–490.

Budianta, M., Chandrakirana, K., & Yentriyani, A. (2015). Yudhoyono's politics and the harmful implications for gender equality in Indonesia. In E. Apsinall, M. Mietzner, & D. Tomsa (Eds.), *The Yudhoyono presidency: Indonesia's decade of stability and stagnation* (pp. 199–216). Institute of Southeast Asian Studies.

Chouliaraki, L., & Fairclough, N. (1999). *Discourse in late modernity: Rethinking critical discourse analysis.* Edinburgh University Press.

Costera Meijer, I., & Groot Kormelink, T. (2015). Checking, sharing, clicking and linking. *Digital Journalism, 3*(5), 644–679.

Derichs, C., Fleschenberg, A., & Hüstebeck, M. (2006). Gendering moral capital: Morality as a political asset and strategy of top female politicians in Asia. *Critical Asian Studies, 38*(3), 245–270.

Duile, T., & Bens, J. (2017). Indonesia and the "conflictual consensus": A discursive perspective on Indonesian democracy. *Critical Asian Studies, 49*(2), 139–162.

Fairclough, N. (1992). *Discourse and social change.* Polity Press.

Fairclough, N. (2003). *Analysing discourse: Textual analysis for social research.* Routledge.

Fairclough, N., & Wodak, R. (1997). Critical discourse analysis. In T. van Dijk (Ed.), *Discourse studies. A multidisciplinary introduction* (Vol. 2, pp. 258–284). Sage.

Fealy, G. (2011). Indonesian politics in 2011: Democratic regression and Yudhoyono's regal incumbency. *Bulletin of Indonesian Economic Studies, 47*(3), 333–353.

Fealy, G. (2015). The politics of Yudhoyono: Majoritarian democracy, insecurity and vanity. In E. Aspinall, M. Mietzner, & D. Tomsa (Eds.), *The Yudhoyono presidency: Indonesia's decade of stability and stagnation* (pp. 35–54). Institute of Southeast Asian studies.

Fleschenberg, A., & Derichs, C. (2011). Women and politics in Asia: A springboard for democracy? A tentative introduction and reflection. In A. Fleschenberg, & C. Derichs (Eds.), *Women and politics in Asia: A springboard for democracy?* (pp. 1–19). Lit Verlag.

Foucault, M. (1991). Governmentality. In G. Burchell, C. Gordon, & P. Miller (Eds.), *The Foucault effect: Studies in governmentality* (pp.87–104). University of Chicago Press.

Gazali, E. (2014). Learning by clicking: An experiment with social media democracy in Indonesia. *The International Communication Gazette, 76*(4–5), 425–439.

Hatherell, M., & Welsh, A. (2017). Rebel with a cause: Ahok and charismatic leadership in Indonesia. *Asian Studies Review, 41*(2), 174–190.

Heryanto, A. (2008). *Popular culture in Indonesia: Fluid identities in post-authoritarian politics.* Routledge.

Kompas.com. (2016). Media profile Kompas.com, August 2016. In Kompas.com (Ed.). Kompas.com.

Lim, M. (2013). Many clicks but little sticks: Social media activism in Indonesia. *Journal of Contemporary Asia, 43*(4), 636–657.

Lim, M. (2017). Freedom to hate: Social media, algorithmic enclaves, and the rise of tribal nationalism in Indonesia. *Critical Asian Studies, 49*(3), 41–427.

Masaki, K. (2007). *Politics, participation and policy: The "emancipatory" evolution of the "elite-controlled" policy process.* Lexington Books.

McRae, D. (2013). Indonesian politics in 2013: The emergence of new leadership? *Bulletin of Indonesian Economic Studies, 49*(3), 289–304.

Melissa, E. (2019). *The internet, social media, and political outsiders in post-Suharto Indonesia: A case study of Basuki Tjahaja Purnama.* [Doctoral dissertation, University of Western Australia]. University of Western Australia Research Repository.

Mietzner, M. (2012). Indonesia's democratic stagnation: Anti-reformist elites and resilient civil society. *Democratization, 19*(2), 209–229.

16 *Introduction*

Mietzner, M. (2014). How Jokowi won and democracy survived. *Journal of Democracy, 25*(4), 111–125.

Mietzner, M. (2015). Reinventing Asian populism: Jokowi's rise, democracy, and political contestation in Indonesia. East West Center.

Muhtadi, B. (2015). Jokowi's first year: A weak president caught between reform and oligarchic politics. *Bulletin of Indonesian Economic Studies, 51*(3), 349–368.

Nilan, P. (2008). Youth transitions to urban, middle-class marriage in Indonesia: Faith, family and finances. *Journal of Youth Studies, 11*(1), 65–82.

Raicheva-Stover, M., & Ibroscheva, E. (2014). *Women in politics and media: Perspectives from nations in transition.* Bloomsbury Academic.

Reisigl, M., & Wodak, R. (2009). The discourse-historical approach (DHA). In R. Wodak & M. Meyer (Eds.), *Methods of critical discourse analysis* (pp. 87–121). Sage Publications.

Robinson, K. (2014). Citizenship, identity and difference in Indonesia. *RIMA Review of Indonesian and Malaysian Affairs, 48*(1), 5–34.

Ross, K., & Sreberny, A. (2000). Women in the house: Media representation of British politicians. In A. Sreberny & L. van Zoonen (Eds.), *Gender, politics and communication* (pp. 79–99). Hampton Press.

Sugiarto, B. (2006). Beyond formal politics: Party factionalism and leadership in post-authoritarian Indonesia [Doctoral dissertation, Australian National University]. Australian National University Open Research Library.

Tapsell, R. (2015a). Indonesia's media oligarchy and the "Jokowi phenomenon". *Indonesia, Apr 2015*(99), 29–50.

Tapsell, R. (2015b). Platform convergence in Indonesia: Challenges and opportunities for media freedom. *Convergence: The International Journal of Research into New Media Technologies, 21*(2), 182–197.

van Dijk, T. A. (1988). *News as discourse.* Lawrence Erlbaum Associates.

van Dijk, T. A. (1996). Discourse, power and access. In C. R. Caldas-Coulthard & M. Coulthard (Eds.), *Texts and practices: Readings in critical discourse analysis* (pp. 84–104). Routledge.

van Dijk, T. A. (1997). What is political discourse analysis? *Belgian Journal of Linguistics, 11*, 11–52.

van Dijk, T. A. (2015). Critical discourse analysis. In D. Tannen, D. Schiffrin & H. Hamilton (Eds.), *Handbook of discourse analysis* (pp. 466–485). John Wiley & Sons.

van Klinken, G. (2014). Introduction: Democracy, markets and the assertive middle. In G. van Klinken & W. Berenschot (Eds.), *In search of middle Indonesia: Middle classes in provincial towns* (pp. 1–32). Brill.

van Leeuwen, T. (2008). *Discourse and practice: New tools for critical discourse analysis.* Oxford University Press.

Weiss, G., & Wodak, R. (2003). Introduction: Theory, interdisciplinarity and critical discourse analysis. In R. Wodak, & G. Weiss (Eds.), *Critical discourse analysis. Theory and interdisciplinarity* (pp. 1–34). Palgrave Macmillan.

Widodo, J., & Kalla, J. (2014). *Jalan perubahan untuk Indonesia yang berdaulat, mandiri dan berkepribadian: Visi misi, dan program aksi.* Jakarta: Sekretariat Nasional Joko Widodo.

Winters, J. (2013). Oligarchy and democracy in Indonesia. *Indonesia, 96*(1), 11–33.

Wodak, R. (1996). *Disorders of discourse.* Addison Wesley Longman.

Wodak, R. (2004). Critical discourse analysis. In C. Seale, G. Gobo, J. Gubrium & D. Silverman (Eds.), *Qualitative research practice* (pp. 185–201). Sage.

Wodak, R. (2013). Critical discourse analysis: Challenges and perspectives. In R. Wodak (Ed.), *Critical discourse analysis* (pp. 19–43). Sage.

Wodak, R., de Cillia, R., Reisigl, M., & Leibhart, K. (2009). The discursive construction of national identity. In R. Wodak, R. de Cillia, M. Reisigl & K. Leibhart (Eds.), *The discursive construction of national identity* (pp. 7–48). Edinburgh University Press.

2 Women and political power in Indonesia

The portrayal of Megawati, Risma, and Susi as prominent social actors in the discourse of Kompas.com not only reflected the ideological tensions of the 2014 presidential election, but also the salient and often precarious position of women in the media and the broader process of democratisation. The historical relationship between the gender order (Connell, 2009) and hierarchical structures of power in Indonesia resulted in the long-term exclusion of most women from active participation in political life. The onset of democracy in 1998 heralded the beginning of major structural reform in Indonesia, which inevitably gave rise to shifts in gender roles, and the increased visibility of women in various aspects of public life, including the media. Where relations of power and gender norms are linked, the process of social-political change invariably produces tensions around issues of gender, including women's participation in the traditionally masculine political realm. Sixteen years since *Reformasi*, Indonesia's political landscape continues to change, and the ideologically charged 2014 presidential election becomes a crucial period for examining the role of women in Indonesian political life and their relationship with the dynamic structures of political power.

To understand the relevance of the discursive representations of the three powerful women to Indonesia's broader social-political transformation, this chapter examines the relationship between gender and historical structures of power in Indonesia, and how it has, and continues to influence women's political participation. Understanding the personal backgrounds of the three women also contributes to a deeper understanding of their significance in media discourse during the 2014 election, as well as the impact of the historical structures of gendered power on both their self-fashioned and mediatised navigation of political power. The link between gender ideology and structures of power, alongside the privileging and preservation of male political power are certainly not unique to Indonesia. This chapter therefore also draws parallels between the experience of women in Indonesia and a broader Asian context to add further evidence when seeking to characterise women's relationship with political power.

DOI: 10.4324/9781003083252-2

Globally, women occupy far less prominent roles in the political space, in terms of quantity and status (Ibroscheva & Raicheva-Stover, 2014, p. 47). Studies of Asian political contexts in particular have revealed that while the explicit expression of political ambition, and the use and abuse of power are acceptable for men, women are expected to downplay their relationship with power, and conform to gendered stereotypes of the loyal wife, good daughter, or nurturing mother in order not to threaten the male status quo (Dalton, 2015; Nichols, 2014b; Ritchie, 2013). A prevailing assumption that women are morally upright, unselfish, and less corruptible also permeates political discourse throughout Asia; however, a failure to transfer their perceived moral capital to moral authority can result in a loss of political credibility (Derichs & Thompson, 2013). This chapter will explore the historical relationship between gender and power in Indonesia as a regulatory force within a broader masculine political agenda, while identifying constraints, tensions, and opportunities for women in the political realm in Indonesia and beyond. It will then introduce Megawati, Risma, and Susi and describe their political careers, making reference to the Indonesian and broader Asian political context.

Gender and power under the new order

Under New Order government from 1966 to 1998, President Suharto maintained a position of absolute power and authority within a patrimonial, highly-centralised system of state power. The acronym KKN (*korupsi, kolusi, nepotisme*) came to define the notorious mode of politics of the regime. Access to power and resources was limited to Suharto's inner circle made up of family members, military elites, and cronies. For the ordinary Indonesian, citizenship was directed towards responsibility to the state, and the fulfilment of the primary goal of national development (*pembangunan*) and the vague nationalist ideology of *Pancasila* (the five principles of nationhood) (Blackburn, 1999; Heryanto, 1995). Surveillance, the ever-present threat of violence and the use of actual violence enforced conformity (Heryanto & Hadiz, 2005; Jackson, 2005; Tan, 2012). While the military formed the all-pervasive internal security apparatus, penetrating both political and civil life (Heryanto & Hadiz, 2005; Pohlman, 2015; Tan, 2012), the seemingly benevolent patrimonial model of the family reinforced the power of the New Order regime, while concealing an underlying violent character of militarised hegemonic masculinity (Robinson, 2009a, p. 68).

Since the independence movement began against the Dutch, Indonesian citizens were constructed as a large organic family to emphasise unity as well as their difference to their colonial oppressors (Boellstorff, 2005, p. 196). Under the New Order, the family became central to political power, and the "family principle," or *azas kekeluargaan* became a pillar of Indonesian citizenship as well as a mode of social control. The "language of the family" became enshrined in state discourse (Shiraishi, 1997, as cited in Boellstorff,

20 *Women and political power in Indonesia*

2005), and a strategy of depoliticization to curb any possible threats to Suharto's power (Melissa, 2019, p. 46). The Suharto government combined ideals of the Javanese elite and western (American) mid-twentieth century values, through which "the happy middle-class nuclear family came to stand for the generic Indonesian moral and social order" (Brenner, 1999, p. 30). The intersection of class and family resulted in the exclusion of the majority of women, as well as poor and working-class men, from meaningful participation in political life (Berman, 1998; Robinson, 2009a). Those who failed to comply with the principles of the family faced harsh social sanctions. The practice of Arche-politics, or the creation of a constitutive, organic ingroup against an outgroup was tied to the model of the family, and left no space for legitimate dissent (Duile & Bens, 2017).

The metaphor of the family produced and reinforced hierarchical relations of power not only within the state, but also between men and women, defining their access to the public realm. The *bapak* (father) was positioned "as the primary source of power," while the *"ibu* (mother) was constructed as a medium of that power" (Suryakusuma, 1996, p. 102). The bapak was granted authority over women, children, and male subordinates by virtue "of his God-given wisdom, self-control, and mastery of emotions" (Nilan, 2009, p. 332). President Suharto embodied the father figure, and arguably managed to remain in power for so long partly through the manipulation of the family. This model enabled Suharto and his government to expand his influence beyond the public arena, and penetrate the private, domestic realm (Brenner, 1998, p. 226).

Women were expected to remain confined to the domestic realm, fulfilling their role as loyal wives and as mothers, or ibu. They were also expected to remain calm and serene in the face of uncertainty and defer to their husband in decision-making processes. Djajadiningrat-Nieuwenhuis (1987) coined the term *ibuism* (lit. "motherism") to define the dominant model of womanhood under the New Order, describing it as "the ideology which sanctions any action provided it is taken as a mother who is looking after her family, a group, a class, a company, or the state, without demanding power and prestige in return" (p. 44). The ideals of self-sacrifice and surrendering personal ambitions for the sake of the family denied women access to power in the New Order state.

The idealised model of femininity was reinforced by cultural and state-level discourses circulated in the media, as well as in state-run institutions. The New Order government invoked the semi-religious term, *kodrat wanita* (women's essential nature determined by God) in official state discourse. This concept became a naturalising force that directed women to their correct biologically determined role as wives and mothers (Blackburn, 2004). Explaining women's social location in terms of their biologically determined destiny effectively denied them access to the public world of the body politic in Indonesia (Robinson, 2009a, p. 120). The culturally salient concept of *malu* (acute awareness of one's social standing and associated conduct) was also exploited to support the social hierarchy and power of the New Order by promoting "correct" gendered conduct and feelings of shame when transgression occurred (Collins & Bahar, 2000).

State institutions upheld a narrow vision of womanhood anchored to reproduction and service to the family. The term "state ibuism" was first coined by Suryakusuma (1987) to describe the role of state institutions in reinforcing women's ultimate role as the mother. In the non-elite realm, the Family Welfare Movement (PKK, *Pembinaan Kesejahteraan Keluarga*) oversaw family planning at the village-level, and entailed surveillance and control of women through their reproductive capacities. At the elite-level, *Dharma Wanita* (lit. women's moral duty) was an organisation established for the wives of civil servants, which Suryakusuma argues defined "women as appendages of their husbands" and "cast female dependency as ideal" (p. 97).

In accordance with the model of Arche-politics, the ideal image of the apolitical wife and mother was defined against contrasting images of the deviant other (Dwyer, 2000, p. 28). By anchoring gendered norms to the state, women who did not fulfil these gendered norms were viewed as a threat not only to the social order, but the symbolic reproduction of the nation (Dwyer, 2000, p. 28). The politically active and autonomous woman became the model of deviance, and was viewed as a destructive and thereby evil force (Tiwon, 1996, p. 65). The sexualised danger of the autonomous woman is in fact a recurring theme throughout Indonesian modern history. These threatening, deviant figures are subject to social sanctions, and even violence, and serve as a warning to others of the consequences of transgression (Brenner, 1998; Hatley, 2002).

The defamation of *Gerwani* (*Gerakan Wanita Indonesia*, or the Indonesian Women's Movement) draws upon this model of deviance, and stands as a historical turning point that signalled women's withdrawal from official political life, and continued throughout the New Order (Dwyer, 2004; Rhoads, 2012; Wieringa, 2002). Prior to the establishment of the New Order government, Gerwani was Indonesia's most politically active and progressive women's group. Aligned with the PKI, (*Partai Komunis Indonesia*, Indonesian Communist Party), Gerwani members campaigned for women's rights since independence. On 30 September—1 October 1965, following an alleged coup attempt by leftist forces within the Indonesian military, Major General Suharto and several supporters moved swiftly to crush the uprising and wrest power and control from the wavering President Soekarno. Six generals and one lieutenant were killed in the clash (Rhoads, 2012, p. 48). Blaming the PKI for the coup, members of the Indonesian military then set out to eradicate members of this political group and their suspected associates. Led by General Suharto, the Indonesian military carried out a massive propaganda campaign, flaming anti-Communist hatred throughout the country. Civilian militias and youth gangs were enlisted nation-wide to carry out the arrests and massacres. While the exact death toll is unknown,

22   *Women and political power in Indonesia*

estimates range from one hundred thousand to three million (Pohlman, 2013, p. 3).

Among the organisations targeted, Gerwani women were blamed for the soldiers' deaths, and singled out and attacked through a campaign of violence and sexual slander. Many were captured and subjected to imprisonment, torture, and sexual violence at the hands of the Indonesian military (Pohlman, 2015). New Order state media began to spread a myth of the morally deviant Gerwani women dancing lewdly around the generals, mutilating their genitals, and gouging out their eyes (Wieringa, 2002, pp. 294–297). The propaganda campaign lasted throughout the regime, and contained a calculated mixture of stories, warnings, and instructions reproduced in film, and in the national school curriculum (Hearman & McGregor, 2007; Pohlman, 2015, p. 7). Ever since the demonisation of the Gerwani, women's political struggles in Indonesia have been associated with sexual debauchery, while politically active women faced the looming threat of being branded as "new Communists" (Wieringa, 2015, p. 11). For elite women, while some managed to obtain positions within political parties through their social networks, these roles generally served the interests of the power elite, and thus did not represent a political threat.

The threat of the autonomous woman is also embedded in Indonesian folklore, such as in the story of Calonarang. Dating back to the Hindu-Buddhist Empire of the 12th century, the allegorical tale portrays a widowed woman who resists male violence through witchcraft (Parker, 2016). In the Balinese Hindu dance drama, Calonarang appears as Rangda—the child-eating demon witch who cyclically threatens the community with disease, pestilence, and death until she is subdued by the righteous, mythical figure of Barong. The demonisation of the autonomous woman is also evident in contexts beyond Indonesia, such as in the case of the former Indian prime minister, Indira Gandhi. After leading India to victory in a war against Pakistan in 1971, Gandhi was declared a hero and a "good woman" by complying to male wishes for war and adhering to her correct role within the male-dominated political game (Hellmann-Rajanayagam, 2013). Later, in the midst of economic turmoil and civic unrest, she made the autonomous decision to declare a state of emergency from 1975 to 1977. During this period, Gandhi's exercise of political power was considered a manifestation of her dark and evil feminine side, and was compared to the destructive Goddess Kali (Hellmann-Rajanayagam, 2013). She was later assassinated on 31 October, 1984 in response to her role in leading an Indian military operation against the Sikh insurgency in Punjab.

Women's political agency in Indonesia

Despite the multiple institutional and cultural restrictions placed on women's active participation in Indonesia, certain historical figures are also celebrated as examples of women's emancipation. Their much-lauded

Women and political power in Indonesia 23

narratives are, however, greatly influenced by the social-political context, and are retold in accordance with masculine structures of power. The story of the *priyayi* (Javanese aristocrat) writer, Kartini has been adopted as an example of women's empowerment in modern Indonesian history, and each year Indonesians commemorate Kartini Day in her honour. Her early struggle for women's access to education and attempts to resist the demands of polygamous marriage in 1900 colonial Java made her a folk hero and a symbol of "Native" enlightenment in a new colonial agenda. At the time, women were subject to severe restrictions on their social movements and received limited education (Smith-Hefner, 2007, p. 393). By virtue of her family's privileged access to educational and social opportunities, Kartini managed to negotiate the demands of aristocratic femininity and achieve a degree of autonomy. Under the New Order, however, rather than focusing on Kartini's resistance and personal autonomy, her story was rearticulated to fit in with the dominant trope of ibuism. Kartini became *Ibu Kartini,* despite having died one day after officially becoming a mother at the age of 25 (Tiwon, 1996, p. 58).

Historical narratives of brave women engaged in battle, such as Galuh Candra Kirana who disguises herself as a man to find her beloved husband in the 14th century Javanese Panji Chronicles, and the real-life Tjut Meutia in her struggle against the Dutch in Aceh are also held up as feminist examples in Indonesia. While highlighting their bravery, their engagement in war reinforces violent hegemonic masculinity as an ideal. Moreover, like Kartini of the New Order, the women are conveniently anchored to marriage or the gendered hierarchy of the family to normalise their autonomous exercise of power. In accordance with the values of ibuism, their defiant stance is justified on the basis of their loyalty to their husband, family, and nation, while remaining dependent on a man for full social representation (Hatley, 1990).

While ubiquitous under the New Order, scholars have also highlighted the limits of the influence of state-sanctioned domesticity upon women's actual lived experiences in Indonesia. Budianta (2002) asserts that it would be misguided "to assume that women's everyday praxis was controlled solely by the state" (p. 20). Elite women were able to take advantage of education and professional opportunities made possible by the elevated social and economic status of their families. For working-class women, the ideal nuclear family and women's passive domestic role contradicted a way of life that has never truly been limited to housewifery (Robinson, 2009a). These non-elite women have managed to navigate the public and private space and the overarching gender norms, operating as key economic actors and decision makers (Brenner, 1998; Dwyer, 2000; Newberry, 2008). Moreover, in a Javanese cultural context, somewhat paradoxically, women have been permitted a range of communicative and behavioural styles as "inferiors," comparatively free from the constraints of social etiquette applied to men who are positioned as their "superiors" (Hatley, 1990; Keeler, 1990).

24 *Women and political power in Indonesia*

The New Order government eventually collapsed in May 1998 at the peak of the Asian financial crisis, which revealed the extent of corruption and economic mismanagement that had engulfed the nation under Suharto's rule. Citizens took to the streets in major capital cities across Indonesia demanding Suharto's resignation and an end to the tyranny of the military. The large-scale civil unrest became destabilised, where initial politically motivated opposition was replaced by mass looting and violence, targeted particularly at the ethnic Chinese community. Eventually Suharto announced his resignation when it became clear that he was unable to remain in control of the nation he once ruled with an iron fist.

In the lead up to his resignation, reminiscent of the politically active Gerwani members, women suddenly emerged in the public space as a highly visible, politically mobilised collective. The *Suara Ibu Peduli* (SIP, Voice of Concerned Mothers) campaign began during the economic crisis that swept the nation at the beginning of 1998 and became a symbol of defiance. Recontextualising the dominant trope of motherhood that had previously excluded women from active political participation, the SIP moved in to occupy the public space to protest the rising cost of household staples and the inability of the government to solve the financial crisis. In Asian political contexts, research suggests that rather than overtly opposing gendered structures of power, women tend to navigate barriers to power by subverting, or even playing upon gender norms (Wang et al., 2008). Women standing up as mothers against the father figure (Suharto) severely disrupted the hierarchical family model of the New Order (Robinson, 2009, p. 152) while remaining within the security of state-sanctioned gender norms.

In contexts of political renewal or opposition, playing upon a gendered identity can become a particularly powerful form of moral capital for women, which emphasises their difference to the entrenched male political elite (Bucciferro, 2014; Fleschenberg, 2013b; Thompson, 2013). When working in opposition to Suharto, SIP women played upon their gendered identity by invoking the image of the suffering mother as a way to touch and move the broader population (Budianta, 2002). Given the history of exclusionary practices against those who defied state-sanctioned gender norms, the adoption of a motherhood identity as a form of political activism became a strategic way of challenging state power, by ostensibly complying with gender norms, but inverting them as a form of political protest.

Despite the initial fervour of Reformsi, since 1998, women's quantitative political representation has remained low. Bessell (2010) claims that the legacy of New Order gendered structures of power has been the largest barrier for achieving gender equality in the national parliament whereby patriarchal norms are reproduced in political processes and within individual political parties. Despite the introduction of a quota system requiring 30% of party candidates to be women, political parties later fail to place their female candidates in winning positions on the ballot, meaning that the quota is never realised at the parliamentary level (Bessell, 2010). In local politics in

Bali, Rhoads (2012) contends that a combination of "cultural, political, and historical factors create a discriminatory political environment" against women (p. 36). She further argues that the quota system will have no effect if these underlying factors are not addressed (p. 36). Budianta et al. (2015) claim that opportunities for women's acceptance as equal participants in Indonesia's democracy depends not only on changes made to legislation and internal political culture but also on broader structural changes in the public domain. The role of the media in facilitating broader social-political change, or sustaining the political order remains largely overlooked.

The small number of women who have achieved political success in Indonesia have received significant levels of public and media attention. They must tread carefully, however, as they navigate a pathway to power in the political realm. For some, as in political contexts across Asia, dynastic family ties have facilitated their entrance into politics, furnishing them with both legitimacy and all-important financial backing. Others follow a more grassroots pathway to power, making use of their social, commercial, religious, and vocational connections (Choi, 2019). Megawati, Risma, and Susi's political careers will be discussed below, outlining how they managed to gain a foothold in the Indonesian political arena and how they shaped their careers.

The political career of Megawati Soekarnoputri

Among the women to make their mark on the Indonesian political scene, Megawati Soekarnoputri stands out as an enduring icon. Born in the Central Javanese city of Jogjakarta on 23 January 1947, she possesses an exceptional political pedigree. Her status and influence span the late New Order and the democratic era. As the daughter of the nostalgic national hero Soekarno, a prominent leader in the independence movement against the Dutch and Indonesia's first president (van Wichelen, 2009), Megawati's political pathway was almost guaranteed. In Asian political contexts, women's access to the male-dominated political arena through a dynastic pathway, typically links them to a martyred father or husband (Fleschenberg, 2013a; Gerlach, 2013a). These women are positioned as bearers of their husband or father's political legacy (Derichs et al., 2006), which means their political participation is motivated by a sense of duty, rather than self-interest. While providing a way into politics, these women often tend to conceal their personal political ambitions and rely on entrenched masculine power (Derichs et al., 2006), as evidenced in the political careers of former South Korean president, Park Geun-hye, and the Burmese opposition leader, Aung San Suu Kyi. Since the beginning of her political career, Megawati has drawn upon the image of her father in her public political engagements, conjuring a romanticised connection to Indonesia's nationalist past.

Megawati holds an extensive political track record, as the chair of the *Partai Demokrasi Indonesia* (PDI, Indonesian Democratic Party) (1993–1998),

26 Women and political power in Indonesia

chair and founder of the *Partai Demokrasi Indonesia-Perjuangan* (PDI-P, Indonesian Democratic Party of Struggle) since its formation in 1998; vice president of Indonesia (1999–2001), and president (2001–2004). Megawati's official political career began in the mid-1980s, through her association with the PDI, a predecessor to the PDI-P. The PDI was one of only two state-approved parties permitted to operate in the New Order (Mietzner, 2012). The ultranationalist PNI (*Partai Nasional Indonesia,* Indonesian National Party) formed the largest component of this party, founded originally by Soekarno in the struggle for independence (Mietzner, 2012b, p. 514). The party's close alignment with Soekarno's legacy was intensified by Megawati's party membership, and gave the PDI a strong ideological foundation (Eklöf, 2003). After gaining prominence in the mid-1980s, by 1993 Megawati was elected as party chair.

Towards the end of the New Order, under Megawati's leadership, the PDI became increasingly critical of the regime, and was by then regarded as a threat to Suharto's enduring power. In 1996, the government and military manoeuvred to oust Megawati from her role, and stormed party headquarters (Eklöf, 2003; Ziv, 2001). In 1998, emerging as the embattled hero of the *wong cilik* (lit. small people), Megawati founded the PDI-P (Ziv, 2001), and became an opposition symbol in the Reformasi movement, from the New Order into the democratic era (van Wichelen, 2009). Megawati's party leadership was significantly strengthened by a style that fitted with a traditional model of motherhood (Blackburn, 2004). Portrayed as a "long-suffering mother at the hands of the Suharto regime, she appeared serene, correct, soft, and reticent, but remarkably resolute in the face of adversity" (Blackburn, 2004, p. 165). The image of the feminine, morally upright leader working in opposition to an immoral political regime can become a rallying point for the people. Parallels can be drawn between Megawati's image and Aung San Suu Kyi's deeply-feminised resistance to the Burmese military junta, where she displayed grace and serenity while under house arrest and leading the National League for Democracy (Fleschenberg, 2013b).

In the early years following the end of the New Order, despite her wide-spread popularity as a figurehead of the Reformasi movement, Megawati faced obstacles to achieving political legitimacy. Indeed, while conforming to traditional gender ideals can provide women with leverage in an opposition role, transferring their perceived moral capital to a position of power can prove challenging (Derichs et al., 2006; Thompson, 2013, p. 158). In 1999, Megawati became vice president, despite her party having won the majority of the parliamentary seats. Soon after, she was appointed to the role of president in 2001 but only as a result of the impeachment of President Abdurrahman Wahid. As the country's first female president in 2001, Megawati was regarded by some as a symbol of women's political advancement (Choi, 2019, p. 229); however, she remained in a precarious position. In the years that would follow, her inability to implement promised reforms damaged her public reputation.

Women and political power in Indonesia 27

In 2004, Megawati's run for the presidency in Indonesia's first direct presidential election became a source of significant ideological contestation. Nationalist groups de-sexualised her through reference to her motherhood identity and daughter of Soekarno, while feminist groups constructed her as an icon of female leadership (van Wichelen, 2006). Certain rival groups, however, called upon so-called Islamic values to challenge Megawati, by claiming that the teachings of Islam did not permit a woman to lead a nation (White & Anshor, 2008). Rather than Islam itself, however, these groups who challenged Megawati engaged Islamic values opportunistically in a bid to gain power, and used her gender as a point of contention within a masculine political domain (Elson, 2010; Rinaldo, 2011; Robinson, 2015; White & Anshor, 2008). Islam has played an ambiguous role in the post-authoritarian Indonesian political landscape, including the regulation of women's political participation (Blackburn, 2019).[1] Overall, the public debate Megawati's leadership reflected the tensions surrounding women's role in the political domain in the early years of Reformasi and the continued presence of gendered structures of power (van Wichelen, 2006).

Megawati was ultimately defeated by Susilo Bambang Yudhoyono (SBY) in 2004, and again in 2009 when she ran for the presidency the second time with Prabowo as her running mate. Her relationship with both SBY and Prabowo has been reportedly strained since these events. After an unimpressive performance as president and two subsequent failed bids for re-election, Megawati's overwhelming popularity underwent significant decline. Drawing further parallels with the fate of Aung San Suu Kyi, rather than the idealised figure of the selfless, duty-bound daughter working from outside the regime for the sake of the common good, some now regard Megawati as an entrenched member of the political elite (Gerlach, 2013b). No longer the people's champion, her personality has become a sticking point for critics, whereby her once heralded reticence is now considered one of her flaws (Gerlach, 2013b, p. 273).

Despite the disenchantment, Megawati remains an enduring figure in the democratic era, sitting at the helm of the PDI-P. The popularity of her party remains stable and admittedly Megawati continues to receive public support from segments of the population. Throughout her career, Megawati has continuously invoked the image of her father as a source of personal legitimacy and her party's identity, which contributes to her resilience. Her ability to form strategic alliances with key political and business figures has further enhanced her durability and influence.

In March 2014, in her role as party chair, Megawati secured the nomination of Jokowi as the PDI-P presidential candidate. She worked closely with him in preparation for the campaign, and helped secure crucial support from political, business, and media groups. While Jokowi's campaign was strengthened by his alliance with the PDI-P and Megawati's connection to her father's legacy (Robinson, 2014), her role in Jokowi's rise did become

28 *Women and political power in Indonesia*

a sticking point. Despite ongoing support from some stalwarts, her motivations for supporting Jokowi were called into question, suggesting that her personal interest in accumulating power influenced her relationship with Jokowi and later, the Jokowi government. Despite the conjecture, Megawati continued to perform her role as party leader, and remained an influential behind the scenes wheeler and dealer.

The political career of Tri Rismaharini

In Southeast Asia, while an elite family background like Megawati's can clear a pathway for women to attain political power, others have managed to launch their political career at the grassroots level, starting out as informal political problem-solvers before moving into mainstream politics (Choi, 2019, p. 235). This is certainly the case for Tri Rismaharini (Risma), who began as a public servant and is now distinguished as the first female mayor of the East Javanese city of Surabaya, Indonesia's second largest city. Born in Kediri, East Java, on 20 November 1961, Risma entered politics from a largely non-political background, as a member of the public service in the Surabaya City Government. Backed by the PDI-P, Risma was elected as mayor in 2010. She held her first tenure in office to 2015 and was subsequently re-elected in December 2015. While differing from the elite pathway to power in terms of privilege and access, Risma's grassroots political career is also imbued with a sense of duty rather than self-interest. Indeed, in Asian political contexts, female leaders are expected to act for the greater good, rather than out of personal interest (Thompson, 2013, p. 156).

Following the decentralisation of political power in the Reformasi period, local politicians have become increasingly influential (Hatherell & Welsh, 2017). For Risma, the importance of duty and local politics intersect. She first earned a reputation as the head of the Surabaya City Sanitation and Parks Office in 2007 for her contribution to the city's development as a green and business-friendly city (Choi, 2019). In recognition of her transformative work, she was named "Person of the Year" in 2007 by the East Java-based daily *Jawa Pos* (Choi, 2019, p. 240). She rose to national fame in her role as mayor of Surabaya and her perceived efforts to improve the lives of the everyday people of Surabaya. As mayor, Risma led initiatives such as the building of public parks and the implementation of education and housing services to the poor (Nurroni & Sulistyawati, 2015; Sahab, 2017).

As mayor of Surabaya, Risma became subject to increasing levels of media attention at the national level in February 2014 following her appearance on the popular television talk show, *Mata Najwa*. During the television interview, Risma shed tears over the pressure she faced in her role and refused to confirm or deny rumours of her plans to resign. Rather than losing credibility, from this point on, Risma became a media darling in local and national printed and electronic media (Sahab, 2017). Immediately after her televised appearance, Risma became a trending topic on Twitter, inspiring the hashtag #saveRisma. She gained widespread public sympathy as a duty-bound, morally-upright leader suffering from politically motivated attempts to undermine her. Despite the rumours of her imminent resignation, Risma continued to lead Surabaya and implemented a number of campaigns to clean up the city and provide more efficient, modern services to the people.

While Risma's dedication to the people undoubtedly upheld the values of feminised duty-bound leadership, she also gained a reputation for her apparently transgressive behaviour, including her *galak* (hot-tempered) personality, and for her "frank and unbending political style" (Choi, 2019, p. 241). She became known for her hands-on, openly emotional approach to tackling threats to the integrity of the city and the well-being of her citizens. Risma targeted a range of offenders with her galak approach, including inefficient public servants, drug dealers, and those caught damaging public facilities. While an apparent violation of traditional gender norms, her hot-tempered behaviour was justified by her apparent motivation to protect the people of her city, much in line with the concept of ibuism discussed above. Moreover, considering the greater range of behavioural forms accessible to women in a Javanese cultural context (Hatley, 1990; Keeler, 1990), Risma's gender opened the door to a widely popular political style. In the immediate political context, political outsiders like Risma were welcomed as changemakers, drawing readily on their difference as well as shock tactics to make their position known (Melissa, 2019). At this time, Jakarta's governor, Basuki Tjahaja Purnama (Ahok) also emerged as another charismatic outsider. Despite his double-minority status as an ethnic Chinese and Christian, Ahok took a vocal and similarly galak stance against entrenched corruption, and challenged prevailing cultural norms, eliciting an initially positive public response (Hatherell & Welsh, 2017).

Risma also expresses a publicly pious appearance by wearing a *jilbab*, a style of headscarf that has been adopted by most Indonesian Muslim women as an expression of religious devotion, particularly since Reformasi (Smith-Hefner, 2007). In democratic Indonesia, women actively navigate the new social, economic, and educational opportunities of the modern public sphere, and often do so within the boundaries of Islamic piety (Smith-Hefner, 2019). While Islamic values were enacted by rivals to stymy Megawati's political career, Islam has also been an enabling factor for many other Indonesian women seeking to enter formal politics (Blackburn, 2019). Certain politicians cultivate a publicly pious image by donning Islamic dress to set themselves apart from their male political rivals as exemplars of Islamic moral values (Dewi, 2015)[2]. More than simply a way of upholding religious norms, women's appearance in the political realm across the world becomes a source of representational and symbolic power, a focal point of media coverage, and a key component of their political persona (Hüstebeck,

30   *Women and political power in Indonesia*

2013a; Ibroscheva & Raicheva-Stover, 2009; Nichols, 2014a, Nichols, 2014b; Voronova, 2014). For Risma, adopting an outwardly pious image supported her political career, as she also drew upon traditional gender norms and emergent political values.

The political career of Susi Pudjiastuti

For Susi Pudjiastuti, the rise of the influential outsider paved the way for her entrance to, and acceptance in the political arena. Born on 15 January 1965, in Pangandaran, West Java, Susi was appointed to the role of minister of Maritime Affairs and Fisheries in October 2014 in the newly-formed Jokowi-Jusuf Kalla presidential cabinet. Like Risma, and unlike Megawati, Susi lacked an elite political "pedigree;" instead, she entered the ministry from an extensive business background in the fishing and aviation industry in which she accumulated significant levels of wealth. Despite her wealth, Susi was generally posited as an anti-elite figure in the Jokowi cabinet who represented a challenge to the status quo. Her perceived lack of pretension, and at times outwardly provocative public persona were largely viewed as a positive sign of political transformation. Bearing similarities to Japan's former foreign minister, Tanaka Makiko, Susi's public image as a nontraditional, outspoken woman positioned her at odds with the cold and aloof male political elite (Hüstebeck, 2013b). She occupied a unique position as one of the eight women appointed to ministerial roles in the Jokowi presidential cabinet, and moreover, as the first ever woman appointed to lead the Ministry of Maritime Affairs and Fisheries.

From the moment of her appointment, Susi's hardworking, supposedly "rags to riches" backstory quickly became the focus of media reports and public discourse across Indonesia, constructing her as a popular yet provocative figure. Susi did not complete middle school (Stevani, 2017). Her lack of education stood out as an anomaly in the traditional realm of the highly-educated political elite.[3] Instead of completing high school, Susi began working as a trader in the seafood industry. As her business expanded, she opened a seafood processing plant, and then founded PT ASI Pudjiastuti Aviation (Susi Air) in 2004 with a small fleet of aircraft to distribute her products nationally (Hamayotsu & Nataatmadja, 2016). Her charter airline company was operating a fleet of 49 aircraft in 2020 (Susi Air, 2020). Susi's lack of education established her as an accessible grassroots figure, while her business success appeared well-deserved, as a product of personal determination and talent rather than elite privilege. This is not to say that Susi's presence in the political realm did not attract criticism; certain elite male figures initially spoke out against her appointment, and later against her policies on the grounds of her lack of experience, education, and foresight.

Susi garnered media attention when she made her first major public appearance at her inauguration ceremony. The media reported on her clothing choice of a traditional-style choice of clothing, wearing a lace *kebaya* and batik *kain* (cloth) as a skirt. Rather than adopting Islamic dress, her choice in clothing instead upheld a traditional, idealised model of womanhood from a bygone era, that some would argue was increasingly eclipsed by the popularisation of Islamic modes of dress. At the inauguration, she was also captured on camera smoking while sitting on the ground outside the main parliamentary building. Susi would go on to be photographed smoking on numerous occasions; a famous image of her smoking while drinking coffee perched upon a paddleboard in the sea circulated the internet in 2017, and quickly became a meme. Her visible dragon tattoo on her ankle also gained immediate attention, as a clear marker of her difference from conservative elite norms, as well as the reticent female elite. Her past marriage to a German man further set her apart from the norm. She frequently engaged in brusque, yet humorous interactions with members of the media at political events, and her uniquely husky voice and laugh made her a perfect contender for a soundbite. It is no wonder that Susi quickly earned the label as *menteri nyentrik*, or the "eccentric minister," in the media.

Similar to Risma, Susi became known for her outspoken style and antagonistic attitude towards perceived threats. In this case, she sought to defend the integrity of the nation, particularly its marine environment. Susi adopted a strong stance against illegal, unreported, and unregulated (IUU) fishing; large-scale trawling in Indonesian waters; transhipment between Indonesian and foreign ships at sea; and slavery in the maritime industry. The implementation of a spectacular militaristic policy of capturing and blowing up predominantly foreign illegal fishing boats caught in Indonesian waters became a particularly powerful symbol of her ministry, her personal image, and the broader agenda of the Jokowi government (Bush, 2016). Intersecting with the post-election aftermath, the dominant discourse of change was replaced by more "inward-looking," nationalist discourses of sovereignty, preservation, and development. Jokowi declared an interest in domestic affairs with a focus "on strengthening Indonesia's maritime infrastructure and reasserting the authority of the state" (Connelly, 2015, p. 1). Overall, like Risma, while ostensibly transgressing the ideal image of the refined and reticent woman, Susi's behaviour in the ministry upheld a predominantly conservative agenda.

Navigating gendered structures of power

This chapter has illustrated the enduring relationship between structures of power and gender norms, the ways in which women in Indonesia have navigated their access to the political realm, and the residual and emergent values that define the scope of their participation. The New Order legacy of the family state channelled men and women into biologically-determined roles to legitimise state power and maintain control over the

32 *Women and political power in Indonesia*

population. The state promoted an ideal model of depoliticised woman-hood confined to the domestic realm, set apart from the deviant model of the politically active, autonomous woman. Because of the entwinement of gender norms and dominant state discourse, transgression not only contravened social norms, but represented a threat to the integrity of the nation.

As in all cases of political transformation, where structures of political power are linked to a hierarchical gender order, social-political change invariably leads to tensions around issues of gender. It also results in an increase in the visibility of women in the political domain. In the democratic era, residual and emergent factors both facilitate and impede women's political participation in Indonesia. Given the historical gendering of the political sphere, women's mere presence in politics constitutes a defiance of established norms, which places them in a precarious position. Given the formidable obstacles to access, women seeking to engage in politics cannot rely on a single, universal formula; instead, they must draw on multiple strategies to gain political leverage, in accordance with the specific local context in which they operate (Yeoh et al., 2002). In Indonesia, conforming to gender norms can enable women to access the political realm, and highlight their difference to an entrenched and unpopular political regime. On the other hand, engaging in a form of norm-breaking behaviour can also facilitate their political participation, positioning them as a change-maker. Ultimately, however, operating in a gendered environment means that a conservative agenda often determines the scope of their political engagement.

News media discourse plays a role in both reflecting and influencing the dynamics of structures of power and determining the scope of women's political participation. The next chapter explains the impact of the news media on the Indonesian political space, along with women's political engagement. It outlines its historical background in the New Order, and the emergent patterns of production and consumption in the democratic era, with specific attention paid to the role of Kompas.com and its portrayal of Megawati, Risma, and Susi.

Notes

1 While Indonesia is widely-known as having the world's largest Muslim population, with almost 90% of Indonesians identifying as Muslim, Indonesian Islam does not represent a unitary movement, nor is there a definitive relationship between state and religion, and the direct relationship between religious belief and political preferences remains tenuous (Pepinsky et al., 2018).
2 Notably, while the majority of female Indonesian Muslims now readily wear the jilbab, or other variations on Islamic veiling practices, the majority of prominent female political leaders at the national level still do not.
3 In Indonesia, education has long been widely accessible to those living in developed areas, while those from poor and rural backgrounds face obstacles to access, creating a stark division between rich and poor (Stein, 2007).

References

Berman, L. (1998). *Speaking through the silence: Narratives, social conventions and power in Java*. Oxford University Press.

Bessell, S. (2010). Increasing the proportion of women in the national parliament: Opportunities, barriers and challenges. In E. Aspinall & M. Mietzner (Eds.), *Problems of democratisation in Indonesia: Elections, institutions and society* (pp. 219–242). Institute of Southeast Asian Studies (ISEAS).

Blackburn, S. (1999). Women and citizenship in Indonesia. *Australian Journal of Political Science, 34*(2), 189–204.

Blackburn, S. (2004). *Women and the state in modern Indonesia*. Cambridge University Press.

Blackburn, S. (2019). How Islam affects the political participation of Indonesian women. In T. W. Devashayam (Ed.), *Women and politics in Southeast Asia: Navigating a man's world* (pp. 68–92). Sussex Academic Press.

Boellstorff, T. (2005). *The gay archipelago: Sexuality and nation in Indonesia*. Princeton University Press.

Brenner, S. (1998). *The domestication of desire: Women, wealth and modernity in Java*. Princeton University Press.

Brenner, S. (1999). On the public intimacy of the New Order: Images of women in the popular Indonesian print media. *Indonesia, 67*, 13–37.

Bucciferro, C. (2014). Michelle Bachelet, President of Chile: A moving portrait. In M. Raicheva-Stover & E. Ibroscheva (Eds.), *Women in politics and media: Perspectives from nations in transition* (1st ed., pp. 217–232). Bloomsbury Academic.

Budianta, M. (2002). Plural identities: Indonesian women's redefinition of democracy in the post-Reformasi era. *RIMA Review of Indonesian and Malaysian Affairs, 36*(1), 35–50.

Budianta, M., Chandrakirana, K., & Yentriyani, A. (2015). Yudhoyono's politics and the harmful implications for gender equality in Indonesia. In E. Aspinall, M. Mietzner, & D. Tomsa (Eds.), *The Yudhoyono presidency: Indonesia's decade of stability and stagnation* (pp. 199–216). Institute of Southeast Asian Studies.

Bush, R. (2016). Indonesia in 2015. *Southeast Asian Affairs, 2016*, 131–144.

Choi, N. (2019). Women's political pathways in Southeast Asia. *International Feminist Journal of Politics, 21*(2), 224–248.

Collins, E., & Bahar, E. (2000). To know shame: Malu and its use in Malay societies. *Crossroads: Interdisciplinary Journal of Southeast Asian Studies, 14*(1), 35–69.

Connell, R. (2009). *Gender*. Polity Press.

Connelly, A. (2015). Sovereignty and the sea: President Joko Widodo's foreign policy challenges. *Contemporary Southeast Asia: A Journal of International and Strategic Affairs, 37*(1), 1–28.

Dalton, E. (2015). *Women and politics in contemporary Japan*. Routledge.

Derichs, C., & Thompson, M. R. (2013). Introduction. In C. Derichs & M. R. Thompson (Eds.), *Dynasties and female political leaders in Asia: Gender, power and pedigree* (pp. 11–26). Lit Verlag.

Derichs, C., Fleschenberg, A., & Hüstebeck, M. (2006). Gendering moral capital: Morality as a political asset and strategy of top female politicians in Asia. *Critical Asian Studies, 38*(3), 245–270.

Dewi, K. H. (2015). *Indonesian women and local politics*. NUS Press.

34 *Women and political power in Indonesia*

Djajadiningrat-Nieuwenhuis, M. (1987). Ibuism and priyayization: Path to power? In E. Locher-Scholten & A. Niehof (Eds.), *Indonesian women in focus: Past and present notions* (pp. 43–51). Foris Publications.

Duile, T., & Bens, J. (2017). Indonesia and the "conflictual consensus": A discursive perspective on Indonesian democracy. *Critical Asian Studies, 49*(2), 139–162.

Dwyer, L. (2000). Spectacular sexuality: Nationalism, development and the politics of family planning in Indonesia. In T. Mayer (Ed.), *Gender ironies of nationalism* (pp. 25–62). Routledge.

Dwyer, L. (2004). Intimacy of terror: Gender and the violence of 1965–1966 in Bali. *Intersections: Gender and Sexuality in Asia and the Pacific* (10).

Eklöf, S. (2003). *Power and political culture in Suharto's Indonesia: The Indonesian Democratic Party (PDI) and decline of the New Order (1986–98)*. Nordic Institute of Asian Studies.

Elson, R. (2010). Nationalism, Islam, 'secularism' and the state in contemporary Indonesia. *Australian Journal of International Affairs, 64*(3), 328–343.

Fleschenberg, A. (2013a). Benazir Bhutto: Her people's sister? A contextual analysis of female Islamic government. In C. Derichs & M. Thompson (Eds.), *Dynasties and female political leaders in Asia: Gender, power and pedigree* (pp. 63–111). Lit Verlag.

Fleschenberg, A. (2013b). Min Laung or fighting peacock? Aung San Suu Kyi's political leadership via moral capital (1988–2008). In C. Derichs & M. Thompson (Eds.), *Dynasties and female political leaders in Asia: Gender, power and pedigree* (pp. 191–245). Lit Verlag.

Gerlach, R. (2013a). Female leadership and duelling dynasties in Bangladesh. In C. Derichs & M. Thompson (Eds.), *Dynasties and female political leaders in Asia: Gender, power and pedigree* (pp. 113–150). Lit Verlag.

Gerlach, R. (2013b). 'Mega' expectations: Indonesia's democratic transition and first female president. In C. Derichs & M. Thompson (Eds.), *Dynasties and female political leaders in Asia: Gender, power and pedigree* (pp. 247–290). Lit Verlag.

Hamayotsu, K., & Nataatmadja, R. (2016). The people's president's rocky road and hazy outlooks in democratic consolidation. *Asian Survey, 56*(1), 129–137.

Hatherell, M., & Welsh, A. (2017). Rebel with a cause: Ahok and charismatic leadership in Indonesia. *Asian Studies Review, 41*(2), 174–190.

Hatley, B. (1990). Theatrical imagery and gender ideology in Java. In J. Monnig Atkinson & S. Errington (Eds.), *Power and difference: Gender in island Southeast Asia* (pp. 177–208). Stanford University Press.

Hatley, B. (2002). Literature, mythology and regime change: Some observations on recent Indonesian women's writing. In K. Robinson & S. Bessell (Eds.), *Women in Indonesia gender, equity and development* (pp.130–143). Institute of Southeast Asian Studies.

Hearman, V., & McGregor, K. (2007). Challenges of political rehabilitation in post-New Order Indonesia: The case of Gerwani (the Indonesian women's movement). *South East Asia Research, 15*(3), 355–384.

Hellmann-Rajanayagam, D. (2013). The pioneers: Durga Amma, the only man in the cabinet. In C. Derichs & M. Thompson (Eds.), *Dynasties and female political leaders in Asia: Gender power and pedigree* (pp. 27–62). Lit Verlag.

Heryanto, A. (1995). *Language of development and development of language: The case of Indonesia.* (Pacific linguistics. Series D–86). Research School of Pacific and Asian Studies, Australian National University.

Heryanto, A., & Hadiz, V. (2005). Post-authoritarian Indonesia. *Critical Asian Studies, 37*(2), 251–275.

Hüstebeck, M. (2013a). Park Geun-hye: The eternal princess? In C. Derichs & M. Thompson (Eds.), *Dynasties and female political leaders in Asia: Gender, power and pedigree* (pp. 353–380). Lit Verlag.

Hüstebeck, M. (2013b). Populist or reformer? Tanaka Makiko. In C. Derichs & M. Thompson (Eds.), *Dynasties and female political leaders in Asia: Gender, power and pedigree* (pp. 321–352). Lit Verlag.

Ibroscheva, E., & Raicheva-Stover, M. (2009). Engendering transition: Portrayals of female politicians in the Bulgarian press. *Howard Journal of Communications, 20*(2), 111–128.

Ibroscheva, E., & Raicheva-Stover, M. (2014). The girls of parliament: A historical analysis of the press coverage of female politicians in Bulgaria. In M. Raicheva-Stover & E. Ibroscheva (Eds.), *Women in politics and media: Perspectives from nations in transition* (1st ed., pp. 47–64). Bloomsbury Academic.

Jackson, E. (2005). *'Warring Words': Students and the state in New Order Indonesia, 1966–1998* [Doctoral dissertation, Australian National University], Australian National University Open Research Library.

Keeler, W. (1990). Speaking of gender in Java. In J. Monnig Atkinson & S. Errington (Eds.), *Power and difference: Gender in island Southeast Asia* (pp. 127–152). Stanford University Press.

Melissa, E. (2019). *The internet, social media, and political outsiders in post-Suharto Indonesia: A case study of Basuki Tjahaja Purnama.* [Doctoral dissertation, University of Western Australia], University of Western Australia Research Repository.

Mietzner, M. (2012). Ideology, money and dynastic leadership: The Indonesian Democratic Party of Struggle, 1998–2012. *South East Asia Research, 20*(4), 511–531.

Newberry, J. (2008). Women's ways of walking: Gender and urban space in Java. In R. Hutchinson (Ed.), *Gender in an urban world* (Vol. 9, pp. 77–102). Emerald Group Publishing.

Nichols, E. G. (2014a). Ultra-feminine women of power: Beauty and the state in Argentina. In M. Raicheva-Stover & E. Ibroscheva (Eds.), *Women in politics and media: Perspectives from nations in transition* (1st ed., pp. 249–264). Bloomsbury Academic.

Nichols, E. G. (2014b). Virgin Venuses: Beauty and purity for "public" women in Venezuela. In M. Raicheva-Stover & E. Ibroscheva (Eds.), *Women in politics and media: Perspectives from nations in transition* (1st ed., pp. 233–248). Bloomsbury Academic.

Nilan, P. (2009). Contemporary masculinities and young men in Indonesia. *Indonesia and the Malay World, 37*(109), 327–344.

Nurroni, A., & Sulistyawati, R. (2015, April 29). Tri Rismaharini wali kota Surabaya: Si pengubah wajah Surabaya. *Republika.co.id.* Retrieved from http://www.repu blika.co.id.

Parker, L. (2016). The theory and context of the stigmatisation of widows and divorcees (*janda*) in Indonesia. *Indonesia and the Malay World, 44*(128), 7–26.

Pepinsky, T. B., Liddle, R. W., & Mujani, S. (2018). *Piety and public opinion: Understanding Indonesian Islam.* Oxford University Press.

Pohlman, A. (2013). Introduction: The massacres of 1965–1966: New interpretations and the current debate in Indonesia. *Journal of Current Southeast Asian Affairs, 32*(3), 3–9.

36 *Women and political power in Indonesia*

Pohlman, A. (2015). *Women, sexual violence and the Indonesian killings of 1965–66.* Routledge.

Rhoads, E. (2012). Women's political participation in Indonesia: Decentralisation, money politics and collective memory in Bali. *Journal of Current Southeast Asian Affairs, 31*(2), 35–56.

Rinaldo, R. (2011). Muslim women, moral visions: Globalization and gender controversies in Indonesia. *Qualitative Sociology, 34*, 539–560.

Ritchie, J. (2013). Creating a monster. *Feminist Media Studies, 13*(1), 102–119.

Robinson, K. (2009). *Gender, Islam and democracy in Indonesia.* Routledge.

Robinson, K. (2014). Citizenship, identity and difference in Indonesia. *RIMA Review of Indonesian and Malaysian Affairs, 48*(1), 5–34.

Robinson, K. (2015). Masculinity, sexuality and Islam: The gender politics of regime change in Indonesia. In L. Bennett & S. G. Davies (Eds.), *Sex and sexualities in contemporary Indonesia* (pp. 51–68). Routledge.

Sahab, A. (2017). Realitas citra politik Tri Rismaharini. *Masyarakat, Kebudayaan dan Politik, 30*(1), 20–34.

Shiraishi, S. (1997). *Young heroes: The Indonesian family in politics.* Cornell Southeast Asia Program Publications.

Smith-Hefner, N. (2019). *Islamizing intimacies: Youth, sexuality, and gender in contemporary Indonesia.* University of Hawaii Press.

Smith-Hefner, N. (2007). Javanese women and the veil in post-Soeharto Indonesia. *Journal of Asian Studies, 66*(2), 389–420.

Stein, E. (2007). Midwives, Islamic morality and village biopower in post-Suharto Indonesia. *Body and Society, 13*(55), 55–77.

Stevani, W. (2017). Kepribadian dan komunikasi Susi Pudjiastuti dalam membentuk personal branding. *Jurnal Komunikasi, 9*(1), 65–73.

Suryakusuma, J. (1987). *State ibuism: The social construction of womanhood in the Indonesia New Order.* [Unpublished Master's thesis, The Institute of Social Studies], The Hague.

Suryakusuma, J. (1996). The state and sexuality in Indonesia. In L. J. Sears (Ed.), *Fantasizing the feminine in Indonesia* (pp. 92–119). Duke University Press.

Susi Air. (2020). *Profile.* Retrieved from https://www.susiair.com/profile.

Tan, L. (2012). Indonesian national security during the Suharto New Order (1965–1998): The role of narratives of peoplehood and the construction of danger. *New Zealand Journal of Asian Studies, 14*(1), 49–70.

Thompson, M. (2013). Presidents and 'people power' in the Philippines: Corazon C. Aquino and Gloria Macapagal Arroyo. In C. Derichs & M. Thompson (Eds.), *Dynasties and female political leaders in Asia: Gender, power and pedigree* (pp. 151–190). Lit Verlag.

Tiwon, S. (1996). Models and maniacs. In L. J. Sears (Ed.), *Fantasizing the feminine in Indonesia* (pp. 47–70). Duke University Press.

van Wichelen, S. (2006). Contesting Megawati: The mediation of Islam and nation in times of political transition. *Westminster Papers in Communication and Culture, 3*(2), 41–59.

van Wichelen, S. (2009). Polygamy talk and the politics of feminism: Contestations over masculinity in a new Muslim Indonesia. *Journal of International Women's Studies, suppl. Special Issue: Gender and Islam in Asia, 11*(1), 173–188.

Voronova, L. (2014). Between two democratic ideals: Gendering in the Russian culture of political journalism. In M. Raicheva-Stover & E. Ibroscheva (Eds.),

Women in politics and media: Perspectives from nations in transition (pp.115–130). Bloomsbury Academic.

Wang, Q., Milwertz, C., Burghoorn, W., & Iwanaga, K. (2008). Introduction. In W. Burghoorn, K. Iwanaga, C. Milwertz, & Q. Wang (Eds.), *Gender politics in Asia: Women manoeuvring within dominant gender orders* (pp. 1–10). Nordic Institute of Asian Studies (NIAS) Press.

White, S., & Anshor, M. (2008). Islam and gender in contemporary Indonesia: Public discourses on duties, rights and morality. In S. White & G. Fealy (Eds.), *Expressing Islam: Religious life and politics in Indonesia.* ISEAS Publishing.

Wieringa, S. (2002). *Sexual politics in Indonesia.* Palgrave Macmillan.

Wieringa, S. (2015). Gender harmony and the happy family: Islam, gender and sexuality in post-Reformasi Indonesia. *South East Asia Research, 23*(1), 27–44.

Yeoh, B. S., Teo, P., & Huang, S. (2002). Introduction: Women's agencies and activisms in the Asia-Pacific region. In B. S. Yeoh, P. Teo, & S. Huang (Eds.), *Gender politics in the Asia-Pacific region* (pp. 1–16). Routledge.

Ziv, D. (2001). Populist perceptions and perceptions of populism in Indonesia: The case of Megawati Soekarnoputri. *South East Asia Research, 9*(1), 73–88.

3 News media and democracy in Indonesia

The Indonesian news media played an unprecedented role in shaping political engagement in the 2014 presidential election, and public perceptions of Megawati, Risma, and Susi's leadership. In the transformation of the political space taking place since the fall of the New Order, both residual and emergent factors influence news media production and consumption, and in turn, shape political discourse. This chapter draws upon scholarly analysis of past and present news media practices to illustrate the transformation of the Indonesian media industry since the end of authoritarianism, and define the parameters in which journalists work. In describing the developments in the Indonesian mediascape, this chapter also introduces the highly influential conglomerate, Kompas Gramedia Group and its online digital news platform, Kompas.com, the source of data for analysis. To conclude, the chapter provides an overview of major topics in the Kompas.com coverage of Megawati, Risma, and Susi during the 24 months surrounding the 2014 presidential election.

The Indonesian news media in transition

Under the New Order, Indonesian journalists operated in a highly restricted environment, where reporting was subject to both formal and informal censorship mechanisms (Sen & Hill, 2007; Tapsell, 2012). The Ministry of Information was the main instrument of propaganda and censorship for the government. Journalists were subject to surveillance and control by the ministry, and media outlets deemed too critical of the government or the president faced bans, while individual journalists faced the threat of incarceration. In addition to the ministry, the military also enforced content guidelines, and journalists faced the threat of violence for reporting on sensitive issues, including the activities of military personnel (Tapsell, 2012, p. 231). Developmental journalism became the desired practice, where journalists were encouraged to selectively focus on positive issues for the sake of national development, and avoid reporting on sensitive issues deemed detrimental to the national interests (Tapsell, 2012).

DOI: 10.4324/9781003083252-3

An overall culture of surveillance permeated newsrooms and became embedded in professional practice (Sen & Hill, 2007; Tapsell, 2012). In order to survive under these conditions, journalists practiced cautious self-censorship, while editors strictly monitored content to avoid raising the ire of the New Order elite. Over time, rather than direct government intervention, the threat of punishment became the most effective mode of press control (Sen & Hill, 2007, p. 207). Within this restrictive environment, Indonesian journalists nevertheless developed strategies to navigate constraints and report on taboo topics. As a way of expressing subtle critique, they employed indirect language including allusions and metaphors, while carefully representing the elite social actors involved in news events to avoid direct accusations of wrongdoing. Stories focusing on victims and discrete episodes rather than thematic events showcased single acts of injustice without directly identifying or criticising the perpetrator or the underlying causes (Steele, 2011). Readers, however, became adept at picking up on these subtle cues and "reading between the lines" (Tapsell, 2012, p. 230).

After the fall of the New Order, the Indonesian mediascape underwent a period of rapid transformation. Indeed, Heryanto and Hadiz (2005) declared that nothing epitomised change in post-1998 Indonesia more than developments in the media industry. In a highly symbolic act, the Ministry of Information was closed down in 1999, and new laws were enacted guaranteeing freedom of media expression. Shortly after, the media became filled with a diversity of voices and images. New print media organisations emerged, jumping from 289 to around 1600 in the early years of Reformasi (Heryanto & Hadiz, 2005, p. 257). In line with the growing Islamic awareness among the population, Islamic publications also proliferated, reflecting the diversity of Islamic beliefs and practices in Indonesia (Weintraub, 2011).

Representations of women in various media forms have functioned as a way of navigating shifting dimensions of power and changing narratives of nationhood, identity, culture, and class since the New Order (Campbell, 2007; Hatley, 1990, 2008; Rinaldo, 2011; Subijanto, 2011; Sunidyo, 1996). In the democratic era, representations of women in the media spotlight have led to controversy and public debate. These controversies have demonstrated the salience of gender in the media to power relations and its relationship to the diversity of values, attitudes, and beliefs circulating in public discourse. In Megawati's bid for the presidency in 2004, for example, the media played a key role in manufacturing divisions between Islamic, nationalist, and feminist social groups, while fuelling the debate over women's political leadership (van Wichelen, 2006, pp. 3–4).

The case of the popular female *dangdut* (grassroots Indonesian pop music) performer, Inul Daratista is another example of the provocative women play in the post-authoritarian media. In 2003 her unique and sexually suggestive

40 *News media and democracy in Indonesia*

style of dancing became a source of public debate fuelled by the mass media. Heryanto (2008) argues that Inul and her on- and off-stage performances became the site of a fierce ideological battle for dominance between liberalism and conservatism in the negotiation of "Indonesian-ness" in the immediate post-authoritarian environment. When examining the role of women such as Inul and Megawati, however, it is important not to overlook their agency in the process, rather than positioning them as passive sites within a masculine framework of nation-building (Jurriens, 2011). Indeed, highlighting the agency of women in public debates can reveal the active role they play in shaping and even resisting the discourses and structures of power around them (Budiman, 2011).

While the media has become a crucial source of the circulation of new ideas, images, and voices in the democratic era, journalistic freedom has become increasingly constrained by elite interests. Replacing the explicit government or military interventions of the New Order, media owners and their alliances with business and political parties now play the dominant role in determining content and reporting styles. These tight relationships reinforce the hegemonic influence of elite interests in the political domain (Haryanto, 2010; Ida, 2009; Wijayanto, 2015). In contrast to Heryanto and Hafiz's optimistic evaluation of the press and its diversity in the early years of Reformasi, by 2010, the number of print media organisations had shrunk, and nine business groups come to control half of the print media and two-thirds of the television stations in Indonesia (Haryanto, 2010).

A dependent relationship now exists between the media, business, and political groups; politicians seeking preferable coverage are known to cultivate relationships with media organisations, while news media conglomerates remain susceptible to external pressures from the political and business interests of the patrons on whom they depend (Heryanto & Hadiz, 2005; Steele, 2013, p. 355). In addition to external pressures, the personal political and business interests of media owners themselves also determine newsroom agendas. For journalists, these intersecting political and business interests restrict their ability to publish content freely, while their professional goals become "subordinate to the market-driven aims of media owners and conglomerates" (Steele, 2011, p. 99). Adding to the mix, an increasingly precarious job market compounds restrictions on journalists worldwide, including Indonesia, which makes them likely to adhere to the agenda of the ownership in order to maintain opportunities to work.

The constraints on journalistic practice are further augmented by legal mechanisms in Indonesia. Despite the initial reforms guaranteeing press freedom, ten years after Reformasi, Indonesia's parliament passed the law regarding electronic information and transactions (ITE) in 2008, which was later updated in 2016. The law contains a provision criminalising defamation and insult on the internet (Balfas, 2014). The vague definition of the defamation within the law means that it can be used opportunistically "against individuals and groups who express [critical] opinions on the internet and social media" (Lim, 2013a, p. 134). The presence of this defamation law, compounded by the ability of powerful individuals to apply it, compels journalists to exercise caution in their reporting.

Indonesian journalists in the democratic era are acutely aware of the constraints in which they operate, but nevertheless express a view of themselves as highly professional, contemporary watchdogs (Hanitzsch, 2006). Evidence gleaned from contemporary reporting practices, however, suggests that while the topics may have expanded to include previous off-limits themes such as corruption and conflict at the elite level, journalists continue to actively self-censor. Bearing similarities to the New Order, reports on contentious issues are characterised by a lack of context, a focus on events rather than underlying causes, and too much privileging of official sources (Steele, 2011). In covering elite-level corruption, for example, while demonstrating a newfound enthusiasm, journalists tend to "scandalise" the cases, focus on sensationalism, and engage in "soap-operafication," rather than exploring the underlying institutional and systemic causes (Kramer, 2013, p. 61). Such coverage can potentially strengthen public support for the anti-corruption movement; however, the superficial nature undermines democratic political engagement (Kramer, 2013). Reporting on corruption typifies the dilemma faced by Indonesian journalists in the democratic era—on the one hand, they seek to satisfy an increasing public demand for transparency and politically compelling content, while on the other they remain at the mercy of the commercial and political interests of their employer.

The emergence of online news media

The digital revolution taking place in Indonesia, much like elsewhere around the world, has become the most recent factor to influence news media practices. Since 2010, the Indonesian press began to undergo a rapid transformation, moving from print production to digital news media platforms. This change took place as the number of internet users increased and the spread of smartphones and cheaper internet rates broadened internet access (Lim, 2013b; Weiss, 2014, p. 102). In 2012, internet users approximated 55 million out of a total population of 240 million (Lim, 2013b, p. 652), and by 2015, this number had grown to 73 million ("Internet users in Indonesia reach 73 million"). By 2013, online media was edging closer towards print media as the preferred source of news, with 72% of web users reportedly accessing their news online (Hamzah, 2013). Despite the changes taking place, a digital divide shaped by wealth, gender, education,

42 *News media and democracy in Indonesia*

infrastructure, and geographical location limits access to the internet. Similar to the typical journalist, members of the urban, educated middle class made up the majority of internet users in 2013, with the bulk of the population still lacking ready access to the internet or sufficient levels of digital literacy (Hamzah, 2013; "Internet users in Indonesia reach 73 million" Lim, 2013b; Melissa, 2019).

As online news media and social media platforms converge, news is now far more spreadable and interactive than ever before, meaning that consumer activity plays an increasingly important role in determining news content in Indonesia (Tapsell, 2015b). Moving away from the traditional model of engagement with the print media, new social and mobile media technologies have influenced the ways readers interact with news, which include monitoring, reading, scanning, clicking, snacking, or sharing (Costera Meijer & Groot Kormelink, 2015). Profit-driven online news agencies in Indonesia readily monitor key indicators of audience interest, such as "trending topics," "clicks," and "shares," and tailor their content accordingly (Tapsell, 2015a, p. 45). The increasing orientation towards consumer interest represents a significant transformation of the traditional "top-down" flow of information from news institutions to the public. While a news text has always needed to present information that reflects general socially-shared knowledge and beliefs of the target readership to achieve intelligibility (van Dijk, 1988, 2000), now more than ever, news content is tailored towards an online reader response. When targeting audience reactions, the overall quality of news suffers, which Miller (2015) argues threatens to produce a democratic deficit. Indeed, the online media environment has been a driving force behind the populist movement and the personalisation of political leadership, through which traits and personality take prominence over issues (Campus, 2010; Garzia, 2011; McAllister, 2007). Simplified messages and a focus on in-group/out-group polarisation in the online media combine with a public demand for strong leadership, through which superficial political engagement flourishes.

The nature of online news media engagement shapes how readers understand important political events and more broadly, their participation in democratic political life. Online audiences tend to view the headline, image, and the lead rather than read the story in-depth (Costera Meijer & Groot Kormelink, 2015). Andrew (2007) theorises that readers who simply view headlines receive different heuristic cues than those who read a news report in detail, which limits their knowledge and understanding of the event. The growing tendency to access online news on a mobile device (Costera Meijer & Groot Kormelink, 2015; Lim, 2013b) further reduces the depth of engagement, as users skim read news stories on their small devices, share, and comment rapidly, as they flit across multiple online media platforms. An absence of digital literacy can also undermine a reader's ability to critically analyse a news report, including its sources and motivations for publication, leading to the sharing of misinformation online and the formation of distorted opinions. While Tapsell (2015a) pointed to the emergence of digitally literate middle-class youth as an actively engaged political force during the 2014 presidential election, the middle class do not always act as a progressive force in Indonesia (Budiman, 2011). In fact, given the short-comings discussed above, engaging with news and political discourse in the online realm may undermine their contribution to democratic outcomes.

Focusing on Indonesian political activism in an online environment, Lim (2013b) argues that participation so far mainly "embraces the principles of a contemporary culture of consumption," which is characterised by simpli-fied narratives and symbolic representations, light package, and a focus on headlines. More recently, Lim (2017) identified the formation of "algorithmic enclaves" as a product of continuous political interaction online. As users seek to express, reinforce, and defend their group-based beliefs, while denigrating the beliefs of others, the ideological groupings become self-perpetuating and sectarianism flourishes (Lim, 2017). Similarly, in the United States during the 2016 presidential election, Mihailidis and Viotty (2017) highlighted the causal link between online news reports targeting audience reactions and the perpetuation of partisan ideologies, which rein-forced boundaries between groups.

Kompas

In line with the rise of digital media technology, Indonesian news media corporations including the Kompas Gramedia Group have moved towards an online platform. Established in the 1980s, the Kompas Gramedia Group emerged as one of three major media conglomerates by the close of the New Order. In the democratic era, it maintains its dominant market presence, made up of several business units, including mass media assets such as the *Kompas* newspaper, Kompas.com, Kompas TV, Sonora Radio, and the popular Gramedia bookstore chain. Established in 1965, the *Kompas* print newspaper is "Indonesia's most prestigious and largest-selling daily print newspaper" (Sen & Hill, 2007, p. 57). The newspaper managed to navigate restrictions and avoid mass bans under the New Order, "through cautious self-censorship on sensitive political issues" (Sen & Hill, 2007, p. 57). Under the ownership of the president director, Jakob Oetama, a member of the ethnic Chinese, Catholic minority, *Kompas* gained a public reputation for accuracy and objectivity geared to middle-class, urban, secular inter-ests (Nilan, 2008, p. 65; Sen & Hill, 2007). The prestigious reputation of *Kompas* endures in the democratic era and consistently attracts the inter-est of the Indonesian political elite who seek to benefit from its coverage. The president director of *Kompas* has been known to receive visits from presidential candidates to negotiate positive coverage of their campaign (Wijayanto, 2015).

44 *News media and democracy in Indonesia*

The Kompas Gramedia group first launched the online newspaper, Kompas.com in 1995; however, its popularity as a news source began to soar only when internet access became more widespread around 2010. Kompas.com differs from the flagship print newspaper, Kompas, in terms of its staff, editorial board, content, and production schedule. Despite the difference between the print and free online version, according to brand psychology theory, the familiarity and perceived quality of the Kompas Gramedia brand is likely to influence readers' perception of Kompas.com (Gabay, 2015). In an increasingly competitive online news environment, journalists are required to provide regular news updates, which are to be uploaded continuously throughout the day and night (Tapsell, 2015a). The rapid production schedule undoubtedly affects the ability of journalists to produce in-depth stories, and instead short articles become the accepted form. Produced expeditiously, these articles at times closely resemble the contents of the government press releases on which journalists often rely as their source of information. Kompas.com is freely available to those with an internet connection, and articles can be shared directly from the website, or through social media platforms without any restrictions, albeit heavily beset by advertising content such as pop-ups and flash animation. Accessing the article on a mobile device reduces the disruptions caused by advertising.

A report published by Kompas.com in 2013 indicated that an average of 21 million people visited the Kompas.com site each month, with a monthly average of 180 million page views (Djumena, 2013). In 2015, the majority of readers were aged between 18 to 34, 74% male, belonged to middle-to upper-middle class socio-economic bracket, and were located in urban areas; 43% of readers resided in the national capital, Jakarta (Kompas.com, 2016). Kompas.com was the third most popular source of online news in Indonesia in 2015, ranked behind Detik.com and Liputan6.com (Alexa.com, 2016). While ranked third in Indonesia, it represents a highly influential news media site due to its affinity with the important urban, middle-class demographic, combined with its association with the reputable Kompas brand.

An overview of Kompas.com coverage of Megawati, Risma, and Susi

Kompas.com positioned Megawati, Risma, and Susi as key social actors in the political climate of the 2014 presidential election. Although Risma and Susi emerged later in the period in focus than Megawati, media coverage of all three women became a crucial component of political reportage, and captured some of the defining events and issues of the era. Over time, the reports built up an impression of the individual actors, while providing broader observations of the processes involved in a change in government and its aftermath.

Megawati Soekarnoputri

Among the three women, Megawati maintained the most consistent media profile as a result of her well-established public prominence. As chair of the PDI-P, the party behind Jokowi's nomination, Megawati was connected most closely to the specific events surrounding the presidential election. From July 2013 to February 2014, Kompas.com focused predominantly on speculation on the identity of the PDI-P presidential candidate, with reports suggesting Jokowi; Megawati's daughter and PDI-P manager, Puan Maharani; or Megawati herself as potential contenders. Megawati was positioned at the centre of the speculation because of her gatekeeping role as party chair, and her rumoured personal political ambitions for another term in the presidency.

After months of ongoing conjecture, in March 2014, Megawati announced Jokowi as the official party candidate. From that moment to June 2014, Kompas.com covered the presidential election campaign in detail. In reports concerning Megawati, Kompas.com focused on her role in guiding Jokowi through the campaign process. Within this time period, the reports also began to speculate on the dynamics of their power relationship and hint at Megawati's underlying thirst for power. Aside from the presidential election campaign, in April 2014, Kompas.com also detailed the role of the PDI-P under Megawati's leadership in other important elections for the national parliament, provincial assemblies, and district assemblies taking place in the lead up to the presidential election. Kompas.com foregrounded Megawati's role as chair issuing instructions to party members running for election. The presidential election in July 2014 became the next major event covered by Kompas.com. Reportage highlighted the darker side of politics, involving bitter political rivalries and rumoured acts of sabotage and smear campaigns. Kompas.com covered the intense final days of the campaign, Election Day, polling results, and the final announcement of the Jokowi-Jusuf Kalla victory.

From the presidential win to the end of June 2015, Kompas.com reports on Megawati focused heavily upon her relationship with the Jokowi government. It covered several political events while implying her excessive influence in decision-making processes. For example, reports on the appointment of Megawati's daughter, Puan Maharani to a ministerial role in October 2014, included reference to Megawati's involvement in the proceedings. In November 2014, Kompas.com reported on the official succession of PDI-P-backed "Ahok" Basuki Tjahaja Purnama to the role of governor of Jakarta after the former governor, Jokowi, ascended to the presidency. As party leader, Kompas.com drew attention to Megawati's gatekeeping role in securing Ahok's selection as governor, as well as details of their more personal social interactions. The nomination of Budi Gunawan for the role of chief of the National Police in January 2015 became a source of controversy in the early months of the Jokowi presidency, inculcating Megawati

46   *News media and democracy in Indonesia*

in controversial presidential decision making. When the Corruption Eradication Commission (KPK) revealed that he was under investigation for corruption[1], reports published by Kompas.com not only reproduced conjecture on Megawati's role in the appointment of Gunawan, but also her alleged attempts to criminalise the KPK to protect her interests.

The final major event covered in the 24-month period involved the PDI-P congress held in Bali in April 2015. Kompas.com focused on Megawati's reinstatement as party chair for another five years, having served in the role since the formation of the party in 1998. The reports called into question the transparency of the internal mechanisms in her reappointment at the congress. Over the entire period, Kompas.com highlighted Megawati's party leadership and her influential role in important political decisions; however, the contents of some reports pointed to her undemocratic use of power.

Tri Rismaharini

Tri Rismaharini was the topic of minor levels of coverage in 2013 in her role as mayor of Indonesia's second largest city, Surabaya. Risma rose to national fame, however, from January 2014, when rumours began to circulate about her potential resignation as a result of political pressure. Coverage in Kompas.com further intensified in February 2014, following her appearance on the popular current affairs talk show, *Mata Najwa,* where her personal struggle was broadcast nationwide. Risma shed tears while talking about her desperate bid to close down the Gang Dolly (Dolly Lane) red-light district in Surabaya, and the internal and external opposition she faced. Thereafter, Kompas.com reported on Risma's personal political struggle against her political opponents who criticised her plans to close Gang Dolly, as well as her troubled relationship with the PDI-P. For the next three months, Kompas.com covered contestation over the closure, and Risma's determination to proceed, protect the children of Surabaya, and ensure the sex workers were redirected to a morally correct path in life. The event culminated with the official closure in June 2014, after which Kompas.com published very few reports on Gang Dolly.

Following this event, Kompas.com focused on Risma's public popularity and potential career advancement. It covered her involvement in a range of episodic activities in modernising Surabaya and protecting citizens, including her use of CCTV technology to monitor the city, the implementation of e-governance, personally cleaning up garbage from the river and streets, defending local parks from damage, and even scolding drug dealers for harming the youth. Kompas.com published reports that drew attention to international recognition of Risma's efforts through the bestowal of awards, such as the Socrates Award for her leadership in the development of Surabaya as a modern and environmentally sound city. Following the presidential election in July 2014, Kompas.com produced speculation that Risma would be nominated for a ministerial position, which was followed immediately by coverage of Risma's rejection of the suggestion. From September 2014 to June 2015, Kompas.com also covered Risma's bid for re-election in the 2015 mayoral election, highlighting the challenges she faced from rivals despite her widespread popularity.

In December 2014, the AirAsia aviation disaster emerged as a major short-term episode in which Kompas.com positioned Risma in a central role. On route from Surabaya to Singapore, an AirAsia passenger jet malfunctioned. When the pilots failed to regain control, it plunged into the Java Sea, killing all 162 people on board. The majority of those killed in the crash originated from Surabaya. Kompas.com foregrounded Risma's performance of duties at the official crisis centre set up at the Surabaya airport, where she aided local victims' families. Overall, patterns in media coverage portrayed Risma in a hands-on role, looking out for the well-being of residents of Surabaya.

Susi Pudjiastuti

Susi emerged later in the Kompas.com coverage than both Risma and Megawati, only following her appointment to the role of minister of Maritime Affairs and Fisheries in October 2014. In the first two months, Kompas.com focused on her unique background as a hardworking entrepreneur who started out selling fish in the market, going on to own a seafood company and her own charter airline, Susi Air. Komapas.com also highlighted Susi's unconventional behaviour, emphasising her difference from the rigid norms of the political elite as well as her public popularity, as discussed in Chapter 2.

From November 2014, Kompas.com began to report on Susi's role in the implementation of ministerial policies. Kompas.com explained in cursory detail that these policies set out to tackle illegal, unreported, and unregulated (IUU) fishing in Indonesian waters; protect natural resources; develop the maritime and fisheries industry; reduce bureaucratic red tape; and empower local fishermen. As part of her broader stance against illegal fishing practices, Kompas.com also provided episodic coverage of the impact of interventions from her ministry, including a ban on transhipment at sea between Indonesian and foreign ships, a ban on trawling for large vessels, the closure of fishing ports for illegal practices, fining fishing companies, along with her stance against slavery. The most visually impactful policy covered in Kompas.com involved blowing up captured illegal fishing vessels overseen by her ministry and the Indonesian Navy.

Kompas.com also covered criticism of Susi. Within the first month of her appointment in October 2014, Kompas.com reports featured the voice of experts who called into question Susi's suitability for a cabinet position due to her lack of qualifications. From this point on, Kompas.com covered criticism of her policies from a range of sources, including regional government,

48 *News media and democracy in Indonesia*

local fishermen, academics, and the national parliament. In January 2015, reports also emerged of anonymous threats made against Susi on the basis of her policies, urging her to resign. Kompas.com habitually covered Susi's direct response to these attacks.

Changing media cultures, changing gendered politics

The online news media has clearly become a new and influential source of political discourse in Indonesia, like elsewhere around the world. Production and consumption habits in an online environment invariably influence the nature of news media discourse, with repercussions for political engagement. In the democratic era, commercial, legal, and political interests intersect in the Indonesian newsroom, prompting journalists to self-censor, bearing some similarities to New Order journalistic practices. Intense competition among news media outlets, rapid production schedules, and demands for immediacy and sensation encourage journalists to tailor their stories to suit a reactive online readership. As a product of a reputable news media group, Kompas.com plays a key role in this new climate of media production and consumption.

For Megawati, Risma, and Susi, their political careers during the 2014 election were shaped in large part by the Indonesian media. As outsiders in the political realm, the three women naturally fulfilled news values of novelty, and their coverage helped support the online news agenda aimed at clicks, likes, comments and shares. While elevating the role of the individual leaders can create intense interest in political issues and prompt reader reactions, such a reporting style can also limit the depth of engagement with events. A focus on the individual politicians can also heighten their level public recognition, but simultaneously increase their subjection to scrutiny. The critical analysis of the discourse produced by the influential mainstream news site, Kompas.com thus becomes a key site for understanding how the news influences the role of women in politics, while reflecting and shaping political discourses of power. The next three chapters present evidence of the multifaceted representations of Megawati, Risma and Susi within Indonesia's shifting arrangements of power, played out in the discourse of Kompas.com.

Note

1 Budi Gunawan subsequently launched a successful legal challenge against the vice chair of the KPK citing a lack of legitimate evidence to investigate him.

References

Alexa.com. (2016). *Kompas.com Traffic Statistics.* Retrieved from https://www.alexa.com/siteinfo/kompas.com

Andrew, B. C. (2007). Media-generated shortcuts: Do newspaper headlines present another roadblock for low-information rationality? *The Harvard International Journal of Press/Politics, 12*(2), 24–43.

Balfas, H. M. (2014). The Indonesian law on electronic information and transactions. *Digital Evidence and Electronic Signature Law Review,* 202–206.

Budiman, M. (2011). The middle class and morality politics in the envisioning of the nation in post-Suharto Indonesia. *Inter-Asia Cultural Studies, 12*(4), 482–499.

Campbell, M. (2007). Mother/non-mother: Ibuism as subtext in the literary works of Ayu Utami. *RIMA Review of Indonesian and Malaysian Affairs, 41*(2), 41–66.

Campus, D. (2010). Mediatization and personalization of politics in Italy and France: The cases of Berlusconi and Sarkozy. *The International Journal of Press/Politics, 15*(2), 219–235.

Costera Meijer, I., & Groot Kormelink, T. (2015). Checking, sharing, clicking and linking. *Digital Journalism, 3*(5), 644–679.

Djumena, E. (2013, May 30). *"Kompas.com," Transformasi untuk semakin dekat dengan pembaca.* Retrieved from http://www.kompas.com

Gabay, J. (2015). *Brand psychology: Consumer perceptions, corporate reputations.* Kogan Page.

Garzia, D. (2011). The personalization of politics in Western democracies: Causes and consequences on leader–follower relationships. *The Leadership Quarterly, 22*(4), 697–709.

Hamzah, S. (2013). New media on the rise in Indonesia. *The Washington Report on Middle Eastern Affairs,* p. 61. Retrieved from https://www.wrmea.org

Hanitzsch, T. (2006). Journalists in Indonesia: Educated but timid watchdogs. *Journalism Studies, 6*(4), 493–508.

Haryanto, I. (2011). Media ownership and its implications for journalists and journalism in Indonesia. In K. Sen & D. Hill (Eds.), *Politics and the media in twenty-first century Indonesia: Decade of democracy* (pp. 104–118). Routledge.

Hatley, B. (1990). Theatrical imagery and gender ideology in Java. In J. Monnig Atkinson & S. Errington (Eds.), *Power and difference: Gender in island Southeast Asia* (pp. 177–208). Stanford University Press.

Hatley, B. (2008). Hearing women's voices, contesting women's bodies in post-New Order Indonesia. *Intersections: Gender and sexuality in Asia and the Pacific, March*(16), 1–14.

Heryanto, A. (2008). *Popular culture in Indonesia: Fluid identities in post-authoritarian politics.* Routledge.

Heryanto, A., & Hadiz, V. (2005). Post-authoritarian Indonesia. *Critical Asian Studies, 37*(2), 251–275.

Ida, R. (2009). Reorganisation of media power in post-authoritarian Indonesia: Ownership, power and influence of local media entrepreneurs. In K. Sen & D. Hill (Eds.), *Politics and the media in twenty-first century Indonesia* (pp. 13–25). Routledge.

Internet users in Indonesia reach 73 million. (2015, 10 March). *The Jakarta Post.* Retrieved from http://www.thejakartapost.com

Jurriens, E. (2011). A call for media ecology. *Indonesia and the Malay World, 39*(114), 197–219.

Kompas.com. (2016). Media profile Kompas.com, August 2016. Retrieved from http://www.kompas.com

50 *News media and democracy in Indonesia*

Kramer, E. (2013). When news becomes entertainment: Representations of corruption in Indonesia's media and the implication of scandal. *Media Asia, 40*(1), 60–72.

Lim, M. (2013a). The internet and everyday life in Indonesia: A new moral panic? *Journal of the Humanities and Social Sciences of Southeast Asia, 169*(1), 133–147.

Lim, M. (2013b). Many clicks but little sticks: Social media activism in Indonesia. *Journal of Contemporary Asia, 43*(4), 636–657.

Lim, M. (2017). Freedom to hate: Social media, algorithmic enclaves, and the rise of tribal nationalism in Indonesia. *Critical Asian Studies, 49*(3), 411–427.

McAllister, I. (2007). The personalization of politics. In R. Dalton & H. Klingemann (Eds.), *The Oxford handbook of political behaviour* (pp. 571–588). Oxford University Press.

Melissa, E. (2019). *The internet, social media, and political outsiders in post-Suharto Indonesia: A case study of Basuki Tjahaja Purnama.* [Doctoral dissertation, University of Western Australia], University of Western Australia Research Repository.

Mihailidis, P., & Viotty, S. (2017). Spreadable spectacle in digital culture: Civic expression, fake news, and the role of media literacies in "post-fact" society. *American Behavioral Scientist, 61*(4), 441–454.

Miller, T. (2015). Unsustainable journalism. *Digital Journalism, 3*(5), 653–663.

Nilan, P. (2008). Youth transitions to urban, middle-class marriage in Indonesia: Faith, family and finances. *Journal of Youth Studies, 11*(1), 65–82.

Rinaldo, R. (2011). Muslim women, moral visions: Globalization and gender controversies in Indonesia. *Qualitative Sociology, 34*, 539–560.

Sen, K., & Hill, D. (2007). *Media, culture and politics in Indonesia.* PT Equinox.

Steele, J. (2011). Indonesian Journalism post-Suharto: Changing ideals and professional practices. In K. H. Sen & D. T. Hill (Eds.), *Politics and the media in twenty-first century Indonesia: Decade of democracy* (pp. 85–103). Taylor and Francis.

Steele, J. (2013). "Trial by the press": An examination of journalism, ethics, and Islam in Indonesia and Malaysia. *The International Journal of Press/Politics, 18*(3), 342–359.

Subijanto, R. (2011). The visibility of a pious public. *Inter-Asia Cultural Studies, 12*(2), 240–253.

Sunidyo, S. (1996). Murder, gender and the media. In L. J. Sears (Ed.), *Fantasizing the feminine in Indonesia* (pp. 120–139). Duke University Press.

Tapsell, R. (2012). Old tricks in a new era: Self-censorship in Indonesian journalism. *Asian Studies Review, 36*, 227–245.

Tapsell, R. (2015a). Indonesia's media oligarchy and the "Jokowi phenomenon". *Indonesia, Apr 2015*(99), 29–50.

Tapsell, R. (2015b). Platform convergence in Indonesia: Challenges and opportunities for media freedom. *Convergence: The International Journal of Research into New Media Technologies, 21*(2), 182–197.

van Dijk, T. A. (1988). *News as discourse.* Lawrence Erlbaum Associates.

van Dijk, T. A. (2000). New(s) racism: A discourse analytical approach. In S. Cottle (Ed.), *Ethnic minorities and the media* (pp. 33–49). Open University Press.

van Wichelen, S. (2006). Contesting Megawati: The mediation of Islam and nation in times of political transition. *Westminster Papers in Communication and Culture, 3*(2), 41–59.

Weintraub, A. (2011). Introduction: The study of Islam and popular culture in Indonesia and Malaysia. In A. Weintraub (Ed.), *Islam and popular culture in Indonesia and Malaysia* (pp. 1–18). Routledge.

Weiss, M. (2014). New media, new activism: Trends and trajectories in Malaysia, Singapore and Indonesia. *International Development Planning Review, 36*(1), 91–109.

Wijayanto (2015). Old practice in a new era: Rasa as the basis of self-censorship in Kompas daily newspaper. *GSTF Journal on Media & Communications (JMC), 2*(2), 66–74.

4 Niche, yet constrained, power: Navigating women's political leadership in Kompas.com

Both mediated and self-fashioned representations of women in politics worldwide exhibit a range of contradictions, dilemmas, and antagonisms as they navigate gender norms and shifting dimensions of political power (Dalton, 2015; Frederick, 2013; Hall & Donaghue, 2013; Lazar, 2005). Recognising the multifaceted nature of power, the historical relationship between gender and power in Indonesia, and the characteristics of the immediate political context, this chapter highlights the pattern of mitigation in the representation of Megawati, Susi, and Risma in Kompas.com discourse. Rather than embedding the leaders in traditional top-down leadership roles, mitigation diminishes the impression of their absolute authority, agency, and control of others, while establishing their difference to the male political norm. The discourse strategies of mitigation have both enabling and constraining effects for the three female leaders in Indonesia's changing social-political context.

As power relations continued to shift and the populist movement intensified over the course of the 2014 presidential election, politicians summoned crowd-pleasing tactics to channel public support (Hatherell & Welsh, 2017; Melissa, 2019; Mietzner, 2015). As this chapter will demonstrate, discourse strategies of mitigation provided Megawati, Risma, and Susi a degree of leverage in this political climate. By constructing their novelty, accessibility, and apparent lack of self-interest, discursive patterns of mitigation increased their popular appeal and legitimised their presence in politics, while creating reader interest. Scholars, however, have turned a critical eye toward discourse practices associated with purportedly more accessible, crowd-pleasing modes of leadership in contexts of social-political transformation. Studies have revealed that these practices can ultimately contradict goals of inclusivity and equality through the subtle reproduction of underlying exclusionary practices, concealed by apparently more friendly, humanised leadership styles (Harrison & Young, 2005; Mayes, 2010; Orellana, 1996; Wodak, 1996). In other words, power relations in contexts of change may continue to exist wearing new masks (Habermas, 1985, pp. 297–298, as cited in Wodak, 1996). Examining the various patterns of the mitigation involved in the representation of Megawati, Risma, and Susi and their

DOI: 10.4324/9781003083252-4

relationship with power in Kompas.com discourse aims to critically investigate its social-political causes and consequences for Indonesia's process of democratic transformation and women's political participation.

As this chapter will illustrate, the practice of mitigation in the Kompas. com discourse can facilitate the female leaders' public appeal by making them appear more accessible in a context of rising populism, but the strategies engaged in the realisation of this practice are inherently gendered. Indeed, scholars working in political contexts worldwide have identified a tendency among women in politics to minimise the impression of their authority and ambition, and instead emphasise their commitment to duty in a bid to appear less threatening to the traditionally male political status quo (Dalton, 2015; Frederick, 2013; Hall & Donaghue, 2013; Lazar, 2005). While enabling their political participation, mitigation can reinforce the gendering of the political realm, where men are allowed pursue power actively, and women are expected to self-censor. Overall, the strategies of mitigation identified in Kompas.com discourse reflect the tensions and opportunities arising from the transformation of Indonesia's political space and the online news media in the democratic era, amidst historical links to gendered structures of power.

Conducted through the lens of van Leeuwen's categories of social actor analysis (2008), this chapter describes two distinct clusters of social actor representations that contribute to the practice of mitigation identified in the analysis of Kompas.com discourse. These clusters form the two major discourse strategies, which are labelled *regulating access* and *constructing spectacle*. The strategy of regulating access erodes the typically dominant hierarchical position expected of political leaders of the traditional elite. Instead, the strategy establishes Megawati, Risma, and Susi's public accessibility, their lack of interest in accruing power as well as their subordination to other elite actors and institutions. The strategy of constructing spectacle contributes to the pattern of mitigation by drawing attention to the leaders' public visibility and novelty. Instead of highlighting their decisive acts of political leadership, it focuses on the women's physical appearance and atypical behaviours. In so doing, the strategy emphasises their marked public status as political outsiders, while lowering their perceived levels of agency and ability to enact direct control of others. The strategies will be explained in detail through illustrative examples, according to their respective *building blocks* consisting of unique combinations of social actor representations that contribute to the formation of the strategy. The functions of these strategies will be discussed in relation to the circumstances of the individual leaders and the Indonesian social-political context.

Regulating access

The strategy of regulating access placed the women in a niche, yet constrained political leadership role that appealed to ostensibly democratic ideals and populist values. Downplaying their relationship power appeared

54 *Niche, yet constrained, power*

to refashion established hierarchical power arrangements between the politicians and members of the non-elite by portraying the women as uniquely accessible, down to earth figures who were untainted by self-interest. The strategy nevertheless upheld aspects of an established gendered hierarchy by downplaying the women's authority, ambition, and agency. The strategy will be discussed according to its key representational building blocks. Illustrative examples from the Kompas.com discourse demonstrate how these representations function to mitigate the leaders' power, and connect to the broader social-political context.

Gendered, familiar, and novel nomination techniques

Through the representational category of nomination, a form of identification through naming practices (van Leeuwen, 2008), Kompas.com established Megawati, Risma, and Susi as distinctive political figures, who were nevertheless kept at a distance from power. In the strategy of regulating access, nomination commonly involved combining honorific titles with diminutives or pseudo-titles (van Leeuwen, 2008) to identify the leaders as accessible and novel individuals. These nomination techniques appealed to populist anti-elite values; normalised the women's presence in the political realm; and lowered their perceived relationship with power. These techniques were particularly prominent in the representation of Risma and Susi. As newcomers, identifying them in such a way contributed to the construction of their endearing public image, while mainstreaming their political agenda. On the other hand, for Megawati, the representations helped navigate her precarious relationship with Jokowi and her continued presence in the political realm.

The use of the formal, honorific title *Ibu* (Mrs, Madam), or more informal, yet still respectful *Bu* (Mrs, Ma'am) attached to a shortened version of the leaders' full name generally upheld their authority, but also expressed a sense of intimacy, especially when used in stories portraying public interaction between Risma or Susi and the public. Excerpt (1) shows the effects of this nomination choice for Susi's political agenda and her relationship with power, portraying her as a publicly accessible figure.

> (1) *"Ibu Susi, Mengapa Ikan di Laut Kita Sering Dicuri? Apa di Laut Mereka Tak Ada Ikan?"*
>
> "Mrs Susi, Why do They Keep Stealing the Fish From Our Sea? Don't They Have Any Fish in Their Sea?"

Taken from the headline, Kompas.com reproduces the voice of a child who addresses her as *Ibu Susi*, and questions her about foreign illegal fishing in Indonesian waters. An adult member of the public addressing a female minister would more likely use the formal term, *Ibu Menteri* (Lit. Madam Minister). The use of *Ibu Susi* in the headline evokes an innocent, light-hearted

Niche, yet constrained, power 55

Table 4.1 Building block 1: Gendered, familiar, and novel nomination techniques

Realisation in the strategy	Function in the strategy	Definitions
Nomination of the women with honorifics such as *Ibu* (Mrs), *Bu* (Mrs), or *Mbak* (Miss) followed by a shortened version of their name	• Establishes a unique, gendered identity • Mitigates their perceived level of authority • Establishes their accessibility • Lowers perceived threat to (male) political order • Normalises their participation in politics by linking their difference to a new agenda	• *Nomination* represents social actors by their name and in terms of their unique social identity. Typically realised by proper nouns, making these social actors clearly identifiable, and well-known through repeated appearances in public discourse
Use of pseudo-titles instead of standard nomination techniques to identify the women	• Establishes the women's novelty and accessibility in contrast to other typical politicians • Creates affinity with the ordinary people based on their unique, approachable identity	• A *pseudo-title* is an alternative, non-official way of referring to a social actor. Simultaneously identifies and classifies the social actor according to a culturally, socially, or politically relevant category

interaction reserved for children addressing adult acquaintances. The report locates the interaction in a public forum about Indonesia's maritime identity and the importance of defending Indonesia's sovereignty at sea. The child-like innocence contrasts against Susi's militaristic stance against illegal fishing. Reinforcing the child's innocence, Kompas.com later describes the his appearance in detail, identifying him as a primary school student dressed in a scout uniform. The representation functions to simultaneously soften Susi's exercise of political power, while normalising her tough stance against illegal fishing, by illustrating both her approachability and the acceptability of her policy even among innocent children. Overall, the positioning of this intimate interaction between a child and a politician within a serious discussion of foreign illegal fishing transcends the barriers between the elite and the public.

Excerpt (2) demonstrates the effect of this nomination technique for Risma and her relationship with power, as a charismatic political leader. The report highlights a humorous evaluation of Risma's personality from a fellow, equally charismatic politician, published as speculation grew over the appointment of the next deputy governor of Jakarta, and the possibility of Risma's ascension to the role. Jokowi's victory in the 2014 presidential election would require him to resign as Jakarta governor, meaning that Deputy Governor Ahok[1] (Basuki Tjahaja Purnama) would replace him, leaving the deputy position open. At the time, both Ahok and Risma

56 *Niche, yet constrained, power*

were gaining public prominence as ground-breaking, charismatic political outsiders who sought to improve their respective cities. The report draws attention to Ahok's rejection of Risma as a candidate on the basis of her excessively strong character, but makes his evaluation appear playful.

> (2) *"Kita cari perempuan saja yang menyejukkan. Tapi, jangan <u>Bu Risma</u> (Wali Kota Surabaya), terlalu galak dia, ha-ha-ha," kata Basuki, di Balaikota Jakarta, Selasa (22/7/2014)*
>
> "We are looking for a woman who has a soothing effect. But, not <u>Mrs Risma</u> (Mayor of Surabaya), she's too grumpy, ha ha ha," said Basuki at Jakarta City Hall, Tuesday (22/07/2014).

In a direct quote, Ahok indicates that he and his team are indeed searching for a female candidate, and at this point refers to Risma through the more familiar title, *Bu Risma* (Mrs. Risma). Ahok, however, proceeds to describe her explicitly as an undesirable candidate based on her *galak* (grumpy, fierce, bad-tempered) personality. While Ahok's unhedged negative evaluation of Risma violates norms of politeness, the more informal, abbreviated title *Bu* combined with the shortened *Risma* alleviates the force of the transgression, by imbuing it with an informal, intimate mood. The direct reproduction of his laughter to follow indicates the humour and irony attached to such a direct assertion, especially given Ahok's well-known explosive personality (Hatherell & Welsh, 2017). The serious matter of the gubernatorial appointment is thus transferred to an intimate and humorous realm, framing the relationship between Risma and Ahok as one built on familiarity and good humour.

In contrast to the personal leverage afforded to Susi and Risma as perceivably likeable, down to earth political newcomers, nomination using Bu functioned slightly differently for Megawati. While having a similar normalising effect, its use helped alleviate the impression of her personal political ambitions, and in particular, the suspected threat she posed to Jokowi's political career. With Megawati as PDI-P chair and Jokowi as both party member, presidential candidate, and later president, the power dynamics of their relationship became increasingly contentious. Early speculation before the presidential campaign focused on Megawati's political ambitions, suggesting that she would run for the presidency for a third time, rather than backing the widely popular Jokowi through her party. Excerpt (3) was published in early 2014 amidst this speculation, but functions to smooth over the suggestion of Megawati's excessive ambition and the apparent threat she posed to the desired political order.

> (3) *Panda: Kata <u>Bu Mega</u>, 2014 Dia Sudah Nenek-nenek*
>
> Panda: <u>Mrs Mega</u> Says in 2014, she's an Old Lady

Niche, yet constrained, power 57

Presented through the voice of "Panda" (later identified as a senior PDI-P member), Megawati is named as *Bu Mega* (Mrs. Mega), and associated with the self-deprecating status of being an "old lady" in an indirect quote. As in the examples above, the use of Bu as an honorific connotes less formality than Ibu, while the shortened version of her name indicates a high level of intimacy. As an experienced, senior female political figure, however, nomination as *Bu Mega* deprives Megawati of her due status. Her apparent self-deprecating identification as an "old woman" (*nenek-nenek*) establishes her recognised incongruity with the role of president on the basis of both her age and gender. Moreover, the filtering of this evaluation through a senior party official reduces her authority in voicing this assessment. Ultimately, this representation lowers the perceived threat Megawati poses to the political realm by downplaying her status, while emphasising her acknowledgement of her incompatibility with a role of greater power.

Kompas.com engaged another, more disparaging nomination technique in the representation of Megawati as a means of lowering the threat she posed to Jokowi and the political order. This technique involved the use of the Javanese title *Mbak* (older sister, Miss) followed by the diminutive, Mega. While Ibu or Bu connote the status of a married woman, Mbak is used generally to address younger, unmarried women, particularly in a Javanese cultural context. The use of Mbak also functions as a form of infantilisation, by denying Megawati's maturity in both age and political experience, particularly in relation to the younger Jokowi. Furthermore, in light of the death of her husband in June 2013, the use of Mbak subtly suggests Megawati's unmarried status. In Indonesia, widows experience acute social stigmatisation. They are viewed as autonomous, yet sexually experienced women and become the object of gossip, jealousy, and general vilification (Parker, 2016, p. 7). Excerpt (4) demonstrates the use of Mbak, and was taken from the headline of an article drawing attention to Megawati's potentially problematic relationship with Jokowi as public support grew for his presidential nomination.

(4) "*Mbak Mega* Tak Pernah Cemburu Sama Jokowi"

"Miss Mega has Never been Jealous of Jokowi"

Presented as a direct quote, an as yet unnamed speaker refers to Megawati as *Mbak Mega* (Miss Mega) and denies her apparent feelings of jealousy for Jokowi. The combination of the stigmatising and infantilising title along with the trivial emotion of jealousy undermines Megawati's authority and potential suitability for the role of head of state. Furthermore, the nomination technique serves to define an asymmetrical power relationship between Megawati and Jokowi, placing Megawati in an inferior role. While undermining Megawati's status, this form of nomination ultimately eliminates the impression of competition between the two figures.

58 *Niche, yet constrained, power*

The use of "pseudo titles" (van Leeuwen, 2008, p. 41) was evident in the representation of Risma and Susi, and functioned to firmly establish their familiarity and acceptance in the public and political realm. For Risma, the title, "the one/woman who is commonly called Risma" (*yang akrab disapa Risma/perempuan yang akrab disapa Risma*) emphasised her level of public accessibility by being "familiarly called Risma." When the classifier, *perempuan* (woman) was added to the pseudo title, Kompas.com foregrounded her gender in addition to her familiarity. The focus on Risma's gender enhanced the impression of her breakthrough status as a woman in the political realm, while mitigating her relationship with power through the portrayal of her accessibility. Excerpt (5) demonstrates the use of this title in a report on a light-hearted public event held in Surabaya to celebrate the Jokowi-Jusuf Kalla (JK) presidential win.

> (5) *Perempuan yang akrab disapa Risma ini mengatakan, pihaknya menghargai kemenangan Jokowi-JK karena itu merupakan pilihan rakyat Surabaya.*
>
> <u>The woman familiarly known as Risma</u> said her party appreciates the Jokowi-JK victory because it represents the choice of the *rakyat* of Surabaya.

Naming Risma according to the pseudo title "the woman familiarly known as Risma" in this context establishes her affinity with and proximity to the general public. In an indirect quote, Risma justifies the Jokowi-JK win as "the choice of the *rakyat* of Surabaya." Risma's use of the historically salient keyword, rakyat (ordinary people) (van Langenberg, 1986) involves the lower-class, yet influential social group in achieving the election outcome, through possessivation in "the choice of the rakyat." Kompas.com thus draws a close connection between Risma and the everyday people.

Impersonalisation in the accumulation of power

Aside from downplaying the women's high status and emphasising their accessibility through nomination, the strategy of regulating access constructed the accumulation of power and success as a process beyond the leaders' direct control. Patterns of impersonalisation involving the removal of the social actor from the portrayal of social actions, were used in the strategy of regulating access to realise this representational goal. Impersonalisation concealed the impression of the leaders' direct participation in the potentially transgressive act of gaining personal political power and presented them instead as humble, unselfish individuals. For women in political contexts across Asia, power is ideally attained and exercised out of a sense of duty and a commitment to the people, rather

Niche, yet constrained, power 59

than personal interest (Choi, 2019; Gerlach, 2013; Thompson, 2013). This idea is also reflected in the residual Indonesian values of *ibuism,* which emphasises duty to others over personal gains. Removing the impression of personal agency in the pursuit and accrual of power thus upholds these gendered values.

Impersonalisation in the strategy of regulating access most commonly took the form of instrumentalisation and abstraction. Instrumentalisation is a form of metonymical objectivation, which involves the representation of a social actor by reference to the instruments with which they perform a social action (van Leeuwen, 2008, p. 46). In politics, this can take the form of a policy, for example. Abstraction, on the other hand, replaces the individual with a quality assigned to them, and adds connotative meaning which serves as an evaluation (van Leeuwen, 2008, p. 47). These two forms of impersonalisation were predominantly possessivised, which included the leader as the "owner" of the instrument or quality represented. Modification through possessivation maintained the leader's human presence in the text, and a limited degree of agency in the events portrayed (van Leeuwen, 2008, p. 33). As the following examples will demonstrate, occurring predominantly in the representation of Risma and Susi's positive achievements and increasing popularity, the impact of these impersonalisations in mitigating the women's direct relationship with power was augmented by additional grammatical operations within the co-text. Reference to the immediate and broader historical context also enhanced the impact of these mitigating operations. The properties of impersonalisation in the strategy of regulating access are described in Table 4.2.

Excerpt (6) is an example of instrumentalisation used to lower the impression of Risma's agency when gaining greater power and authority. It applies to speculation over her potential promotion to a ministerial position in the new Jokowi presidential cabinet.[2] While the pattern of representation reflects Risma's public popularity, it also demonstrates the absence of her direct involvement in the accrual of power and prestige.

(6) <u>*Nama Wali Kota Surabaya Tri Rismaharini*</u> *digadang-gadang menjadi salah satu <u>nama</u> yang akan mengisi pos Menteri Pendayagunaan Aparatur Negara dan Reformasi Birokrasi (PAN-RB) atau Menteri Pekerjaan Umum (PU) dalam kabinet Jokowi mendatang.*

Mayor of Surabaya, <u>Tri Rismaharini's name</u> is hoped to be one of the <u>names</u> that will fill the post of Minister of Administrative and Bureaucratic Reform (PAN-RB) or the Minister of Public Works (PU) in the forthcoming Jokowi cabinet.

Through possessivised instrumentalisation, Kompas.com positions *Nama Wali Kota Surabaya* (The Mayor of Surabaya's name) rather than

60 *Niche, yet constrained, power*

Table 4.2 Building block 2: Impersonalisation in the accumulation of power

Realisation in the strategy	Function in the strategy	Definitions
Impersonalisation through possessivised instrumentalisation	• Instrumentalisation downplays their perceived level of participation in the pursuit and accrual of power and popularity • Lowers their threat to the political order • Creates an impression that duty motivates leadership rather than self-interest • Possessivation maintains the leaders' presence in the discourse and their association with power and popularity; however, conceals their agency in the process of accumulating it • The concealment of agency suggests that leadership was thrust upon them, rather than pursued because of personal ambition	*Impersonalisation* removes identifiable human characteristics from the discourse in the portrayal of a social actor or action. *Instrumentalisation* is a form of impersonalisation. Objectifies social actors by reference to the instrument instead of the person through which a social action is performed (e.g., a pen, policy, etc.) *Possessivation* portrays a social actor as the "owner" of an object, while the object, whether human or non-human, is transformed into a possession or "thing." This process generally semi-activates the owner as the participant in the social action, while the possessivised object is passive. Possession is indicated by word order in Indonesia, where the possessor follows the object.
Impersonalisation through possessivised abstraction	• Foregrounds the leader's positive traits associated with their popularity • Conceals their agency in the accrual of power and popularity • Duty rather than self-interest appears to motivate the leader • Possessivation maintains the association between the leader and the positive traits, but conceals their agency in the accumulation • Leadership qualities appear natural and innate, rather than something pursued and developed because of personal ambition	*Abstraction* is another form of impersonalisation. The social actor is objectified by reference to a quality assigned to them, rather than represented directly as the human participant. Abstraction serves to evaluate, as well as distance the social actor from direct participation in events. *Possessivation* as defined above.

Niche, yet constrained, power 61

Risma herself as the participant in the social process of both gaining greater power and receiving public support. *Nama Wali Kota Surabaya* is passivised, as the phenomenon in the mental process of being "hoped for" (*digadang-gadang*) in relation to the act of "filling" (*mengisi*) a potential ministerial position. The agent responsible for this mental process of "hoping" remains suppressed through passive agent deletion, constructing an impression of universal consensus, without the need to specify the source.

Possessivised abstraction also functioned to obfuscate the leaders' role in the accumulation of power, while providing a positive evaluation of their traits. While possessivation maintained the link between the leader and the quality denoted in the representation, Kompas.com consistently activated the abstract quality rather than the individual in the social process. This foregrounding of positive characteristics contributed to the construction of a form of popular character-based leadership that was devoid of an explicit drive for external validation. Excerpt (7) comes from a report focusing on the endorsement of Risma's leadership by an external, authoritative political figure.

(7) *Ketua Umum Partai Solidaritas Indonesia (PSI), Grace Natalie memberikan apresasi atas <u>keberhasilan Walikota Surabaya Tri Rismaharini</u> <u>dalam membanguan kota terbesar nomor dua di Indonesia</u> menjadi maju dan sejahtera.*

Chair of the Indonesian Solidarity Party (PSI), Grace Natalie has shown appreciation for <u>Mayor of Surabaya, Tri Rismaharini's</u> <u>success</u> in <u>developing the second largest city in Indonesia</u> to be advanced and prosperous.

While possessivised abstraction in "Mayor of Surabaya Tri Rismaharini's success" highlights her positive attributes, her "success" rather than Risma herself is positioned as the recipient of PSI chair, Grace Natalie's *apresiasi* (appreciation). While Kompas.com maintains Risma's participation in the discourse through possessivation, her actual role in receiving appreciation remains minimised through abstraction. The infinitival clause that follows, "in developing the second largest city..." continues the concealment of Risma's direct agency in the achievement of positive outcomes for the city, thus constructing her as a humble, yet highly effective leader.

Excerpt (8) also provides a positive evaluation of Susi, while obscuring her agency in receiving public support through abstraction. In this case, Kompas.com represents Susi in terms of her quality of "determination" (*tekad*). Furthermore, in the clause that follows, "to sink the boats of foreign fish thieves," Susi remains the implied agent as in the example of Risma above. Through abstraction and the use of a passive sentence structure, her

62   Niche, yet constrained, power

"determination," rather than Susi herself becomes the recipient of support from the local fishermen of Bengkulu.

(8) _Tekad Menteri Kelautan dan Perikanan Susi Pudjiastuti untuk menenggelamkan kapal asing pencuri ikan di perairan Indonesia didukung penuh oleh nelayan Bengkulu._

The determination of Minister of Maritime Affairs and Fisheries, Susi Pudjiastuti to sink the boats of foreign fish thieves in Indonesian waters is supported fully by Bengkulu fishermen.

Negotiating power in interaction with the political elite

The discursive representations discussed so far have focused predominantly on the individual leaders, with minor reference to their engagement with others. Keeping in mind that representations of social actors in texts "can reallocate roles and rearrange the social relations between the participants" (van Leeuwen, 2008, p. 32), the portrayal of the leaders in interaction with other social actors and groups warrants further attention, as it becomes a way of interrogating underlying relations of power among social groups. The negotiation of power roles among social actors can result in more democratic outcomes by relaxing barriers to power and provide the space for more inclusive participation (Wodak et al., 2011). Nevertheless, the evidence in the discourse indicates a prevailing reluctance to significantly challenge arrangements of power at the very top, the continued subordination of both the female leaders and the ordinary people to higher institutional authority.

The representations of the leaders' interactions in the strategy of regulating access predominantly involved members of the elite and institutions, members of the media, and the ordinary people. Beginning with the portrayal of interaction with the political elite, Table 4.3 outlines how Kompas.com positioned the women in a mix of active and passive roles, which defined the limits of their personal power along with their deference to elite, institutional power. In contrast to the female leaders, members of the political elite and the institutions to which they belonged were portrayed consistently in an active role.

This pattern of interaction was evident in the portrayal of Risma in relation to her potential resignation in February 2014 due to political pressure. Despite, or perhaps because of the ongoing representations of Risma's vulnerability, her popularity skyrocketed at the time, with expressions of public support for her emerging across the country in the online and offline realms. In Excerpt (9), different role allocations to Risma to that of the PDI-P elite define her vulnerability and subordinate position within the party hierarchy.

(9) _Hasto menekankan, PDI-P akan melindungi Risma dari tekanan dan kepentingan politik apa pun._

Hasto stressed that the PDI-P will protect Risma from any political pressures and interests.

Niche, yet constrained, power 63

Table 4.3 Building block 3: Negotiating power in interaction with the political elite

Realisation in the strategy	Function in the strategy	Definitions
Female leaders: • Intermittent activation in self-oriented mental and behavioural processes • Passivation in interaction with elites • Individualised and nominated *Elites:* • Activated in mental and verbal processes in concurrence with the silencing of female leaders • Individualised and nominated	• Activation in mental and behavioural processes limits agency, but shows human side • Passivation shows limitations of their agency and dependence on others • Passivation indexes the relative power of members of the elite or institutional power compared to the individual leaders • Individualisation and nomination maintain their social identity and prominent status • Activation in social processes on behalf of female leaders establishes their authority • Establishes the dependence of the female leaders on these figures and the institution • Individualisation and nomination showcase their social identity and status as members of the elite	*Activation* establishes the social actor in the role of the agent responsible for a social process, which can be further categorised according to process type. *Verbal processes* are communicative actions involving a speaker, which are sometimes accompanied by the specification of a listener, or receiver of the information *Material processes* have a physical, transformative impact on human/non-human objects, involving an actor and a goal or target of the action. Represents the actor as the dynamic force in the activity *Mental processes* relate to thoughts and feelings, and involve a sensor and an optional phenomenon of the thoughts and feelings *Behavioural processes* focus on the performance of a behaviour, which is generally grammatically intransitive, without a direct human/ non-human grammatical object. *Passivation* can represent the social actor as *subjected* to the actions of others, positioning them as the goal or target of material actions; or *beneficialised*, positioned at the receiving end of a social action directed toward them, such as a verbal instruction *Individualisation*, as the name suggests, portrays social actors as individuals as opposed to a member of a collective *Nomination* identifies the social actor by name and/or title (see Table 4.1)

64 *Niche, yet constrained, power*

Kompas.com activates PDI-P Vice Secretary Hastro in the verbal process of "stressing, emphasising" (*menekankan*). As an indication of his status and authority, Kompas.com identifies Hastro elsewhere in the report according to this full name and title. His verbal activation in this case places him in a commanding communicative role in contrast to Risma's silence. The PDI-P as an institution is activated in the material process of "protecting" Risma (*melindungi Risma*). The activation of the PDI-P as the protector of a passive Risma illustrates the power of the institution in contrast to her vulnerability. Combined with the topic of her potential resignation, these differentiated role allocations emphasise Risma's dependence on the party and her lack of personal interest in holding onto power.

In the case of Megawati, the activation of powerful members of the political elite relative to her positioning in a passive role also served to mitigate the impression of her interest in power. In this case, however, the representations functioned to negate the salacious rumours of her power-seeking behaviour, and by extension, the threat she posed to the political order. This representation was particularly beneficial to navigating her precarious relationship with Jokowi, as well as negative perceptions surrounding her long-term, uninterrupted leadership of the PDI-P. Published in the context of ongoing controversy over her return to the PDI-P leadership for another five years, Excerpt (10) demonstrates how strategic role allocation regulated Megawati's relationship with Jokowi, as well as perceptions of her long-term leadership.

(10) *Ketua Umum DPP PDI Perjuangan Megawati Soekarnoputri sangat terkejut mendengar presiden terpilih Joko Widodo memintanya kembali menjadi ketua umum PDI-P untuk periode 2015–2020.*

Chair of the PDI-P Megawati Soekarnoputri was very <u>surprised</u> to hear that President-elect Joko Widodo <u>requested</u> her to return as the chair of the PDI-P of the 2015–2020 period.

Kompas.com activates Megawati in the intransitive behavioural process of being "surprised" (*terkejut*), while activating Jokowi in the verbal process of "requesting her" (*memintanya*) to return to the party leadership. Portraying Megawati in a self-oriented act of being surprised, and as the recipient of Jokowi's request places her in a subordinate role. Moreover, the activation of Jokowi in his request to Megawati to remain in the leadership role removes the impression of her personal desire to perpetuate her own power. Instead, Kompas.com allocates the responsibility to the president, who ultimately holds the greatest decision-making power in the country within a socially-accepted, hierarchical chain of decision making.

Niche, yet constrained, power 65

Negotiating power in interaction with the media

Kompas.com also portrayed the three leaders in interaction with members of the media, which provided some evidence of the democratisation of relations between this social group and the elite, or at least in relation to Megawati, Risma, and Susi. The direct representation of the media in social interaction with the female leaders provided insight into the self-perception of journalists and their role in Indonesian political life, including how they relate to politicians. These Kompas.com representations of the two groups in interaction de-emphasised and emphasised agency strategically. Members of the media were positioned in a range of active and passive roles in relation to the female leaders, who were similarly activated and passivised at strategic moments. Kompas.com also tended to portray members of the media as an assimilated and functionalised group, represented in terms of their primary activity of gathering news, as an indication of their professionalism.

Excerpt (11) shows members of the media in interaction with Risma after rumours of her potential resignation circulated, and demonstrates the strategic navigation of power relations between the two sides.

(11) *Pasca-meredanya polemik rencana mundur sebagai Wali Kota Surabaya, Tri Rismaharini masih takut diwawancara awak media. Saat ditunggu wartawan di Kampus Universitas Indonesia (UI), Jakarta, Kamis (6/3/2014), Risma sempat berlindung di belakang Buya Syafii Maarif.*

Following the dissipation of the issue of plans to resign as Mayor of Surabaya, Tri Rismaharini is still scared of being interviewed by media crew. When awaited by reporters at the University of Indonesia (UI), Jakarta, Thursday (06/03/2014), Risma hid behind Buya Syafii Maarif.

Kompas.com represents the media as a functionalised collective group, referring to them as *awak media* (media crew) and its members as *wartawan* (reporters). Functionalisation here indicates their professionalism, organised for the legitimate purpose of news gathering. In contrast to the collective media group, Risma is identified by her full name and title, establishing her prominent status as an individual. In terms of grammatical role allocation, Kompas.com activates the media in the verbal process of "interviewing," and in the material process of "waiting for" Risma, who is the object of their activities. In contrast to the portrayal of the media engaging in professional activities, Kompas.com activates Risma in the mental process of being "scared" (*takut*) and the behavioural process of "taking shelter" (*berlindung*), establishing her agency only in relation to personal vulnerability, while indexing the relative professionalism and

66　*Niche, yet constrained, power*

Table 4.4 Building block 4: Negotiating power in interaction with the media

Realisation in the strategy	Function in the strategy	Definitions
Female leaders • Intermittent activation in behavioural, verbal and mental processes • Passivised as beneficialised receivers of the verbal processes of the media • Individualised, nominated	• Activation in behavioural processes highlights their unusual public actions, and novelty • Activation in mental processes provides access to their inner thoughts and vulnerabilities • Activation in verbal processes maintains their degree of authority, as well as a sense of ease in dealing with the media • Passivation indicates a degree of vulnerability at the hands of the media	*Activation* and *passivation* as described in Table 4.3
Media • Intermittent activation in verbal processes in interaction with the leaders • Passivation as beneficialised receivers of leaders' verbal processes • Collectivised, functionalised	• Activation in interaction with the female leaders demonstrates a sense of ease in engaging directly with the political elite • Passivation, however, demonstrates their role as recipients of information from the elite, and the limits of their agency • Collectivisation shows their size and formidability as a group, while concealing individual identities and autonomy • Functionalisation in terms of their occupation indicates their professionalism, acting within the guidelines of their occupation	*Activation* and *passivation* as described in Table 4.3 *Collectivisation* portrays social actors as members of groups rather than as individuals, but does not quantify the size of the group. A form of assimilation. *Functionalisation* represents social actors as the "doer" of an activity or role, such as an occupation.

power of reporters. Kompas.com, however, regulates their power relationship by representing the media actions in passive form, in which Risma is "interviewed" (*diwawancarai*) and "awaited" (*ditunggu*) by journalists. Downplaying the agency of members of the media indicates a degree of continued deference to Risma's authority, while nevertheless cautiously eroding hierarchical boundaries between the two through the portrayal of more open interactions.

As evidence of a more explicit transformation of power relations between the media and the elite, at a lower structural level of the same report,

Kompas.com not only activates the media, but also positions them as the subject of the active sentence, as shown in Excerpt (12).

(12) *Untuk dapat <u>mewawancarai</u> Risma, wartawan <u>meyakinkannya</u> untuk tidak perlu takut. "Tidak apa-apa, Bu. Tidak usah takut," kata <u>seorang wartawan televisi</u>.*

In order to interview Risma, reporters <u>reassured</u> her there was no need to be afraid. "It's okay, *bu*. No need to be scared," said <u>a television reporter</u>.

Reporters are activated in the verbal processes of both "interviewing Risma" (*mewawancarai Risma*) and "reassuring her" (*meyakinkannya*). Risma is positioned at the receiving end of both verbal processes. The replication of this intimate, one-on-one interaction between the media and a passive Risma potentially erodes a perceived power dichotomy separating the elite and non-elite. The lower-level concealment of this representation, however, indicates a reluctance to overstep unspoken boundaries explicitly. This portrayal ultimately provides tentative evidence of the changing relationship between the media and the elite, and contributes to Risma's accessible and humanised, yet vulnerable public image.

Like Risma, the portrayal of the relationship between Susi and the media also demonstrated a degree of intimacy. Susi's appointment to the role of minister in October 2014 attracted significant media attention, which continued throughout her time in office. Published nine months after her appointment, Excerpt (13) initially activates Susi, but later places her in a passive role when in interaction with the media.

(13) *Menteri asal Pangandaran Jawa Barat itu <u>mengatakan</u>, anggota DPR justru sering menyebut Susi Pudjiastuti adalah media darling, <u>pemberitaannya</u> selalu bagus. Padahal, Susi malah <u>merasa</u> sering <u>dipojokkan media</u>. <u>Ranah privacy-nya</u> kadang <u>dijadikan</u> ranah publik <u>oleh media</u>.*

The Minister from Pangandaran, West Java <u>said</u> that members of the People's Representative Council often claim that Susi Pudjiastuti is a *media darling*, <u>the news about her</u> is always good. In fact, <u>Susi feels</u> that she is often <u>cornered by the media</u>. <u>Her private life</u> is sometimes <u>made public by the media</u>.

Quoting Susi indirectly, Kompas.com first activates her in a verbal process, where she speaks of herself in third person and iterates apparent assertions by members of the mid-level elite regarding her status as a *media darling*. Members of the media are impersonalised as *pemberitaan* (the news). Kompas.com then activates Susi in the mental process of "feeling"

68   Niche, yet constrained, power

(*merasa*) where she expresses the opinion that she is "often cornered by the media" (*dipojokkan media*). In this instance, while Kompas.com positions Susi in an agentive role, her agency occurs in relation to the self-oriented act of "feeling." Moreover, through a form of self-fashioned passivation, Susi positions herself in a subordinate role as the goal of the media's material process of cornering her. The activation of the media and subordination of Susi continues in the sentence that follows. In this case, "her private life" (*ranah privacy-nya*) rather than Susi herself becomes the goal in the media's material process of "being made public" (*dijadikan ranah public*). Overall, while this excerpt portrays Susi in a partly passivised role relative to an active media, several representational choices mitigate the impact of the media's incursion into Susi's authority, thus only partially eroding hierarchical relations between the two.

Negotiating power in interaction with the ordinary people

Kompas.com also portrayed the female leaders in interaction with the ordinary people, and the elements of this building block are illustrated in Table 4.5. Role allocations and social actor representations in this case highlighted niche modes of interaction, whereby members of the public were shown participating in political life and gaining access to the female leaders. Reflecting a degree of change to the boundaries of the political realm, this aspect of the strategy demonstrated some fluidity in the interactions between the female leaders and members of the public. The ordinary people were portrayed with varying degrees of activation and passivation; aggregation as a quantified collective; and functionalisation, by reference to their social role. Cases of individualisation and identification of members of the public also occurred, but only on rare occasions.

Excerpt (14) describes the abrupt rise of Risma's public popularity following her appearance on the popular talk show, *Mata Najwa,* which sparked rumours of her pending resignation and the birth of the social media hashtag campaign, #saverisma. Here Kompas.com portrays the online interaction regarding Risma, portraying her and members of the public in a mix of active and passive roles.

> (14) *Wali Kota Surabaya Tri Rismaharini menarik perhatian warga media sosial saat tampil dalam acara Mata Najwa di Metro TV, Rabu (12/2/2014) malam. Kata kunci "Bu Risma" menjadi "Indonesia trending topic" atau topik yang banyak diperbincangkan warga Indonesia di Twitter*
>
> Mayor of Surabaya, Tri Rismaharini attracted the attention of citizens of social media when she appeared on the program, *Mata Najwa* on Metro TV, Wednesday (12/02/2014). The keyword, "Bu Risma" became an "Indonesia trending topic" or a topic that is talked about a lot by Indonesian citizens on Twitter.

Table 4.5 Building block 5: Negotiating power in interaction with the ordinary people

Realisation in the strategy	Function in the strategy	Definitions
Female leaders • Activated in verbal and mental processes • Passivised as beneficialised receivers of the verbal processes of the public • Impersonalised	• Activation in these processes demonstrates the leaders' agency in engaging with the public, by interacting freely and sharing their thoughts and feelings openly. • Activation also indicates some easing of boundaries between the elite and non-elite realms as the public gain access to the leaders' thoughts and feelings, or interact in verbal or other communicative exchanges with the leaders • Passivation, however, limits the leaders' agency, highlights their susceptibility to public scrutiny, and narrows the perceived power distance between the leader and the public. • Impersonalisation inhibits the leaders' direct participation in events.	*Activation* and *passivation* defined in Table 4.3 *Impersonalisation* defined in Table 4.2
Ordinary people • Mix of activation and passivation in verbal processes in interaction with leaders • Aggregated • Functionalised • Collectivised • Occasionally individualised	• Activation in verbal processes in interaction with the leaders demonstrates the agency of members of the public in approaching them, and suggests the erosion of communication barriers • Passivation as beneficiaries of verbal processes from the leaders, however, show limits of their role, and willingness to accede to the elite • Aggregation according to quantity demonstrates size and formidability, but limits individual autonomy and establishes consensus • Functionalisation according to social role indicates social belonging and legitimacy • Collectivisation homogenises the public and political opinion, and support of the female leaders • Individualisation showcases active participation in political discourse, and provides a degree of enhanced social status • Individualisation of stereotypical working-class figures however, limits the scope of their political participation	*Activation* and *passivation* defined in Table 4.3 *Aggregation* occurs when a social actor or group is represented as a quantity, which, like collectivisation, is a form of assimilation *Functionalisation* and *collectivisation* defined in Table 4.4 *Individualisation* defined in Table 4.3

70 *Niche, yet constrained, power*

Kompas.com first activates Risma in the material process of "attracting attention" (*menarik perhatian*), placing her in an agentive role responsible for her rise in popularity. In contrast to an individualised Risma, the public are functionalised according to their "citizenship" in the realm of social media (*warga media sosial*, citizens of social media). This form of representation extends the role of citizenship from the public sphere to encompass the online realm. Following initial individualisation, Kompas.com then impersonalises Risma, referring to her as a "keyword," and then as an impersonalised "trending topic." The public are then functionalised as "Indonesian citizens" and positioned as the agent responsible for establishing Risma as a trending topic, by having "talked about" her. Their agency, however, remains contained by portraying the act in passive voice. While activating the public and establishing a niche role as dual citizens of the online and offline realms, their role in interacting with Risma and collaborating in the construction of her popularity remains limited.

Kompas.com also aggregated members of the public as a large group in interaction with the individualised leaders. Quantification of members of the public as a large group created an impression of significant public support; however, also obscured the impression of individual autonomy among them. In Excerpt (15), Kompas.com aggregates and activates the public in response to Susi's arrival in their far off, coastal community.

(15) *Ratusan warga mengerumuni Menteri Perikanan dan Kelautan RI Susi Pudjiastuti ketika dirinya tiba di Tongke-tongke Sinjai, Sulawesi Selatan, Selasa (16/12/2014). Warga di Sinjai tampak gembira menyambut Menteri Susi datang ke daerah yang berjuluk "Sinjai Bersatu" itu. Saat dikerumuni, Susi berkali-kali tersenyum lebar ke arah warga.*

Hundreds of citizens crowded around Minister of Fisheries and Maritime Affairs Susi Pudjiatuti when she arrived at Tongke-tongke Sinjai, South Sulawesi, Tuesday (16/12/2014). Citizens in Sinjai appeared happy to greet Minister Susi when she arrived at the area titled "United Sinjai." When surrounded, Susi smiled repeatedly in the direction of citizens.

By referring to "hundreds of citizens" (*ratusan warga*), Kompas.com engages aggregation to create an impression of consensus in support of Susi (van Leeuwen, 2008, p. 37). It also constructs the people as a large horde. This representational choice evokes a historical connection to the New Order vision of the people as an apolitical, "floating mass" (Anderson, 1990). The subsequent functionalisation of members of the public as "citizens," casts them in a more socially and politically empowered role, as opposed to the antiquated concept of the passive floating mass. The discourse thus

Niche, yet constrained, power 71

constructs members of the public somewhat contradictorily as a large consenting collective, with a small degree of political empowerment drawn from their status as citizens. Members of the public are also activated in response to Susi's arrival; however, only for the purpose of showing support as they "crowded around" her. Kompas.com portrays Susi as a simultaneously popular yet potentially vulnerable public figure through passivation, positioned at the centre of the crowd. Despite being surrounded and outnumbered by members of the public, Kompas.com activates Susi in the behavioural process of "smiling" in the direction of citizens, as an indication of her benevolence.

The strategy of regulating access also contained occasional moments of the individualisation and activation of ordinary members of the public in interaction with the leaders. While foregrounding their agency and identity demonstrated individualised participation in the political realm and a degree of equal footing with the individualised leaders, activation for the sole purpose of showing support resulted in a narrow scope for active political participation, and the minimal erosion of hierarchical relations of power. In Excerpt (16), for example, Kompas.com identifies and directly quotes an individual, working-class fisherman who speaks on behalf of other fishermen in his area. He lends his support to Susi and her program of sinking illegal fishing vessels.

(16) *"Kami mendukung penuh langkah Ibu Susi tenggelamkan kapal pencuri ikan di laut Indonesia. Kami juga pernah membakar kapal yang mengambil ikan menggunakan trawl (pukat harimau), dan merusak karang, termasuk anak-anak ikan," kata Rustam, seorang nelayan di Pasar Malabero, Kota Bengkulu, Selasa (25/11/2014).*

"We fully support Mrs Susi's steps to sink the boats of the fish thieves in Indonesian waters. We have also previously set fire to a boat that took fish using a trawl net and destroyed the reef, including fish fry," said Rustam, a fisherman in Malabero Market, Bengkulu City, Tuesday (25/11/2014).

When identifying the source of the direct quote, Kompas.com nominates the fisherman informally by a single name, "Rustam," and functionalises him by occupation, before locating him in the context of a fish market. These representations establish his working-class status. Given that Susi was known to sell fish at the beginning of her career, the representation also draws parallels between the two figures, and more broadly, between the non-elite and the elite. When first individualising Rustam in a direct quote, he refers to a collective group through the first-person exclusive plural pronoun, *kami* (we/us/our). This group is activated in the mental process of completely "supporting" (*mendukung*) Susi and her efforts. They are later activated in the material process of "setting fire" to an illegal fishing boat.

72 *Niche, yet constrained, power*

These actions demonstrate support for Susi's aggressive ministerial agenda, and a willingness to implement the strategy at the grassroots level. Kompas. com nevertheless maintains a hierarchy between the fishermen and Susi by positioning "Mrs Susi's steps" (*langkah Ibu Susi*) as the direct phenomenon of their mental process of "supporting," rather than Susi herself. While individualising and activating a member of the working class demonstrates participation in the political realm, it ultimately contributes to the perception of Susi's popularity and reinforces class boundaries.

Constructing spectacle

In the mitigation of power, the second strategy of constructing spectacle established the women's novelty in the political realm, by foregrounding their unconventional public behaviour and aspects of their physical appearance, in contrast to the normative image of the traditional male political elite. Such representations were bound to attract reader interest and enhance the commercial appeal of the Kompas.com reports. While establishing the women's novelty, this strategy also limited their agency by placing them in an objectified, yet highly visible position. The study of visibility in discourse represents a key area in the analysis of inclusion and exclusion, as well as the gendered dimensions of power (Simpson & Lewis, 2005). Invisibility is "aligned with power for groups through their occupancy of a normative position" (Simpson & Lewis, 2005, p. 1270). Visibility, on the other hand increases susceptibility to scrutiny, and thereby social control. Studies have shown that a focus on femininity and women's attributes mark them as different to the unmarked norm of masculinity, and thereby highly visible in the political realm (Adcock, 2010; Anderson et al., 2011; Dunaway et al., 2013; Ibroscheva & Raicheva-Stover, 2009).

Women's visibility is known to create both political obstacles and opportunities (Ustinoff, 2005; van Acker, 2003; Walsh, 2000). For those who were previously "hidden from view" and are now "struggling for recognition," visibility can have positive links with power (Simpson & Lewis, 2005, p. 1270). In oppositional political contexts in Asia, female leaders such as Aung San Suu Kyi in Burma, Gloria Arroyo in the Philippines, Tanaka Makiko in Japan, and Park Geun-Hye in South Korea have all sourced value in the visible state, where their feminine difference helped transform them into icons of change (Bucciferro, 2014; Fleschenberg, 2013; Hüstebeck, 2013; Thompson, 2013). The long-term effectiveness of this approach once the women enter power, however, has been called into question. Some inevitably succumb to the status quo, or fail to transfer their initial moral capital to political capital (Derichs & Thompson, 2013). The building blocks of the strategy of constructing spectacle will be described below in terms of their properties of social actor representations, and their functions in relation to the individual women and the surrounding social-political context.

Niche, yet constrained, power   73

Activation in unconventional social processes

Constructing spectacle emphasised Megawati, Risma, and Susi's marked status in the political realm, granting them some leverage in a changing political environment, while nevertheless limiting the scope of their agency. In this strategy, Kompas.com frequently activated the women in behavioural and material social processes associated with their norm-breaking behaviour and feminine appearance. Table 4.6 details the features of this building block in the strategy of constructing spectacle. In an Indonesian context, particularly in the bounds of hegemonic Javanese culture that permeates the political realm, members of the elite are traditionally expected to display high levels of refined (*halus*) behaviour, which functions as an index of their power and potency (Anderson, 1990). A failure to conform to normative halus behaviour, by behaving brashly, showing emotion, or voicing dissent can erode their power. Within these strict class-related behavioural conventions, women have been permitted a greater range of behavioural styles to that of men as a result of their predetermined inferior status. In the surrounding context of change, engaging in transgressive behaviour may help to emphasise the female leaders' status as breakthrough changemakers. While having greater manoeuvrability, however, engaging in norm-breaking behaviour can reinforce their subordinate status (Berman, 1998).

When examined through the lens of transitivity, the portrayal of the leaders' behavioural and material actions only had a direct impact on themselves. Such forms of activation inhibited the display of their control over others, a key element in the indexation of social power (van Dijk, 1996). Other social actors were portrayed in a relatively implicit role, most commonly as an unseen, ubiquitous observer, while positioning the female leaders as the observed phenomenon. While generating interest, representations mitigated the women's relationship with power, while lowering their perceived threat to masculine structures of political power. The properties of this building block are listed below and will be explained through illustrative examples thereafter.

As minister of Maritime Affairs and Fisheries, Susi's unconventional character along with her policy of blowing up illegal fishing vessels in Indonesian waters received abundant media attention. The capturing and sinking of illegal fishing boats became a vivid expression of her bold ministerial agenda, which was anchored to a newfound expression of national sovereignty within the Jokowi government (Connelly, 2015). Published four months after her appointment, the Excerpt (17) locates Susi's norm-breaking behaviour in the midst of the equally provocative act of blowing up and sinking an illegal fishing vessel.

> (17) *Selain <u>tertangkap</u> kamera fotografer Tribun Batam sedang <u>bersantai</u> dan <u>merokok</u> di atas KRI Barakuda, Senin (9/2/2015), ia juga <u>terlihat santai melakukan stretching</u> atau peregangan dengan kaki ditarik ke belakang dan diangkat ke atas.*

74 *Niche, yet constrained, power*

Table 4.6 Building block 1: Activation in unconventional social processes

Realisation in the strategy	Function in the strategy	Definitions
Female leaders activated in behavioural, material, and relational processes that affect themselves, but not others	• Activation in self-oriented behaviour establishes norm-breaking, outsider status but limits agency through intransitivity • Activation in material processes associated with clothing and appearance highlights visibility and limits agency • Activation in relational process focuses on their appearance and attributes only • Overall, cannot index power due to absence of another social group as a grammatical object • Limits perceived threat to political order	*Activation, behavioural process* and *material process* defined in Table 4.3 A *relational process* involves representing the social actor as the carrier of an attribute or value. Indicated by a verb that assigns a value to the carrier
Passivised as the phenomenon of a pervasive gaze	• Reinforces status as the object of pervasive scrutiny • Inhibits freedom to act without limits	*Passivation* defined in Table 4.3. In this case, the leaders are the phenomenon of the mental process of seeing, performed by a ubiquitous, yet undefined social force
Inversion of social practices	• Emphasises typically feminine, and therefore norm-breaking behaviour in the context of political leadership • The juxtaposition of the women's gender against the masculine political realm legitimises an agenda of change and difference, but does so indirectly	*Inversion* involves the portrayal of two seemingly opposing social practices occurring naturally in the one discursive text. This has the effect of challenging social norms indirectly by normalising opposing actions in a certain context.

> Aside from being <u>caught</u> by the camera of a *Tribun Batam* photographer <u>relaxing</u> and <u>smoking</u> on the HMS Barakuda, Monday (09/02/2015), <u>she</u> was also <u>seen doing stretching</u> relaxedly with [her] <u>leg pulled behind and lifted upwards</u>.

Taking place against the imposing backdrop of a navy warship, Kompas. com activates Susi in the unconventional behavioural processes of "relaxing and smoking" (*bersantai dan merokok*), and in the self-oriented process of "doing stretching" (*melakukan stretching*). Kompas.com overlaps Susi's idiosyncratic behaviour with the detonation of the illegal fishing boat by the Indonesian Navy. In this regard, her apparent transgression of norms carried out in conjunction with Indonesia's defiant new stance against illegal fishing epitomises difference and change, rather than bad behaviour. Moreover, the specification of Susi's relaxed demeanour in the process functions to further normalise the situation and indicate her confidence.

While establishing Susi's agency in the performance of the unconventional, yet highly symbolic social actions above, Kompas.com positions her as the grammatical object in the processes of being "caught" (*tertangkap*) and "seen" (*terlihat*). The act of being "caught" by an impersonalised camera constrains her agency, implies a transgression of norms, and emphasises her exposure to surveillance. When referring to Susi's act of stretching, the stative verb "seen" does not identify an agent involved, which creates a sense of universal access to her as an object of surveillance. While constructing Susi as a prominent agent of difference and defiance, she remains subject to the ubiquitous public gaze, with limited agency.

Activation in material processes relating solely to physical appearance, including clothing choices, also contributed to the construction of the women's public visibility. While activating the women in the act of wearing clothing, the act only affected the self, and provided no means of indexing power. Reference to clothing choices also drew attention to their appearance, rather than their agency as political leaders. As part of the emphasis on their visibility, Kompas.com also positioned the women as the agent in a relational process which highlighted their attributes. The process was often indicated by the verbs, *tampak* or *tampil* (to appear, appeared) to emphasise the women's susceptibility to the public gaze. Kompas.com did not identify a specific viewer when discussing their appearance, implying that the women were subject to surveillance by a pervasive, yet unseen force.

In the case of Megawati, Kompas.com activated her in these appearance-related material and relational processes as another way of negotiating the dynamics of her relationship with Jokowi and regulating the nature of her participation in politics. These representational techniques emphasised Megawati's susceptibility to public scrutiny based on her appearance and impeded her ability to enact direct influence on others, particularly Jokowi. Excerpt (18) describes Megawati's appearance during her attendance at

76 *Niche, yet constrained, power*

the inauguration of Vice President Jusuf Kalla, following the presidential election.

(18) *Dengan <u>mengenakan</u> baju berwarna merah dan rok dengan warna sama, Megawati <u>tampak nikmat</u> mengikuti jalannya proses pelantikan.*

<u>Wearing</u> a red shirt and a skirt of the same colour, Megawati <u>appeared</u> to <u>enjoy</u> joining in the process of inauguration.

Kompas.com first activates Megawati in the material process of "wearing a red shirt and skirt," establishing her self-oriented agency, while drawing attention to the trivial matter of her clothing at an important political event. Through the relational clause, "Megawati appeared to enjoy..." (*Megawati tampak nikmat...*) and in particular, the use of the verb, "appeared" (tampak) establishes Megawati's exposure to public scrutiny. While highlighting her visibility, the verb "appeared" does not specify an agent responsible for viewing Megawati, thus constructing her and her actions as a phenomenon observable by all. Limiting her agency while establishing her subordination to the public gaze in this case lowers the potential threat she poses to the power of the presidency.

Kompas.com also foregrounded the female leaders' involvement in highly visible public expressions of emotion that clashed with the formal norms of halus behaviour associated traditionally with the male political elite. Foregrounding the women's emotion took place through activation in behavioural processes, and through the use of relational clauses focusing on visual perception. The violation of the behavioural conventions and the limitation of agency enabled Kompas.com to distance the women from power, while establishing a political niche relevant to their personal political circumstances. In the case of Risma, the Kompas.com portrayal of Risma's public display of emotion on national television during her appearance on talk show, *Mata Najwa,* cast her in a vulnerable, yet niche political role. Excerpt (19) foregrounds Risma's display of emotion, by activating her in the politically unconventional behavioural processes of "crying" and "sobbing."

(19) *<u>Risma sempat menangis</u> saat bertutur tentang kisah anak-anak yang menjadi pekerja seks komersial di kawasan Dolly, Surabaya. Sambil <u>terisak</u>, Risma tak kuasa menjawab pertanyaan Najwa tentang apa yang terjadi dengan remaja perempuan yang ia jumpai di sana.*

<u>Risma cried</u> when talking about the story of children who had become commercial sex workers in Dolly, Surabaya. While <u>sobbing</u>, Risma was not able to respond to Najwa's question about what will happen to the young girls she met there.

Niche, yet constrained, power 77

Kompas.com connects Risma's actions to the social practice of motherhood and the values of ibuism, by associating her emotional display with the supposed plight of children living in the Gang Dolly red light district. Framing her emotional response in relation to the needs of innocent children serves to legitimise her display of emotion, and by extension her political leadership by reference to maternalism. For Risma, Kompas.com does not distance her from power entirely. Despite highlighting her display of public vulnerability, reference to children as an even more vulnerable, subordinate social group serves as a subtle index of her own (maternal) power.

Somatisation

The strategy of constructing spectacle also engaged the objectivation technique of somatisation, which contributed to Susi, Megawati, and Risma's public visibility, and the removal of their personal agency. Through somatisation, Kompas.com represented the women "by means of reference to a part of their body" (van Leeuwen, 2008, p. 47). This representational choice concealed their human identity and their direct participation in the events portrayed in the news discourse. Possessivation of the body parts (for example, Megawati's eyes) maintained the women's presence, but nevertheless limited their agency. Table 4.7 outlines the features of this building block in the Kompas.com discourse. The implications of somatisation

Table 4.7 Building block 2: Somatisation

Realisation in the strategy	*Function in the strategy*	*Definitions*
Women somatised	• Highlights the women's visibility, vulnerability, and susceptibility to scrutiny • Limits their direct participation in the social actions in the news texts • Text producer navigates cultural taboos talking about women's bodies • Empowers the reader as the voyeur, disempowers the women as the object of voyeuristic scrutiny	*Somatisation* is a form of impersonalisation realised through metonymic objectivation. In this case it involves the representation of social actors by reference to a part of their body. The body, or part of the body, thus becomes the participant in the social event rather than the human
Possessivised	• Maintains the women's presence in the discourse as the owner of their body • Nevertheless, limits their direct level of participation in the events described	*Possessivation* as defined in Table 4.2

78   *Niche, yet constrained, power*

were tied to the individual political circumstances of the female leaders, as well as the broader political climate, which both helped and hindered their political careers. Notably, this strategy occurred far more commonly in the representation of Megawati and Susi. The lack of attention paid to Risma's physical appearance may be explained by an acknowledgement of her outward expression of Islamic piety, as symbolised by her wearing of the *jilbab* (Islamic headscarf) and the modest covering of her body, which has become the norm for Muslim women in modern Indonesia (Smith-Hefner, 2007; Smith-Hefner, 2019). The properties and functions of somatisation are explained below, followed by a discussion of a series of illustrative examples.

The first example of the function of somatisation in Excerpt (20) was derived from a report describing a shocking painting of Susi displayed at an art exhibition. The painting depicts Susi clad in a leather bikini top, leather gloves, a mermaid tail, and angel wings, with a machine gun in her right hand, and a large sword attached to her back. A photograph of the painting accompanied the news report. In the context of contestation over the female body, the presence of conservative political norms, and rising Islamic conservatism in Indonesia (Robinson, 2009), the sexy, partially nude image of Susi defies conventions. The evocation of aggression through the sword and machine gun, however, also channels the longstanding pervasive influence of the military and its use of violence as a mode of power. It may even go further, conjuring a romanticised image of the cross-dressing female warrior, Galuh Candra Kirana of the 14th century Panji Chronicles.

> (20) *Di atas kanvas, Susi tampil mengejutkan. Tubuhnya seksi dan berekor ikan duyung.*
>
> On canvas, Susi appears shocking. Her body is sexy with a mermaid tail.

Kompas.com emphasises Susi's visibility, and makes the point of locating her "on canvas," which de-personalises the subjective evaluation of her appearing "shocking." Next, through somatisation, Kompas.com refers to "her body" rather than Susi herself in a relational-attributive clause, as the carrier of the trait of being "sexy." Susi's body, rather than Susi herself then becomes the possessor of the mermaid tail. Thus, while the provocative image contributes to the construction of Susi's public persona as a ground-breaking leader, the discourse alienates her from the scene. Somatisation also enables Kompas.com to navigate the potential transgression of cultural norms involved in the evaluation of a woman, not to mention a cabinet minister, in terms of her sexualised appearance.

In the case of Megawati, somatisation functioned to mitigate the impression of her power and authority, by removing her as a human agent from the social practice of leadership and turning attention to her body. Excerpt (21) was taken from a report covering the anniversary of the establishment of the PDI-P. Kompas.com reported on Megawati's delivery of a speech, and the emotional reaction conveyed in her eyes.

(21) _Mata_ Megawati _terlihat_ berkaca-kaca.

Megawati's eyes appeared to well with tears.

Through somatisation Kompas.com suppresses Megawati's power and authority associated with the act of delivering an important speech in her role as party leader, by replacing Megawati with "her eyes," which in turn, become the object of public scrutiny. Megawati's eyes are positioned as the object of the act of being "seen" (terlihat), which establishes her subjection to physical scrutiny, and thereby, her vulnerability. Kompas.com activates her eyes in the behavioural process of "welling with tears" (_berkaca-kaca_), which emphasises her emotion, but reduces her direct human presence in the act.

For Risma, on the rare occasion that Kompas.com used somatisation to represent her, it functioned in conjunction with the portrayal of her self-sacrifice in the performance of duty. In the context of the AirAsia airline disaster, Kompas.com depicted Risma selflessly serving the needs of local Surabayans. In Excerpt (22), Kompas.com engages somatisation to draw attention to her weary appearance following a week of ongoing service at the airport crisis centre.

(22) _Tri Rismaharini sedikit bernafas lega. Bersepatu kets Nike diskon akhir tahun dipadu baju dinasnya, dia duduk meluruskan kakinya di kursi Posko Wartawan. Masker dibiarkan terjuntai di leher. Kedua tangannya tidak lepas menggenggam gelas karton berisi teh hangat sembari sesekali menyeruputnya._

Tri Rismaharini breathed a small sigh of relief. Wearing end of year discounted Nike joggers matched with her departmental uniform, she sat stretching her legs in a chair at the Journalist Command Post. A mask was left hanging around [her] neck. Both of her hands did not let go of a paper cup filled with warm tea while taking sips now and then.

Kompas.com first establishes Risma's agency in relation to self-oriented behavioural processes by focusing on her act of "breathing a sigh of relief" (_bernafas lega_), as well as her act of wearing discount footwear, to maintain her image as an ordinary person. Henceforth, Kompas.com downplays Risma's human presence at the scene through somatisation. Referring to a "mask left hanging around [her] neck" (_masker dibiarkan terjuntai di leher_) Kompas.com portrays Risma as an object of scrutiny. Through passive agent deletion in the verb, "left," Kompas.com suppresses Risma's agency in relation to the placement of the mask, and instead directs attention to her

80 *Niche, yet constrained, power*

body. The elimination of the possessive pronoun, *nya* (her) in relation to her neck further alienates Risma from the scene by concealing her "ownership" of her body. In the next sentence, Kompas.com refers to "both her hands" (*kedua tangannya*) which are activated in the material process of "not letting go" (*tidak lepas menggenggam*) of a paper cup." While possessivation here establishes Risma as the owner of her hands, the focus on, and activation of her hands undermines her personal agency. Finally, through the use of the agentless non-finite clause, "while taking sips now and then" (*sesekali menyeruputnya*) Kompas.com excludes Risma as the agent from this process of drinking tea. By reducing her to parts of her body, Risma is thus constructed as a vulnerable object of public scrutiny who was directly absent in the expression of agency. This form of representation served to emphasise her selflessness, both literally and figuratively, as she dutifully attended to people in need.

Discourse, female leadership, and niche power

Kompas.com strategically mitigated the female leaders' relationship with power, both as individuals and in interaction with key groups within a context of social-political change and rising populist sentiment. The women were allocated to a lower status role with limited personal agency, which defied conventions for typical political leaders, while upholding gender norms. These strategies of mitigation nevertheless enhanced their public appeal, or at the very least, helped normalise their presence in the political realm. In the strategy of regulating access, nomination techniques downplayed the women's status, while increasing their accessibility. These representations symbolised an expansion of the democratic political space to accommodate a more intimate form of leadership, particularly for Risma and Susi. In the case of Megawati, nomination according to an informal title combined with a diminutive served to downplay the impression of her political power and the perceived threat she posed to political order and Jokowi, while facilitating her continued political leadership.

Possessivised instrumentalisation and abstraction served to censor the perception of the women's political ambition by suppressing the impression of their agency in the pursuit or accumulation of power and popularity. While possessivation maintained the presence of the three women in the discourse, the foregrounding of the instruments or qualities associated with their leadership functioned to disengage the women from the process of gaining power and popularity. In accordance with traditional expectations of women in politics in Asia, power appeared to be thrust upon them, rather than deliberately sought out for personal gain. Abstraction added positive connotations to the actions of Risma and Susi when evaluating their leadership, while restricting their agency.

When examining social actors in interaction, the analysis revealed a partial erosion of hierarchical relations of power. While other members of

Niche, yet constrained, power 81

the elite were continuously activated, particularly in verbal processes, the women were often silent, or placed in a passive role. The silencing of the women while other members of the elite spoke on their behalf indicated to the reader that the women were still dependent on other powerful (male) figures for full representation. Passivation of the female leaders in interaction with members of the elite functioned to establish their subordinate status and dependence on others for support in the performance of their role, despite their powerful leadership position.

The representation of the individual political figures in interaction with the media provided evidence of the navigation of power relations between these two important political forces. The media were commonly portrayed as a collectivised group and functionalised in terms of professional activity, as evidence of the strength in numbers and their perception of professionalism. While demonstrating some activation of the media and passivation of the female political figures, direct activation of the media was largely relegated to a lower structural level of news reports. Overall, the interrelationship between the media and the leaders appeared cooperative.

The analysis also revealed that the ordinary people played a participatory role in political life in interaction with the female leaders. The depth of their engagement was, however, limited. Direct interaction with the leaders related primarily to the expression of support rather than criticism. Furthermore, impersonalisation of the public in relation to the leaders abstracted their human agency from the interaction. Aggregation of the ordinary people served as a demonstration of the expression of political opinion; however, it limited the scope for active political participation beyond the expression of support. Rare cases of individualisation of members of the general public took place in relation to the display of support while emphasising their subordinate status to the elite leader.

The portrayal of women's agency in relation to their unconventional behaviours and physical appearance emphasised their "marked" status in the political realm. Kompas.com established the three leaders as icons of public spectacle, while the role of the voyeur in the process was never made explicit, leaving the leaders susceptible to wide-scale public surveillance. The implications of these portrayals of visibility depended largely on the immediate context and associated political activities in which the women were engaged. When associated with protective actions for the benefit of the community, highly visible, unconventional public behaviour served to legitimise their agendas. The inversion of norms symbolised a transformation of the democratic political space to accommodate a new version of political leadership. This supposed transformation, however, came at the expense of the women's agency and ability to enact direct control over others.

Somatisation alienated the female leaders from their professional social practices and transformed them into objects of scrutiny. The focus on the body rather than the individual also emphasised their human vulnerability. In reporting on the image of Susi as a half-naked mermaid, somatisation

82 *Niche, yet constrained, power*

also achieved goals of sensationalism, while navigating norms of propriety. The ongoing implicit presence of the agent in the act of viewing their bodies constructed the women in a highly visible public role, accessible to everyone. This form of representation resulted in disempowerment, which nevertheless also served strategic purposes. For Megawati, it had the effect of placing her in a less dominant role as party leader, and as a subordinate relative to Jokowi, which resulted in the disambiguation of their power relationship. While normalising her relationship with Jokowi, this subordination ultimately resulted in her political immobilisation. Overall, Kompas.com cast the women as unique icons of difference in the context of political and social change, while lowering their perceived status, limiting their agency, and emphasising their difference to the unwritten male political norm.

While to some extent the representations indicated a symbolic transformation of the political order towards more democratic outcomes, the ongoing limits on the women's status and agency were evident in the discourse. Their novelty in the political realm was firmly established in the strategies of regulating access and constructing spectacle, which both contributed to the commercial appeal of the news reports and the gendering of the political realm. While women's difference may work in favour of a populist agenda promoting a superficial promise of change, emphasising their incongruity while undermining their ability to act freely in the social-political order reinforces the gendering of the political realm, and limits their true emancipation.

Notes

1 Ahok was appointed to the role of governor after Jokowi became president in 2014. He was later imprisoned for blasphemy in 2017.
2 Ultimately, Risma remained in her role as mayor of Surabaya.

References

Adcock, C. (2010). The politician, the wife, the citizen, and her newspaper. *Feminist Media Studies, 10*(2), 135–159.

Anderson, B. (1990). *Language and power. Exploring political cultures in Indonesia.* Cornell University Press.

Anderson, J., Diabah, G., & hMensa, A. (2011). Powerful women in powerless language: Media misrepresentation of African women in politics (the case of Liberia). *Journal of Pragmatics, 43*, 2509–2518.

Berman, L. (1998). *Speaking through the silence: Narratives, social conventions and power in Java.* Oxford University Press.

Bucciferro, C. (2014). Michelle Bachelet, President of Chile: A moving portrait. In M. Raicheva-Stover & E. Ibroscheva (Eds.), *Women in politics and media: Perspectives from nations in transition* (1st ed., pp. 217–232). Bloomsbury Academic.

Choi, N. (2019). Women's political pathways in Southeast Asia. *International Feminist Journal of Politics*, *21*(2), 224–248.

Connelly, A. (2015). Sovereignty and the sea: President Joko Widodo's foreign policy challenges. *Contemporary Southeast Asia: A Journal of International and Strategic Affairs*, *37*(1), 1–28.

Dalton, E. (2015). *Women and politics in contemporary Japan*. Routledge.

Derichs, C., & Thompson, M. R. (2013). Introduction. In C. Derichs, & M. R. Thompson (Eds.), *Dynasties and female political leaders in Asia: Gender, power and pedigree* (pp. 11–26). Lit Verlag.

Dunaway, J., Lawrence, R. G., Rose, M., & Weber, C. R. (2013). Traits versus issues. *Political Research Quarterly*, *66*(3), 715–726.

Fleschenberg, A. (2013). Min Laung or fighting peacock? Aung San Suu Kyi's political leadership via moral capital (1988–2008). In C. Derichs & M. Thompson (Eds.), *Dynasties and female political leaders in Asia: Gender, power and pedigree* (pp. 191–245). Lit Verlag.

Frederick, A. (2013). Bringing narrative in: Race-Gender storytelling, political ambition, and women's paths to public office. *Journal of Women, Politics & Policy*, *34*(2), 113–137.

Gerlach, R. (2013). 'Mega' expectations: Indonesia's democratic transition and first female president. In C. Derichs & M. Thompson (Eds.), *Dynasties and female political leaders in Asia: Gender, power and pedigree* (pp. 247–290). Lit Verlag.

Habermas, J. (1985). *Der Philosophische Diskurs der Moderne: Zwölf Vorlesungen*. Suhrkamp Verlag.

Hall, L., & Donaghue, N. (2013). 'Nice girls don't carry knives': Constructions of ambition in media coverage of Australia's first female prime minister. *British Journal of Social Psychology*, *1*(52), 631–647.

Harrison, C., & Young, L. (2005). Leadership discourse in action: A textual study of organizational change in a government of Canada department. *Journal of Business and Technical Communication*, *19*(1), 42–77.

Hatherell, M., & Welsh, A. (2017). Rebel with a cause: Ahok and charismatic leadership in Indonesia. *Asian Studies Review*, *41*(2), 174–190.

Hüstebeck, M. (2013). Park Geun-Hye: The eternal princess? In C. Derichs, & M. Thompson (Eds.), *Dynasties and female political leaders in Asia: Gender, power and pedigree* (pp. 353–380). Lit Verlag.

Ibroscheva, E., & Raicheva-Stover, M. (2009). Engendering transition: Portrayals of female politicians in the Bulgarian press. *Howard Journal of Communications*, *20*(2), 111–128.

Lazar, M. (2005). *Feminist critical discourse analysis: Gender, power and ideology in discourse*. Palgrave Macmillan.

Mayes, P. (2010). The discursive construction of identity and power in the critical classroom: Implications for applied critical theories. *Discourse & Society*, *21*(2), 189–210.

Melissa, E. (2019). *The internet, social media, and political outsiders in post-Suharto Indonesia: A case study of Basuki Tjahaja Purnama*. [Doctoral dissertation, University of Western Australia], University of Western Australia Research Repository.

Mietzner, M. (2015). *Reinventing Asian populism: Jokowi's rise, democracy, and political contestation in Indonesia*. East-West Center.

84 *Niche, yet constrained, power*

Orellana, M. (1996). Negotiating power through language in classroom meetings. *Linguistics and Education, 8*, 335–365.

Parker, L. (2016). The theory and context of the stigmatisation of widows and divorcees (*janda*) in Indonesia. *Indonesia and the Malay World, 44*(128), 7–26.

Robinson, K. (2009). *Globalization of culture-sex and sexuality*. Routledge.

Simpson, R., & Lewis, P. (2005). An investigation of silence and a scrutiny of transparency: Re-examining gender in organization literature through the concepts of voice and visibility. *Human Relations, 58*(10), 1253–1275.

Smith-Hefner, N. (2007). Javanese women and the veil in post-Soeharto Indonesia. *Journal of Asian Studies, 66*(2), 389–420.

Smith-Hefner, N. (2019). *Islamizing intimacies: Youth, sexuality, and gender in contemporary Indonesia*. University of Hawaii Press.

Thompson, M. (2013). Presidents and 'people power' in the Philippines: Corazon C. Aquino and Gloria Macapagal Arroyo. In C. Derichs & M. Thompson (Eds.), *Dynasties and female political leaders in Asia: Gender, power and pedigree* (pp. 151–190). Lit Verlag.

Ustinoff, J. (2005). The many faces of political Eve: Representations of Queensland women parliamentarians in the media. *Queensland Review, 12*(2), 97–106.

van Acker, E. (2003). Media representations of women politicians in Australia and New Zealand: High expectations, hostility or stardom. *Policy, Organisation & Society, 22*(1), 116–136.

van Dijk, T. A. (1996). Discourse, power and access. In C. R. Caldas-Coulthard & M. Coulthard (Eds.), *Texts and practices: Readings in critical discourse analysis* (pp. 84–104). Routledge.

van Langenberg, M. (1986). Analysing Indonesia's New Order state: A keywords approach. *RIMA Review of Indonesian and Malaysian Affairs, 20*(2), 1–47.

van Leeuwen, T. (2008). *Discourse and practice: New tools for critical discourse analysis*. Oxford University Press.

Walsh, C. (2000). *Gender, discourse and the public sphere*. [Doctoral dissertation, Sheffield Hallam University], Sheffield Hallam University Research Archive.

Wodak, R. (1996). *Disorders of discourse*. Addison Wesley Longman Limited.

Wodak, R., Kwon, W., & Clarke, I. (2011). 'Getting people on board': Discursive leadership for consensus building in team meetings. *Discourse & Society, 22*(5), 592–644.

5 Between the individual and the institution: Augmenting power in an established hierarchy

In the midst of the intense battle for power in the 2014 presidential election, leadership became increasingly personalised, and the charismatic individual came to embody hopes for change and political renewal while drawing upon crowd-pleasing populist techniques. The personalisation of political leadership is not unique to Indonesia, but is widely recognised as a trend in liberal democracies worldwide, whereby the individual becomes the central focus of political communication, facilitated to a large extent by media discourse (Campus, 2010; Garzia, 2011; McAllister, 2007). As iterated throughout this book, female political leaders naturally stand out by virtue of their difference to the male political norm. When individual leaders become the focal point of political discourse, women's difference can prove to be an advantage. As demonstrated in the previous chapter, representations of individual female leaders can highlight their novelty, visibility, and accessible non-elite status. Somewhat paradoxically, alongside the approachable image of the leader, the so-called political strongman also plays a role in populist movements. Women's role in this enigmatic form of leadership remains largely unexplored, and this chapter contributes new knowledge to the role of female political leaders not only in the Indonesian context, but in populist movements worldwide. This new knowledge is derived from a critical analysis of Megawati, Risma, and Susi's representation in the Kompas. com discourse.

In contrast to the previous chapter, this chapter shows how Kompas. com discourse augments the three leaders' relationship with power, imbuing them with agency and authority to act upon others atop a hierarchy of power. Given the preoccupation with the individual leaders, the individual may be expected to overshadow the political institution they represent (Karvonen, 2010, p. 4). This chapter demonstrates, however, that social actors are also imbued with "an institutional role, and their discourses are often backed by institutional power" (van Dijk, 1993, p. 27). Thus, in the practice of augmentation in Kompas.com discourse, the portrayal of the iconic female leaders also invokes impersonalised sources of power, such as the city, nation, party, or ministry. A co-dependent relationship

DOI: 10.4324/9781003083252-5

86 *Between the individual and the institution*

emerges, whereby the women become the recognisable face of the institution, while institutional power pervades, and underpins their authority and actions.

This chapter describes the two major discourse strategies of augmentation identified in the Kompas.com discourse. These strategies are labelled *personification* and *institutionalisation*. Formed by co-occurring clusters of social actor representations, the strategies reflect the importance of both individualised and institutionalised power to the three leaders' political participation in Indonesia. The strategy of personification represents the leaders at the helm of an institution, as a recognisable individual acting with legitimate authority relative to other subordinate social actors as an index of their power. In a gendered twist, their powerful actions are justified by the performance of duty, the sake of the common good, and the protection of the party, city, or nation. The strategy of institutionalisation constructs a sense of synergy between the leader and the institution, but subsumes the women's seemingly personal exercise of power under the institution. The two strategies identified are often mutually constitutive in that they habitually appear together in a single news report. The strategies occur most commonly when covering the women's practice of leadership, including the implementation of policies and the provision of guidance or protection to other subordinate social actors and groups.

Personification

The strategy of personification brings the identity and agency of the individual leader to the fore, and constructs the women as the identifiable, agentive "face" of impersonal political institutions—a key element of personalised leadership (Whimster, 2004). Occurring predominantly in the headline and lead, the strategy places the women in an elevated position of authority and agency relative to members of certain subordinate social groups, as an indication of their status within a hierarchy. For a news media institution operating in the competitive online environment, focusing on the women as the unique, recognisable face of a political institution also has the potential to increase the commercial appeal of the news reports, and prompt greater online engagement. Personification in Kompas.com discourse involves three major building blocks made up of unique sets of social actor representations that work together in varying combinations to establish the three leaders as authoritative, agentive icons. The building blocks of the strategy will be introduced hereafter.

Individual nomination and activation

A range of nomination techniques served to represent the three individual women in the strategy. These techniques included formal, semiformal, and unique "pseudo-titles" (van Leeuwen, 2008, p. 40) that established their

Between the individual and the institution 87

renowned public status and authority as well as their legitimacy. These titles also worked in conjunction with the structures of news texts in the headline and lead to establish a clear link between the leaders' identity and their subsequent activation in authoritative social processes. Kompas. com frequently used semiformal nomination in the headlines, naming the leaders according to a single component of their full name. Rather than eroding power, as studies of women in politics have previously suggested (Bucciferro, 2014; Ibroscheva & Raicheva-Stover, 2009; Robson, 2000), single-name nomination in the headlines in an Indonesian context[1] served as evidence of their prominence, as an identifiable "household name." Indeed, famous political figures throughout Indonesia's history have been nominated primarily by a single component of their name, an abbreviation or acronym.

This naming pattern was followed by full, formal nomination in the lead sentence, and consistently accompanied by activation in authoritative verbal, material, and mental processes, establishing the women as both identifiable and agentive leaders. Kompas.com also used "pseudo-titles" (van Leeuwen, 2008, p. 41) as an alternative nomination technique used elsewhere in news reports to identify the high-status leaders, which reinforced their legitimacy and individuality. From a stylistic point of view, variation in nomination enhanced reader engagement with the news reports by avoiding repetition. For Megawati and Susi, a pseudo-title commonly reconciled their successful past identities with their present political leadership roles. For Risma, it established her status as a unique, ground-breaking leader. The components of their representational building block are presented in Table 5.1.

Examples of semiformal nomination combined with activation in authoritative social processes in the headlines are presented below. The examples illustrate how the combination of semiformal nomination in the headline and activation in authoritative actions establish Megawati, Risma, and Susi's identity and agency from the beginning.

> (1) <u>*Megawati*</u> *Peringatkan Calon Kepala Daerah untuk Hindari Masalah Hukum*
>
> <u>Megawati</u> Warns Regional Head Candidates to Avoid Legal Issues
>
> (2) <u>*Susi*</u> *Sebut Kebijakannya Bikin Perikanan Negara Tetangga Terpukul*
>
> <u>Susi</u> Says her Policy has Caused a Blow to Fisheries in Neighbouring Countries

Subsequent formal nomination by full name and title in the lead signalled the authority and command behind their recognisable faces. Formal nomination combined with activation in influential actions reinforced the

88 *Between the individual and the institution*

Table 5.1 Building block 1: Individual nomination and activation

Realisation in the strategy	*Function in the strategy*	*Definitions*
Semiformal nomination to identify the individual women in headline, formal nomination in lead	• Semiformal nomination in the headline establishes their well-known public status while denoting some authority • Formal nomination in the lead grants the leader full status in preparation for subsequent description of their actions	*Semiformal nomination* represents social actors by a portion of their name and title *Formal nomination* represents social actors by their full name and official title *Individualisation*, as the name suggests, portrays social actors as individuals as opposed to a member of a collective *Lead* is the first sentence of the news report
Use of pseudo-titles instead of standard nomination techniques to identify the women	• Establishes the leaders' exceptionality and authority • Justifies their participation in the political realm on the basis of their exceptionally successful track record	A *pseudo-title* is an alternative, non-official way of referring to a social actor. Simultaneously identifies and classifies them according to a culturally, socially, or politically salient category
Prominent activation of individual leaders in verbal, material, and mental processes	• Activation in verbal processes establishes the leaders' authoritative, spokesperson role • Activation in material processes indicates their control of others and ability to intervene in the political order • Activation in mental processes shows their personal investment and authenticity in leadership by reference to thoughts and feelings. Indicates the desired moral order	*Activation* occurs when social actors are represented as the active, dynamic force in an activity. Activation is categorised by social process types, which have different characteristics and outcomes. *Verbal processes* are communicative actions involving a speaker, which are sometimes accompanied by the specification of a listener, or receiver of the information *Material processes* have a physical, transformative impact on human/non-human objects, involving an actor and a goal or target of the action. Represents the actor as the dynamic force in the activity *Mental processes* relate to thoughts and feelings, and involve a sensor and an optional phenomenon of the thoughts and feelings

Between the individual and the institution 89

authority and status of the leaders. The following examples are taken from the leads corresponding to the two headlines presented above:

(3) *Ketua Umum DPP PDI-Perjuangan Megawati Soekarnoputri meng-ingatkan calon kepala daerah yang direkomendasikan PDI-P agar tidak mengandalkan mesin partai*

Chair of PDI-P Megawati Soekarnoputri has reminded regional head candidates recommended by the PDI-P not to rely on the party.

(4) *Menteri Kelautan dan Perikanan Susi Pudjiastuti menunjukkan ekspr-esi gembira ketika ditemui wartawan, Kamis (6/11/2014).*

Minister of Maritime Affairs and Fisheries Susi Pudjiastuti expressed happiness when met by reporters, Thursday (6/11/2014).

The use of pseudo-titles is a noteworthy addition to the strategy of personification, in that it not only highlights the individual leaders' unique identity, but also underpins their legitimate claim to power. Turning first to Megawati, Kompas.com occasionally identified her by the pseudo-title, *Presiden kelima RI* (the fifth President of the Republic of Indonesia). This title emphasised Megawati's legitimacy and authority through reference to her historically powerful position as a former head of state, while overlooking her current position as PDI-P chair. Kompas.com consistently coupled this nomination technique with direct or indirect reference to her father, Soekarno and his legacy, which further legitimised her claim to power through her dynastic roots. Excerpt (5) includes both the headline and the lead as an example of this nomination technique:

(5) *Megawati Pesan ke Jokowi Bawa "Roh" KAA Kembali*

Presiden ke-5 RI Megawati Soekarnoputri menyesali semangat Konferensi Asia-Afrika yang dihasilkan pada 1955 tidak terulang dalam peringatan ke-60 yang digelar tahun ini.

Megawati Messages Jokowi to Reignite "Spirit" of KAA

Fifth President of the Republic of Indonesia, Megawati Soekarnoputri regrets that the enthusiasm of the Asian-African Conference achieved in 1955 was not repeated at the 60th anniversary held this year.

In an indirect quote of Megawati, Kompas.com refers to the historical 1955 Asian-African Conference (KAA) hosted by her father, Soekarno[2],

90   *Between the individual and the institution*

and Megawati's request to Jokowi to "reignite" the spirit of this conference in the present day. Naming Megawati as the "Fifth President of Indonesia" in the lead anchors her present-day authority as party leader to her previous role of power. Reference to her father also imbues her request to Jokowi with legitimacy, creating an impression of equality rather than competition between former president, Megawati and the current, widely popular president, Jokowi.

Reference to Susi's past also took place through nomination in Kompas. com discourse, which enhanced the legitimacy of her individual claim to power and her breakthrough character. Despite having resigned from her role as president director of her namesake company, Susi Air when she became minister, Kompas.com named her colloquially as the "boss of Susi Air." This representational choice added an extra dimension to Susi's identity as a minister by foregrounding her leadership experience beyond the political realm. By reference to her successful business background, Susi stood out from other politicians, as an individual changemaker in the new government. Excerpt (6) engages this representational choice when covering Susi's request to the army and national police to support her campaign to sink illegal fishing boats. This policy stood out as a radical, blatantly aggressive approach to tackling illegal fishing and protecting the Indonesian fishing industry and marine environment.

(6) *<u>Bos Susi Air</u> itu mengatakan, <u>Presiden</u> mendukung wacana menenggelamkan semua kapal pencuri ikan. Dengan demikian, Presiden juga meminta bahwa TNI dan Polri harus mendukung rencana tersebut. "Pokoknya, TNI dan Polri harus mendukung kami," ucap Susi.*

The boss of Susi Air says the President supports the idea to sink all the ships of the fish thieves. In this regard, the President also requested that the Army and National Police must support this plan. "Basically, the Army and National Police must support us," states Susi.

Appearing at a lower level of the report, after naming Susi according to her official title, the alternative title, *Bos Susi Air,* provides her with an alternative source of legitimacy in addition to her ministerial role. Derived from her prior non-political leadership experience, the pseudo-title compliments Susi's breakthrough agenda. Drawing upon her past identity also places her in contrast to the traditional institutional power of the military and police she seeks to influence. Through nomination, both Susi and President Jokowi occupy positions of the highest authority, while the military and national police are placed in a subordinate position in the text, and are urged to cooperate with them. Susi thus appears in a legitimate position of complete control.

Between the individual and the institution 91

While Megawati and Susi were identified according to their exceptional past roles in the strategy of personification, Kompas.com emphasised Risma's exceptional present-day identity, by nominating her as the "first female mayor of Surabaya." This nomination choice distinguished Risma from other leaders, and contributed to the construction of her image as an outsider and a changemaker. Excerpt (7) below demonstrates the use of this nomination technique. The excerpt originated from a report covering Risma's monitoring of the closure of the Gang Dolly red light district through CCTV technology from her office. Both the closure of Gang Dolly and the use of CCTV fall into the agenda of change and modern development for the sake of Surabaya citizens. The lead foregrounds Risma's exceptionality through a combination of nomination and her rejection of the supposed standard leadership practices of receiving oral reports in favour of a more hands-on modern surveillance system.

(7) *Wali Kota Surabaya Tri Rismaharini tidak ingin hanya mendapatkan laporan lisan tentang situasi dan suasana kota yang dipimpinnya. <u>Wali kota perempuan pertama Surabaya</u> itu ingin melihat kondisi riil situasi kota meski hanya dari ruang kerjanya.*

Mayor of Surabaya Tri Rismaharini does not only want to receive oral reports on the situation and condition of the city she leads. <u>The first female mayor of Surabaya</u> wishes to see the real-life situation of the city even if it is only from her office.

Kompas.com also emphasised the women's power by portraying them as the main agents responsible for leadership-related activities in the headline and lead. The process of activation "occurs when social actors are represented as the active, dynamic forces in an activity" (van Leeuwen, 2008, p. 33). The highest rate of activation among the three individuals in the headline and lead occurred in verbal, material, and mental processes. Activation in verbal processes as part of the strategy of personification contributed to the impression of the leaders' powerful role as a "mouthpiece" of ideology and strategy, and as a commander of subordinates. Indeed, discourses that have a directive pragmatic function, such as commands, threats, laws, regulations, instructions, and more indirectly, recommendations and advice can help achieve direct control of action (van Dijk, 1989, p. 27).

Excerpt (8) demonstrates the initial activation of Megawati in the headline in verbal processes, highlighting her authoritative role in communicating party ideology.

(8) <u>*Megawati:*</u> *Ideologi PDI-P adalah Pancasila 1 Juni 1945*

Ketua Umum DPP PDI Perjuangan Megawati Soekarnoputri kembali <u>menegaskan</u> bahwa ideology partainya adalah Pancasila 1 Juni 1945.

92   *Between the individual and the institution*

> *Ia menyampaikan, ideologi partai itu telah ditetapkan pada Kongres II PDI-P tahun 2005.*

> Megawati: PDI-P Ideology is the 1 June 1945 Pancasila

> The Chair of the PDI-P, Megawati Soekarnoputri has again asserted that the ideology of her party is the 1 June 1945 Pancasila. She conveyed that the ideology of the party was established in the 2015 PDI-P Congress II.

Through the use of the colon in the headline,[3] and activation in the verbal process of "asserting" (*menegaskan*) in the lead, Kompas.com positions Megawati in the role of communicator, defining the ideology of her party. Reinforcing her deep-rooted political authority, Megawati associates the party ideology explicitly with *Pancasila* (Indonesia's five principles of nationhood) established by her father Soekarno at the time of independence. Her voice and party leadership are legitimised by reference to nationalist sentiment and the sacred legacy of her father.

Similar to Megawati, Excerpt (9) also activates Risma in an authoritative communicative role in defining the identity of the city she represents.

> (9) *Wali Kota Surabaya Tri Rismaharini mendeklarasikan Kota Surabaya sebagai Kota Literasi.*

> Mayor of Surabaya Tri Rismaharini has declared the City of Surabaya as the City of Literacy.

Through the act of "declaring" (*mendeklarisikan*), Risma takes on the primary role of publicly defining the new Surabaya's new identity as the "City of Literacy," in line with municipal council plans to improve literacy levels among the youth. Her declaration thus supports an agenda of change and support for the well-being of the ordinary people.

Activation in verbal processes also emphasised the leaders' commanding role in controlling the actions of subordinates, particularly in the implementation of rules and policies. Kompas.com constructed these moments of authoritative command as evidence of a particular style of strong leadership that benefited the greater good. Excerpt (10), for example, activates Megawati in the process of "warning" (*peringatkan*) party members to avoid corruption in the headline. Given the popularity of the anti-corruption movement among civil society (Gazali, 2014; Schutte, 2012), Megawati's authoritative command is justified by concern for the public good.

> (10) *Megawati Peringatkan Caleg Terpilih PDI-P Jangan Korupsi*

> Megawati Warns Elected PDI-P Legislative Candidates, don't do Corruption

Between the individual and the institution   93

Activation of the three women in material processes, or the performance of a physical action with an intended goal, also occurred commonly in the strategy of personification. Material processes are important to understanding the exercise of power in relationships among social actors and groups, in that they reveal "who does what to whom" (Nunez-Perucha, 2011, p. 110). In the strategy, activation in material processes positioned the women in two major roles: As "forceful," and as "soft" leaders.

Representation of the women as forceful leaders involved activation in destructive processes such as "ending," "destroying," and "eradicating" undesirable social practices. This form of activation was most prominent in the representation of Risma and her attempts to eradicate bad elements from Surabaya, and Susi in her stance against illegal, unreported, and unregulated (IUU) fishing. Despite activation as forceful leaders, their actions were justified on the basis of protecting the public. Risma's direct involvement in an agenda to clean up Surabaya became particularly evident in the coverage of the closure of Gang Dolly red light district. In Excerpt (11), the headline activates Risma as the individual involved the material process of "closing" or "ending" (*tutup*) Gang Dolly.

(11) *Risma Tutup Cerita Gemerlap Lokalisasi Prostitusi Dolly*

Risma Ends Sparkling Story of Dolly Red Light District

Excerpt (12) positions Susi in a similarly powerful role in the headline, activating her in the process of "taking tough action" (*tindak tegas*) against slavery as part of her broader stance against IUU fishing.

(12) *Menteri Susi Tindak Tegas Praktik Perbudakan pada Usaha Perikanan*

Minister Susi Takes Tough Action against Slavery Practices in Fishing Industries

Kompas.com also activated the leaders in "softer" material processes, such as protecting, encouraging, and helping mainly subordinate individuals or social groups. In these cases, the women were portrayed in a constructive, nurturing role. Wodak's (1997) study of female leadership discourse, however, also revealed the use of "soft" maternal discourse strategies as a way of disguising the exercise of authority and control over others to achieve desired outcomes. In Kompas.com reports, these soft actions took place consistently in relation to a vulnerable social group, as an index of the female leaders' power. The headline below activates Megawati in the process of "pushing" or "encouraging" (*mendorong*) women to enter the

94   *Between the individual and the institution*

political realm. The activation of Megawati in relation to women as a collective, positions her in a hierarchical role as a model for women not yet brave enough to enter the realm of politics.

(13) *Megawati <u>Dorong</u> Perempuan Berani Berpolitik*

Megawati <u>Pushes</u> Women to Dare to do Politics

Activation in mental processes in the strategy of personification provided insight into the intentions, desires, and in turn, underlying values of each leader. Activation in mental, rather than simply material processes also signalled the leaders' personal investment in the practice of leadership as a service to the public, creating a sense of authenticity. Excerpt (14) portrays Risma's desire to see citizens of Surabaya improve their literacy, activating her in the act of "wanting" (*ingin*). The focus on Risma's desire presents her as a political leader who values education as an aspect of development. Moreover, her expression of desire is oriented towards achieving positive outcomes for citizens, rather than herself.

(14) *Risma <u>Ingin</u> Warga Surabaya Gemar Membaca dan Menulis*

Risma <u>Wants</u> Citizens of Surabaya to Enjoy Reading and Writing

In the case of Susi, the representation of what she does and does not want in Excerpt (16) below demonstrates the values that underpin her leadership. Kompas.com first activates her in the rejection of ceremonial practices associated with government programs. In the lead, Susi is activated in an expression of desire for programs that actually help the community. This representation of Susi's desire intersects with populist politics of the era and the discourse of change, which focused to some extent on the role of individual leaders in expanding public welfare programs (Mietzner, 2015, p. 47), and their difference to the stagnant, self-serving political elite.

(15) *Susi: Saya <u>Tidak Mau</u> Diundang Hanya untuk Berikan "Kertas"*

Susi mencontohkan, dia <u>ingin</u> program bantuan yang diberikan pemerintah kepada masyarakat bisa langsung diterima tanpa potongan.

Susi: I <u>Don't Want</u> to be Asked to Just Hand out Pieces of Paper

Susi gave the example that she <u>wants</u> aid programs provided by the government to be received directly [by the community] without any cuts.

Between the individual and the institution 95

Establishing individual power in contrast to mid-range elites

Power is not only indexed through personal agency, but by reference to other social groups in interaction. In conjunction with individual nomination and activation, Kompas.com highlighted Megawati, Risma, and Susi's personal power through contrasting representations of subordinate groups, consisting primarily of mid-level political elites and the ordinary Indonesian people (*rakyat*). For the mid-level elite, collectivised representation concealed their distinct social identity in contrast to the individual leaders. Functionalisation also portrayed them in terms of the activity they perform; namely an occupation or role (van Leeuwen, 2008, p. 42), thus determining the nature of their participation in the event. Kompas.com represented political subordinates as the audience of the leaders' verbal processes, and thus in a passive role (van Leeuwen, 2008).

Excerpt (16) establishes Susi's ministerial power through a contrasting portrayal of her as an individualised, agentalised leader, interacting with a collective group of mid-range political elites.

(16) *Menteri Kelautan dan Perikanan Susi Pudjiastuti menyempatkan diri untuk memperkenalkan filosofi hidupnya kepada jajaran direktorat jenderal dan kepala bagian di kementerian di sela rapat koordinasi, Selasa (28/10/2014).*

Minister of Maritime Affairs and Fisheries Susi Pudjiastuti has taken the time to <u>introduce her philosophy</u> on life to <u>the ranks of the directorate general and ministerial section chiefs</u> in between coordination meetings, Tuesday (28/10/2014).

Published in the weeks following her appointment, through contrasting categorisation choices and grammatical roles, Kompas.com positions Susi in an individual commanding role relative to a group of subordinate political figures who take on the role as passive listeners. Kompas.com identifies Susi through formal nomination and activates her in the verbal process of "introducing" her philosophy on life. In contrast to Susi's activation, the collectivised and functionalised group of mid-level elites are positioned as her audience.

Political subordinates were also possessivised (van Leeuwen, 2008), constructed as the "property" of the female leader. The portrayal of less powerful political groups as property functioned to distinguish hierarchical relations of power and reinforce the leaders' control of others. For Risma, in the aftermath of the AirAsia crash, Kompas.com concentrated on her individual response at the crisis centre, including her overseeing of staff. While the previous chapter demonstrated how Kompas. com discourse showed her self-sacrifice and vulnerability, Excerpt (17) below shows how she exerts control over her staff, who are established as

96 *Between the individual and the institution*

Table 5.2 Building block 2: Establishing individual power in contrast to mid-range elites

Realisation in the strategy	Function in the strategy	Definitions
Female leaders Individualised through nomination, activated	• Establishes individual authority • Combined with contrasting representation of subordinate groups reinforces authority • Contrasting representations reinforce a social-political hierarchy	*Individualised nomination* and *activation* defined in Table 5.1
Mid-range elites • Collectivised as a group • Functionalised according to professional role • Possessivised as the "property" of the leaders • Passivised, beneficialised recipients of leaders' statements/ orders	• Collectivisation homogenises group, creates consent, removes individual voices • Functionalisation defines the scope of their participation in politics according to their professional duties • Being possessivised as property of the leaders indicates that they are under the control of the leader, demonstrates leaders' power • Passivation in relation to leaders' verbal processes places them in the role of listener, and not commander. Required to respond to commands, not give them.	*Collectivisation* portrays social actors as members of groups rather than as individuals, but does not quantify the size of the group. A form of assimilation. *Functionalisation* represents social actors as the "doer" of an activity or role, such as an occupation. *Passivation* can represent the social actor as *subjected* to the actions of others, or *beneficialised*, placed at receiving end of a social action directed toward them, such as a verbal instruction *Possessivation* portrays a social actor as the "owner" of an object, while the object, whether human or non-human, is transformed into a possession or "thing." This process generally semi-activates the owner as the participant in the social action, while the possessivised object is passive. Possession is indicated by word order in Indonesia, where the possessor follows the object. *Aggregation* occurs when a social actor or group is represented as a quantity, which, like collectivisation, is a form of assimilation *Classification* represents social actors according to established social categories, such as age and gender

Between the individual and the institution 97

subordinates. Despite the portrayal of her unique, self-sacrificing leadership style, Kompas.com also reproduces a New Order dichotomy between the leader and subordinates.

(17) *Selain <u>memantau</u> pekerjaan <u>anak buahnya</u> yang menjaga posko khusus Pemkot Surabaya, wali kota perempuan pertama Surabaya itu juga berusaha menemui satu per satu keluarga penumpang yang tercatat sebagai penduduk Kota Surabaya.*

Besides <u>monitoring</u> the work of <u>her subordinates</u> taking care of the Surabaya Municipal Government command post, the first female mayor of Surabaya has also made the effort to meet with the families of passengers listed as residents of Surabaya one by one.

Risma is activated in the somewhat authoritarian-sounding process of "monitoring" (*memantau*) the work of her staff, whom Kompas.com names according to the old-fashioned term, *anak buah* (subordinate—lit. child, or offspring), a relic of the hierarchical social order of the New Order familial state (Shiraishi, 1997). Kompas.com positions these social actors as "her subordinates" (*anak buahnya*), whereby possessivation works to index Risma's power over them.

In the case of Megawati, when portraying her relationship with party cadre, Kompas.com constructed a similar hierarchical relationship between the two. Excerpt (18) below demonstrates the representation of this relationship through contrasting representations.

(18) *Megawati merasa kesal mana kala ada <u>kader partainya</u> yang memohon bantuan karena tersandung masalah hukum. Bagi Megawati, semua kader PDI-P seharusnya tahu batasan dan tidak boleh menabrak aturan hukum, terlebih dalam segala praktik korupsi.*

Megawati feels annoyed whenever <u>her party cadre</u> request help because they are caught up in legal issues. For Megawati, all PDI-P cadre should know their limits and are not allowed to break the law, especially in the practice of corruption in any form.

Kompas.com first activates and individualises Megawati in the mental process of "feeling annoyed" (*merasa kesal*). Kompas.com identifies the source of annoyance as a functionalised and possessivised group, named as "her party cadre" (*kader partainya*). Although these social actors are activated in the verbal process of "requesting help," their possessivation and functionalisation according to a subordinate role within the party constrains their agency and status, while enhancing Megawati's relative power over them. In the sentence that follows, Kompas.com reproduces Megawati's commanding role and party cadres' subordination as she iterates the correct

98 *Between the individual and the institution*

behaviour for party members, stating that "all PDI-P cadre should know their limits..." (*semua kader PDI-P harus tahu batasan...*).

Establishing individual power in contrast to the ordinary people

The representation of the ordinary people also provided a strong point of contrast through which to define the relative power of the three leaders. While the previous chapter suggested that public-elite boundaries were undergoing some transformation, the strategy of personification reinforced a hierarchical difference between the leaders and the public. Table 5.3 explains how this power hierarchy was realised within the strategy. Like members of staff, the ordinary people were rarely individualised, but were predominantly collectivised and functionalised. Kompas.com also obscured their identity through aggregation, subsuming their unique identities, and quantifying them as numbers. Through occasional classification, Kompas.com represented them according to generic social categories, such as age and gender, which ultimately reinforced their subordinate status (van Leeuwen, 2008, p. 42). Kompas.com also commonly allocated these social actors to passive roles at the receiving end of the actions of the individual leader. Rare cases of activation occurred only after initial passivation, and ultimately functioned to reinforce the power of the leaders.

Excerpt (19) was published as speculation surrounding the PDI-P presidential nomination began to emerge. The report foregrounds Megawati's goal of promoting youth leadership within the PDI-P, which potentially assuages fears of her ambition to run again for the presidency, while reinforcing her powerful role as party leader by reference to a subordinate social group.

> (19) *Ketua Umum Partai Demokrasi Indonesia Perjuangan Megawati Soekarnoputri, mengaku selalu berupaya <u>mendorong anak muda</u> untuk menyiapkan diri <u>menjadi pemimpin</u>, sehingga bisa <u>meneruskan cita-cita proklamasi</u>.*
>
> Chair of the Indonesian Democratic Party of Struggle, Megawati Soekarnoputri has admitted that she always makes the effort to <u>push young people</u> (lit. young children) to prepare themselves to <u>become leaders</u>, so [they] can <u>continue the goals of proclamation</u>.

While Megawati is individualised, nominated, and activated in the verbal process of "admitting" (*mengaku*) and the material process of "pushing" (*mendorong*), Kompas.com represents those subjected to Megawati's action as a collective group classified as "young people." As a social category, the youth are ranked at a much lower level to the members of the political elite (Parker & Nilan, 2013). Describing them as *anak muda* (young people— lit. young children) rather than the more politically-infused term, *pemuda* (youth) emphasises their subordinate status. While considered political

Between the individual and the institution 99

Table 5.3 Building block 3: Establishing individual power in contrast to the ordinary people

Realisation in the strategy	Function in the strategy	Definitions
Female leaders Individualised, nominated, and activated in verbal and material processes	• Individualisation and nomination establish authoritative identity • Activation in verbal processes positions leaders in authoritative spokesperson role, and ability to address others freely • Activation in material processes indicates the leaders' transformative ability to intervene in the lives of others, and thus indicates their greater power	*Individualised nomination* defined in Table 5.1 *Activation* defined in 5.1
Ordinary people: • Collectivised as a group • Aggregated as a large number • Classified according to working-class or vulnerable social status • Functionalised according to social role • Passivised • Possessivised • Conditionally individualised	• Collectivisation homogenises members of the public, creates consent, and removes individual voices • Aggregation removes individual identity, suggests size without need for specificity • Classification indicates the subordinate status of the people, and their lower status justifies their reliance on the leaders for help • Functionalisation channels the activities of the people into prescribed social roles • Passivation indicates lack of agency • Possessivation shows their lack of autonomy, and subjection to the control of more powerful forces Individualisation creates a human-interest story, but only occurs on the condition of subordination in the events portrayed	*Collectivisation, aggregation, classification, functionalisation, passivation* and *possessivation* all defined in Table 5.2

100 *Between the individual and the institution*

subordinates, the youth have long been regarded as a potential source of political action in Indonesia (Jackson, 2005). Their subjection in relation to Megawati's process of pushing, however, reinforces a power asymmetry between the PDI-P leader and the youth. While initially subjected, the subsequent activation of the youth in the process of "becoming leaders" (*menjadi pemimpin*) is evidence of their potential political value, but only takes place only following their subjection. Furthermore, through agent elimination, the agent responsible for ultimately "continuing the goals of proclamation" is obscured and thus becomes an ambiguous process. Megawati ultimately takes on a leading role in directing the youth and expressing party ideology, while they bend to her will.

Kompas.com also portrayed Risma in a powerful role, directing the future outcomes for residents of Surabaya. As the closure of Gang Dolly approached, Kompas.com drew attention to her individual efforts to ensure the wellbeing of the residents of the red light district, while regulating their activities. In Excerpt (20), through the aggregation and passivation of the residents and the contrasting individualisation and activation of Risma, Kompas.com constructs an asymmetrical power relationship between the two.

(20) *Wali Kota Surabaya Tri Rismaharini <u>mengirim</u> <u>sejumlah warga</u> di eks lokalisasi prostitusi Dolly untuk belajar tentang batu mulia atau akik ke Pacitan dan Kalimantan.*

Mayor of Surabaya Tri Rismaharini <u>has sent a number of residents</u> from the former Dolly prostitution zone to learn about precious stones in Pacitan and Kalimantan.

Here, Risma "sends" (*mengirim*) the residents of Gang Dolly to a vocational educational course. The differentiated grammatical roles clearly define Risma's power and agency, and diminish that of the residents who are subjected to her action. Moreover, Kompas.com aggregates these residents according to the indefinite quantifier, *sejumlah* (a number of). Aggregation thus conceals their identity while emphasising Risma's. Furthermore, through reference to a vague quantity of social actors, Risma's efforts appear substantial without providing specific evidence.

Rare cases of individualisation and nomination of the ordinary people took place in the strategy of personification. This representational operation occurred in human interest stories that functioned as a small scale "case study" of the leaders' good deeds. In such examples, despite identifying these social actors, Kompas.com positioned them in a passive role. This practice was most common in the portrayal of Risma. As a local level politician, Risma's leadership focused more on grassroots engagement. Excerpt (21) describes Risma's efforts to return an Indonesian migrant worker trapped by her employers in Malaysia. Indonesian migrant workers are still predominantly women who work in the informal sector. Many of them experience exploitation, sexual violence, trafficking, and criminalisation (Komnas Perempuan, 2014).

> (21) *Wali Kota Surabaya Tri Rismaharini mengaku tidak mudah memulangkan warganya, Anies Deka Sany (21), yang terkatung-katung di Malaysia, untuk kembali ke Tanah Air.*
>
> Mayor of Surabaya Tri Rismaharini has <u>admitted</u> that it was not easy <u>returning her citizen,</u> Anies Deka Sany (21), to her homeland, who was in limbo in Malaysia.

Kompas.com activates Risma in the verbal process of "admitting" and the material process of "returning" (*memulangkan*) "her citizen" (*warganya*) to Indonesia. While Kompas.com nominates the citizen formally as Anies Deka Sany, through possessivation she becomes "property" of Risma. Moreover, by portraying her as the goal in the process of Risma's act of "returning" her, Kompas.com positions Anies in a passive role, dependent on Risma's intervention. Rather than highlighting Anies' struggle in Malaysia, the complete report continues to foreground Risma's role in helping her, perpetuating a relationship of dependence between vulnerable citizens and their strong, yet caring leader. A similar weak-strong dichotomy between the leader and citizens is evident in the strategy of *constructing threat*, discussed in Chapter 6.

Institutionalisation

While personification gave the impression that the female leaders were the individuals responsible for important political actions, institutionalisation alluded to the pervasive role of institutions, such as the party, city, or national government in determining political outcomes. Indeed, news values about newsworthiness do not only display "attention for and the interests of various elite actors, but also institutions" (van Dijk, 1989, p. 26). Frequently coinciding with the first strategy of personification, institutionalisation served to anchor the personal power of the individual leaders to institutional power, while giving the institutions a recognisable, commercially viable "face."

Institutionalisation was thus commonly realised through the consecutive, interchangeable activation of the leader and the institution in shared social processes, and through impersonalised representations of social actors and their actions, often in the form of objectifications or nominalisations. While the standard concept of institutionalisation involves impersonalised representations of social actors in terms of their institutional belonging, this strategy in Kompas.com reports incorporated the additional practice of consecutive activation. Together, both forms of representation collapsed

102   *Between the individual and the institution*

the distinction between the leader and the institution, and mystified the true agency and identity of those responsible for political actions. This process of mystification in Kompas.com reports removed space for dissent, while reinforcing hierarchical relations of power and the gap between the public and the elite.

Consecutive activation of the individual and the institution

Consecutive activation generally foregrounded the individual leaders as agents in the headline and lead through personification, before reconfiguring their participation in events through the activation of institutions they represent in a shared social process. The elements of this building block are illustrated in Table 5.4. Given the influence of headlines in determining topical content and influencing recall (van Dijk, 1988), the initial positioning of the leaders as the individual agent in the headline created the impression of power emanating from individual to institution. Occurring predominantly in the representation of political newcomers, Risma and Susi, this collective representation of agency created a sense of synergy between the leader and the organisation. In this regard, while Kompas.com foregrounded the identity of the individual leaders, their ability to act, influence others, and achieve social outcomes took place in alignment with the institution. Overall, this form of representation served to support the authority of the three leaders and give institutions a recognisable public face, all while maintaining the underlying pervasiveness of institutional power behind their leadership.

Table 5.4 Building block 1: Consecutive activation of the individual and the institution

Realisation in the strategy	Function in the strategy	Definitions
Consecutive activation of individual leaders and institutions in shared social processes	• Establishes synergy between the individual and institution • Mutually reinforces their power • Endows institutions with a recognisable human face • Mystifies agency and responsibility for social actions • Adds commercial appeal to the story, making institutions more personalised	*Activation* defined in Table 5.1 A novel variation on van Leeuwen's SFL-derived concept of activation, *consecutive activation* involves initial activation of either the individual leader or the institution in a social process, followed by activation of the counterpart in the same or similar social process. E.g., Activation of the leader in a mental process in the headline, followed by activation of the city in the same or similar mental process elsewhere in the report

Between the individual and the institution 103

A highly illustrative example of consecutive activation can be found in excerpt (22) which combines the headline and lead of a report documenting the final stage in the closure of Gang Dolly.

(22) *Risma <u>Tutup</u> Cerita Gemerlap Lokalisasi Prostitusi Dolly*

> *Rabu (18/6/2014) ini bakal menjadi hari yang bersejarah bagi warga Surabaya dan dunia prostitusi. Sebab, lokalisasi yang konon terbesar di Asia Tenggara, yakni lokalisasi Dolly, <u>ditutup oleh pemerintah Kota Surabaya</u>.*

Risma <u>Ends</u> Sparkling Story of Dolly Red Light District

> This Wednesday (18/6/2014) will become a historical day for the citizens of Surabaya and the world of prostitution. This is because the red-light district known apparently as the largest in Southeast Asia, that is, Dolly, will be <u>closed by the Surabaya Municipal government</u>.

The headline discussed previously as Excerpt (11) first individualises Risma and activates her in the material process of "ending/closing" (tutup) the story of Dolly red light district. In contrast to the headline, the lead passage positions the "Surabaya Municipal government" as the agent responsible for the closure of Gang Dolly, activated in the same material process of "closing" Dolly. The sharing of the same material process between Risma and the municipal government establishes synergy between the individual and the institution, adding certainty to the imminent closure while strengthening the perception of Risma's leading role.

Kompas.com also merged Susi's agency with the Ministry of Maritime Affairs and Fisheries. Excerpt (23) demonstrates the exchange of agency from the headline to the lead. Based on Susi's address to the National Movement for the Protection of Natural Resources, the headline first activates Susi in the material process of "cooperating" (*gandeng*) with the widely popular Corruption Eradication Commission KPK to implement "Jokowi's maritime vision." In contrast to the headline, the lead activates the institution of Maritime Affairs and Fisheries in the similar material process of "synergising" (*bersinergi*) with the KPK to implement this vision, thus assimilating Susi's agency and personal vision with the institutional authority of the ministry, which creates an impression of coherence between the two, as well as their mutual support for President Jokowi.

(23) *Kawal Visi Kelautan Jokowi, Menteri Susi <u>Gandeng</u> KPK*

> *Kementrian Kelautan dan Perikanan (KKP) <u>bersinergi</u> dengan Komisi Pemberantasan Korupsi (KPK) dalam upaya mengawal visi*

104　*Between the individual and the institution*

> *Presiden Joko Widodo (Jokowi) menjadikan laut sebagai masa depan peradaban bangsa.*

Guarding Jokowi's Maritime Vision, Minister Susi <u>Cooperates</u> with KPK

The Ministry of Maritime Affairs and Fisheries (KKP) is <u>synergising</u> with the Corruption Eradication Commission (KPK) in an effort to implement the vision of President Joko Widodo (Jokowi) to transform the sea into the future of civilisation of the nation.

Impersonalisation of social actors and institutions

Institutionalisation also took place through the impersonalised, de-agentalised representations of social actors and their actions. This practice frequently followed the initial identification and activation of the individual leaders, and involved a transfer of personal agency from the individual to the impersonal realm of the political institution. The abstraction of human agency in impersonalising representations eliminates the factors of modality and tense, which removes any questions of certainty, while constructing an ahistorical, continuous reality around social events (Fairclough, 2001). Such representations blur lines of responsibility, conceal divisions, or weaknesses in political activities, and thereby contribute to the manufacture of consent (Fairclough, 2003). Impersonalisation permeates the language of bureaucracy, a social practice that is defined by "the denial of responsibility and governed by impersonal procedures which are impermeable to human agency once put in place" (van Leeuwen, 2008, p. 47). Bureaucratic discourses construct complicity and reciprocal power relations which are crucial to underpinning and maintaining institutional and hierarchical power arrangements (Iedema, 1998).

Impersonalisation in the case of institutionalisation was realised in two ways. First, through the metonymic objectivations of spatialisation and instrumentalisation, Kompas.com portrayed social actors by means of reference to a *place* or *instrument* "closely associated with their person, or with the action in which they were engaged" (van Leeuwen, 2008, p. 46). Secondly, impersonalisation was achieved through the use of grammatical operations that eliminated human agency, namely, nominalisation and passive agent deletion. The omission of agency and tense avoided the need to specify actual responsibility or allocate a timeline to implement planned actions. Table 5.5 explains the elements that form this building block and its particular functions.

Beginning with spatialisation, Kompas.com created an impression of synergy and consensus between the leader, the space they govern, and the inhabitants of this space. Activation of spaces was particularly influential in that it played upon either nationalist or localist sentiment; two key ideological concepts of citizenship and political discourse in the post-authoritarian

Table 5.5 Building block 2: Impersonalisation of social actors and institutions

Realisation in the strategy	Function in the strategy	Definitions
Spatialisation	Spatialisation establishes consensus among leader, government, nation/city, and population by removing human identity, and subsuming it within a place. Individual agency thus disappears, and it appears, for example, that the city is representing the will of the people.	*Spatialisation* is an impersonalising metonymic representation that represents social actors by means of reference to a place in which they are closely associated (e.g., a country or city). The place becomes the social actor rather than the human.
Instrumentalisation	Instrumentalisation maintains detached, impersonal authority and obfuscates agency by removing human identity. The instrument becomes the main actor in the event portrayed, subsuming human agents within.	*Instrumentalisation* is another impersonalising metonymic representation of social actors by reference to a tool or object with which they perform an activity (e.g., a policy)
Nominalisation	Nominalisation of actions erases human agency, responsibility, modality, and temporality. Confounds the role of the individual, institution, and broader society, leading to consent through mystification	*Nominalisation* is an impersonalising linguistic operation that transforms a verb into a noun, and in so doing, suppresses important information such as agency, modality, and tense. E.g., *pembangunan* (development), derived from the transitive verb, *membangun* (to build).
Passive agent deletion	Passive agent deletion removes the human agent responsible, thus generalising the performance of actions, or concealing the identity of the agent	*Passive agent deletion* is another linguistic operation that omits the agent responsible for a social action conveyed in the verb. Realised in Indonesian by word order: object + verb, and attaching the *di-* or *ter-* prefix to the verb, while omitting the agent

era (Robinson, 2014). While constructing an impression of inclusivity and consensus among inhabitants, it led to a great deal of ambivalence surrounding the allocation of roles to the government, nation or city, and citizens, leading to a potentially more coercive form of power (Fairclough, 2000, pp. 34–35). A salient example of the role of spatialisation at the local

106 *Between the individual and the institution*

level can be found in Excerpt (24) below, which comes from the same report as Excerpt (22), covering the closure of Gang Dolly.

> (24) *Mulai hari ini, <u>Kota Pahlawan</u> ini <u>ingin</u> mengubah sebutan kota seribu Pekerja Seks Komersial (PSK) dengan kota budaya. <u>Wali Kota Tri Rismaharini menginginkan</u>, saat orang berbicara soal Surabaya, bukan lokalisasinya yang disebut-sebut, tapi budayanya.*
>
> Today <u>the City of Heroes</u> wishes to change its nickname from the city of a thousand Commercial Sex Workers to the city of culture. <u>Mayor Tri Rismaharini hopes</u> that when people speak of Surabaya, they don't mention the red-light district, but rather, its culture.

In this excerpt, Kompas.com activates the city of Surabaya and Risma in a shared social process. Named according to its patriotic historical title, *Kota Pahlawan* (City of Heroes), dating back to the Indonesian National Revolution, this label channels both contemporary localist and historical nationalist sentiment. Kompas.com activates the "City of Heroes" in the mental process of "wishing/hoping" (*menginginkan*) to change its supposed unofficial title, from "city of a thousand commercial sex workers" (*kota seribu Pekerja Seks Komersial*) to the "city of culture" (*kota budaya*). The agency and identity of the individual residents of Surabaya are subsumed under the title of the city to create the impression of consensus on the desire for the closure. Kompas.com demonstrates consensus between both Risma and the city by activating her in the similar mental process of "hoping" (*menginginkan*) in the next sentence.

On a national level, reference to Indonesia, and by extension all its inhabitants, blurred the demarcation between the vision of the leader and the ordinary people, constructing an impression of participatory democracy while simultaneously concealing alternative, dissenting voices. In Excerpt (25), through spatialisation, Megawati refers to a leadership crisis taking place in Indonesia.

> (25) *Megawati menuturkan, <u>Indonesia</u> kini tengah mengalami krisis pemimpin berkarakter.*
>
> Megawati stated that <u>Indonesia</u> is currently experiencing a leadership crisis (lit. a crisis of leaders of good character).

Indonesia is activated as the "senser" in the mental process of "experiencing" (*mengalami*) a leadership crisis, which inculcates all citizens in this process. Failure to agree thus renders the individual as a "non-citizen." Published in the context of the imminent presidential election, this assertion functions as an indirect endorsement of the presidential candidate, Jokowi as a solution to this perceived crisis. The actual crisis

Between the individual and the institution 107

to which Megawati refers, however, remains vague and a product of her own opinion.

In addition to the impersonal representational choice of spatialisation, Kompas.com engaged instrumentalisation to portray social actors by reference to the instruments through which they performed a task (van Leeuwen, 2008, p. 46). This representational choice often co-occurred with passive agent deletion and nominalisation. It functioned to construct impersonal authority, obfuscate agency and responsibility, and minimise room for dissent through generalisation. Excerpt (26) demonstrates how instrumentalisation follows the initial individual activation of Risma to construct a seamless link between individual and institutional authority in relation to the modern practice of e-governance in Surabaya, and more implicitly, control of the population. This process of impersonalisation avoids the specification of details of the program, while removing space for doubt about its effectiveness.

(26) *Di dalam seminar,* <u>*Risma mempresentasikan*</u> *bahwa* <u>*mekanisme*</u> <u>*kerja Pemkot Surabaya*</u> *banyak* <u>*dilakukan*</u> *dengan berbasis elektronik. Misalnya, kata Risma,* <u>*pengurusan izin pembangunan usaha*</u>

In the seminar, <u>Risma explained</u> that many of the <u>mechanisms of the Surabaya Municipal Government</u> are <u>done</u> on an electronic basis. For example, said Risma, the <u>organisation of business development permits</u>.

Following the personification of Risma, Kompas.com engages the strategy of institutionalisation, which results in the concealment of agency and individual identity. Kompas.com first realises this by reference to the instrumentalised *mekanisme kerja* (mechanisms) of the municipal government. Rather than a social actor, these "mechanisms" are enacted in the agentless passive verb, *dilakukan* (done). Agency remains suppressed when specifying Risma's example of business permits through nominalisation in *pengurususan* (the organisation of) and *pembangunan* (the development of). This grammatical operation transfers these tasks to the impersonalised domain of bureaucracy. Nominalisation also lends a sense of timelessness to the performance of these tasks, while concealing individual responsibility. While Risma does the explaining, the allocation of roles and the process of carrying out the tasks remains hidden.

Excerpt (27) portrays Susi and her apparent concern for the well-being of working-class fishermen. In the representation of her leadership of the Ministry of Maritime Affairs and Fisheries, Kompas.com emphasised Susi's proximity to the people, and in this case, her concern for the rights of vulnerable, traditional working-class fishermen (*nelayan*). The excerpt describes Susi's response to complaints from local fishermen regarding the impact of large fishing boats in their waters. The grammatical operations

108　*Between the individual and the institution*

of nominalisation and passive agent deletion, however, also result in the obfuscation of power and responsibility.

(27) *Perlindungan terhadap nelayan kecil, lanjut Susi, diharapkan bisa diwujudkan dalam bentuk Perda (peraturan Daerah) di masing-masing daerah. Perda ini dibuat agar para nelayan memiliki hak di wilayahnya.*

The protection of small fishermen, continued Susi, is hoped to be able to be realised in the form of local regulations in each region. These regulations are made so that the fishermen have rights in their area.

A close reading of the text reveals that while Kompas.com emphasises Susi's identity, the actual agent responsible for protecting the fishermen remains suppressed. The use of the nominalisation, *perlindungan* (protection), and the agentless passives, *diharapkan* (hoped), *diwujudkan* (realised), and *dibuat* (made) obscure the social actor responsible for protecting fishermen and implementing regulations. By suppressing agency, it becomes possible to present crowd-pleasing ideas about future actions, while avoiding the need to provide a timeline or allocate clear roles and responsibilities for implementing them.

In Excerpt (28), though initial individualisation, subsequent nominalisation, and passive agent deletion, Kompas.com transfers agency from an individualised Megawati to the impersonalised realm of political ceremony. Covering Megawati's attendance at an awards event, the transfer of agency from the individual politician to the ceremonial echoes the New Order preference for ritual and ceremony as a source of power (Pemberton, 1994). In a typical pattern of personification, the headline and lead sentence first identify and activate Megawati in the material process of "giving" (*memberikan*) an award to an aggregated and functionalised group of women. In sequence thereafter, a series of nominalised process nouns, *pemberian* (bestowal), *penghargaan* (award), and *peringatan* (commemoration) suppress the agency of all participants involved and turns the focus to the process and instruments associated with the ceremony. The agentless passive verb, *diperingati* (commemorated) further excludes social actors from direct participation in the event.

(28) *Ketua Umum DPP PDI Perjuangan Megawati Soekarnoputri memberikan penghargaan Sarinah Award kepada 10 perempuan berprestasi. Pemberian penghargaan itu merupakan rangkaian dari peringatan Hari Ibu yang diperingati setiap tanggal 22 Desember.*

The Chair of the PDI-P Megawati Soekarnoputri handed out the Sarinah Award to 10 high-achieving women. The bestowal of the award "represented part of the commemoration of Mother's Day, commemorated every 22 December.

Establishing and legitimising the women leader's authority

The analysis revealed two key strategies through which Kompas.com augmented and legitimised the female leaders' relationship with power. Through these strategies, Kompas.com reproduced hierarchical power arrangements, positioning the leaders both explicitly and implicitly in the top-down exercise of power over subordinates. Personification drew attention to the individual as the clearly identifiable agent at the helm of a political institution, predominantly realised in the headline and lead. Semiformal and formal nomination techniques established the women's popularity as well as their authority. Pseudo-nominations functioned to legitimise, rather than diminish their power by emphasising their unique strengths and personal history that qualified them for a leadership position.

From a commercial perspective, Kompas.com reports attracted reader interest by accentuating the women's individual role in political actions, which gave the public the impression of a more personalised approach to leadership and encouraged greater affinity with the politician. Establishing the individual leaders as agents in the headline and lead exemplified their prominent role in political processes. Activation in verbal, material, and mental processes encompassed the range of possibilities in their leadership within a hierarchical social power network. Activation in verbal processes foregrounded their roles in communicating and enforcing rules, commanding others, and disclosing their personal philosophies. Activation in material processes demonstrated their ability to take a tough stance against unwanted elements for the sake of the well-being of citizens. Activation in mental processes exposed the leaders' intentions and desires behind their actions, including their feelings and thought processes, which contributed to the process of humanisation, arguably enhancing their popularity and commercial appeal in the online media environment. As a clear index of their power, the establishment of the individual leaders' agency also took place through reference to subordinate social groups. Kompas.com generally suppressed the agency and identity of these subordinate social actors through passivation, collectivisation, functionalisation, and classification. This caused the reproduction of an elite-dominated hierarchy and elite-non-elite dichotomy.

Considering the relationship between gender and political power, the representation of the women as top-down sources of power may have the potential to break down the gender binary defining access to the political realm (Bedi, 2016). When women adopt a political persona of authority commonly reserved for men, they take on a transgressive and possibly transformative stance. In the case of Indonesia, however, this transgressive stance appeals to the populist discourse of change, while drawing upon masculine political norms as a resource of power recreates New Order authoritarian power structures. When portraying the women as agents, with the ability to affect others, Kompas.com certainly indexed their power; however, the social

110 *Between the individual and the institution*

actors acted upon were included on the basis of their membership of a subordinate social group relative to the female leaders.

Personification functioned collaboratively with institutionalisation, creating an illusion of the positive "humanised" portrayal of the leader, that was ultimately linked to an established institution. Consecutive activation of the individual and institution in news reports constructed an impression of consensus between the leader, institution, and broader society, a core value of Indonesian political leadership (Irawanto et al., 2011), while removing room for dissent. Within this strategy, spatialisation constructed a seamless impression of consensus between the leader, nation or city, and its inhabitants. Such a representation was likely to rouse localist or nationalist sentiment and provoke reader engagement, while silencing dissenting voices. Reference to instruments rather than human agents disguised individual human agency and transformed the process of governance to an impersonal social practice. Nominalisation and passive agent deletion also worked to mask human agency and responsibility in the performance of government-related actions, and constructed the government in a pervasive role of power.

Discourse mediates and reproduces an ideological framework that can legitimise or transform existing power relations and hierarchies, which are linked to the exercise and maintenance of power relations (Chiapello & Fairclough, 2002; van Dijk, 1989). From an institutional perspective, the foregrounding of the individual in political discourse can signify a shake-up of traditional power arrangements. The blurring of lines between the individual and the institution in Kompas.com reports, however, also subtly reproduced an authoritarian framework of power, and maintained top-down power arrangements. Indeed, concealing clear markings of agency and responsibility for political actions can remove a space for alternative voices, and helps the government claim consensus (Mulderrig, 2011, p. 566). Drawing attention to the women concealed the cold institutional authority of government, yet the discourse reproduced a model of leadership based on a dominant-subordinate dichotomy, and one based on the manufacture of consent.

Notes

1 In Indonesia the categories of "given personal name" or "family name" are often indistinct.
2 Held in 1955, the conference represented a symbolic first meeting between the leaders of many newly independent Asian and African nations following centuries of colonial rule. It became an important historical event announcing Indonesia's newfound independence, and its global importance under Soekarno's leadership.
3 In the Indonesian news media, a colon following the individual's name in the headline functions as shorthand activation in a verbal process. This practice appeared commonly in the data.

References

Bedi, T. (2016). *The dashing ladies of Shiv Sena: Political matronage in urbanizing India*. SUNY Press.

Bucciferro, C. (2014). Michelle Bachelet, president of Chile: A moving portrait. In M. Raicheva-Stover & E. Ibroscheva (Eds.), *Women in politics and media: Perspectives from nations in transition* (1st ed., pp. 217–232). Bloomsbury Academic.

Campus, D. (2010). Mediatization and personalization of politics in Italy and France: The cases of Berlusconi and Sarkozy. *The International Journal of Press/Politics, 15*(2), 219–235.

Chiapello, E., & Fairclough, N. (2002). Understanding the new management ideology: A transdisciplinary contribution from critical discourse analysis and new sociology of capitalism. *Discourse & Society, 13*(2), 185–208.

Fairclough, N. (2000). *New labour, new language?* Routledge.

Fairclough, N. (2001). Critical discourse analysis as a method in social scientific research. In R. Wodak & M. Meyer (Eds.), *Methods of critical discourse analysis* (pp. 121–138). Sage.

Fairclough, N. (2003). *Analysing discourse: Textual analysis for social research*. Routledge.

Garzia, D. (2011). The personalization of politics in Western democracies: Causes and consequences on leader–follower relationships. *The Leadership Quarterly, 22*(4), 697–709.

Gazali, E. (2014). Learning by clicking: An experiment with social media democracy in Indonesia. *The International Communication Gazette, 76*(4–5), 425–439.

Hatherell, M., & Welsh, A. (2017). Rebel with a cause: Ahok and charismatic leadership in Indonesia. *Asian Studies Review, 41*(2), 174–190.

Ibroscheva, E., & Raicheva-Stover, M. (2009). Engendering transition: Portrayals of female politicians in the Bulgarian press. *Howard Journal of Communications, 20*(2), 111–128.

Iedema, R. A. M. (1998). Institutional responsibility and hidden meanings. *Discourse & Society, 9*(4), 481–500.

Irawanto, D. W., Ramsey, P. L., & Ryan, J. C. (2011). Tailoring leadership theory to Indonesian culture. *Global Business Review, 12*(3), 355–366.

Jackson, E. (2005). *'Warring Words': Students and the state in New Order Indonesia, 1966–1998* [Doctoral dissertation, Australian National University], Australian National University Open Research Library.

Karvonen, L. (2010). *The personalisation of politics: A study of parliamentary democracies*. ECPR Press.

Komnas Perempuan. (2014). *National Human Rights Institution independent report on the review of Indonesian report on the implementation of the International Covenant on economic, social and cultural rights in Indonesia*. (National Human Rights Institution Independent Report).

McAllister, I. (2007). The personalization of politics. In R. Dalton & H. Klingemann (Eds.), *The Oxford handbook of political behaviour* (pp. 571–588). Oxford University Press.

Mietzner, M. (2015). *Reinventing Asian populism: Jokowi's rise, democracy, and political contestation in Indonesia*. East-West Center.

Mulderrig, J. (2011). Manufacturing consent: A corpus-based critical discourse analysis of New Labour's educational governance. *Educational Philosophy and Theory, 43*(6), 562–578.

112 *Between the individual and the institution*

Nunez-Perucha, B. (2011). Critical discourse analysis and cognitive linguistics as tools for ideological research: A diachronic analysis of feminism. In C. Hart (Ed.), *Critical discourse studies in context and cognition* (pp. 97–118). John Benjamins.

Parker, L., & Nilan, P. (2013). *Adolescents in contemporary Indonesia.* Routledge.

Pemberton, J. (1994). *On the subject of "Java".* Cornell University Press.

Robinson, K. (2014). Citizenship, identity and difference in Indonesia. *RIMA Review of Indonesian and Malaysian Affairs, 48*(1), 5–34.

Robson, D. (2000). Stereotypes and the female politician: A case study of Senator Barbara Mikulski. *Communication Quarterly, 48*(3), 205–222.

Schutte, S. (2012). Against the odds: Anti-corruption reform in Indonesia. *Public Administration and Development, 32*(1), 38–48.

Shiraishi, S. (1997). *Young heroes: The Indonesian family in politics.* Cornell Southeast Asia Program Publications.

van Dijk, T. A. (1988). *News as discourse.* Lawrence Erlbaum Associates.

van Dijk, T. A. (1989). Structures of discourse and structures of power. In J. Anderson (Ed.), *Communication yearbook 12* (pp. 18–59). Sage.

van Dijk, T. A. (1993). Principles of critical discourse analysis. *Discourse Society, 4,* 249–282.

van Leeuwen, T. (2008). *Discourse and practice: New tools for critical discourse analysis.* Oxford University Press.

Whimster, S. (2004). *The essential Weber: A reader.* Routledge.

Wodak, R. (1997). *Gender and discourse.* Sage.

6 Courting controversy: Women as icons of contestation

Relations of power are highly mobile (Foucault, 1991), and are continually shaped and reshaped through interactions and struggles among social actors across a diverse range of articulatory practices (Masaki, 2007, p. 34). Given women's long-term depoliticisation in Indonesia, their presence in the post-authoritarian public realm can naturally disrupt the status quo, turning political women into icons of contestation. This chapter examines the discursive representation of Megawati, Risma, and Susi at the centre of contestation as the third major facet of their relationship with power portrayed in Kompas.com discourse. As power relates to the "control exercised by a group, organisation, or its members over the actions, and/or minds of others" (van Dijk, 1996), the practice of contestation in discourse is viewed as the use of language that attempts to disrupt or destabilise relations of power, and gain or regain control of the actions or minds of social actors in a power hierarchy. Contestation becomes particularly apparent in contexts of social-political change, where multiple social groups attempt to redefine or defend existing relations of power based on their interests. In the process, certain texts and events "accentuate difference, conflict, polemic, a struggle over meaning, norms, [and thereby] power" (Fairclough, 2003, p. 42).

The news media and more recently, the digital news media play an undeniable role in fuelling a discursive cycle of contestation. Profit-oriented reporting practices aiming for a reactive response and greater online engagement both reflect and influence contemporary political discourse (Hasell & Weeks, 2016; Lim, 2017; Shin et al., 2016; Turner, 2018). In the timeframe of the 2014 election, a shift towards polarisation became evident in both online and offline discourse in Indonesia, closely associated with the rise of populism (Ahlstrand, 2020; Lim, 2017). The construal of rumours, scandal, and conflict involving members of the political elite in Indonesia constitutes a particularly newsworthy event (Ahlstrand, 2020). Kompas. com journalists, like other Indonesian journalists, however, must operate within a range of commercial, professional, and legal constraints, including a legacy of self-censorship from the Suharto era, as discussed in Chapter 3 (Haryanto, 2010; Tapsell, 2012; Wijayanto, 2015). In this chapter, the residual and emergent practices of the online news media, gender, and politics

DOI: 10.4324/9781003083252-6

114   *Courting controversy*

come together in the construal of contestation over the course of the 2014 presidential election.

In discourse oriented towards conflict and difference, power can be viewed as the "transformative capacity of human action to intervene in a series of events and alter their course" (Fairclough, 2003, p. 41). As this chapter will show, however, while Kompas.com positions the women in situations of discursive opposition, the texts do not contain explicit counter-discourses that challenge or transform entrenched structures of power. While the portrayal of contestation in Kompas.com covers conflict, criticism, transgression, rumours, speculation, and retort, through the ambiguous use of language and the strategic positioning of social actors, Kompas.com merely alludes to discursive struggle, while positioning the women as central characters in the events. This mode of representation fulfill the commercial goals of the news media by attracting reader attention, while ultimately consolidating hierarchical relations of power.

The three major discursive strategies that realise the practice of contestation in Kompas.com texts are labelled *constructing threat, alluding to controversy*, and *managed responses*. Constructing threat construes a vague enemy *other* threatening vulnerable victims, which legitimises the power of the leader and her capacity to protect the weak. Alluding to controversy insinuates conflict and transgression, while minimising the direct impact of the controversy on the elite social actors involved, leaving the readers to interpret the events according to their pre-existing knowledge and opinions. The strategy of managed responses focuses on either the leaders' defensive or proactive response to criticism based on their supposed transgressions. The manner in which their response is conveyed has a legitimising or delegitimising effect on the leaders' and their relationship with power. These three key strategies will be explained in detail to follow, including their respective building blocks of social actor representations, and their function in this rather superficial process of contestation within the context of shifting political values and media practices.

Constructing threat

The strategy of constructing threat in Kompas.com reports involves the division of an in-group and an enemy out-group, in which the out-group threatens the integrity and well-being of the in-group through their transgressive actions. The leaders are positioned at the centre, in a protective role to restore the social order and defend the weak. Wodak (2015) identifies the construction of a threat as a key populist tactic particularly favoured by right wing political groups as a source of power and control. Reference to "various real and imagined dangers," constructs fear among the community, while scapegoats labelled as the other are "blamed for threatening our societies," and reinforce the power of the in-group (p. 1). The practice of othering creates a hierarchical differentiation between the included and excluded (Wodak, 2008). In a similar vein, Arche-politics has been the cornerstone of the political identity of the Indonesian state since the New Order, whereby a constitutive outside enemy is used to define and maintain the internal political order (Duile & Bens, 2017, p. 145). The construction of a threat group in Indonesia contributes to a narrative of "state-making" and "people-making" that determines origins and defines national identity against the other (Tan, 2012). This practice appears to have transferred seamlessly to the populist agenda of the 2014 presidential election, with a focus on the power of individual leaders to intervene and defend the integrity of the nation (Melissa, 2019, p. 47).

Through oppositional discourse and an appeal to fear and uncertainty, the strategy enticed a reactive response against the enemy from readers, while legitimising the leaders' position and use of power within the broader hierarchical structures of power. Intersecting with traditional gender norms, the women were constructed as prominent icons in a protective role, determined to maintain the social order. The strategy consists of a distinct set of social actor representations identified through the application of van Leeuwen's framework of social actor analysis, with reference to Indonesia's surrounding social-political context. The members of the out-group are generally portrayed anonymously, as a largely non-human collective associated with deviant acts detrimental to the wellbeing of the nation. Meanwhile, the Indonesian population are portrayed as passive victims, and placed in a vulnerable social category. Amidst this strong-weak dichotomy, Kompas.com portrays Megawati, Risma, and Susi as clearly identifiable, agentive individuals, who provide a source of security for the nation or local community. These representational choices enable Kompas.com to construe a situation of fear and danger, eliminate sympathy for the threat group, and perpetuate the hierarchical dependence of the ordinary people on the political elite.

Constructing a pervasive threat group

Kompas.com employed a range of representational techniques to allude to the presence of a formidable threat group and associate it with deviant activities. The representational techniques managed to convey a sense of fear, while avoiding direct responsibility for accusations of wrongdoing though the strategic obfuscation of identity and agency. The components of this building block are listed below. Given the multifaceted nature of this building block, its components will be explained in increments.

The practice of indetermination (van Leeuwen, 2008, p. 39) became a salient feature of the representation of the threat group, which denies social actors a clear social identity and instead anonymises them. This representational choice obscured the distinction between a real or imagined threat, and contributed to a sense of fear in the community based on uncertainty. Only in the case of Susi did Kompas.com indicate the identity of the threat group, supportive of a nationalist agenda to protect Indonesia from foreign

116   *Courting controversy*

Table 6.1 Building block 1: Constructing a pervasive threat group

Realisation in the strategy	Function in the strategy	Definitions
Indetermination of threat group members	• Conceals identity • Creates a sense of pervasiveness as a non-specified, yet coercive force • Eliminates the need to provide supporting evidence through reliance on vagueness, while avoiding direct accusations and liability	*Indetermination* represents social actors as undefined, anonymous individuals or groups. Often realised through indefinite pronouns
Aggregation	• Enhances the perceived size of the threat, but avoids the need to specify the exact number	*Aggregation* occurs when a social actor or group is represented as a quantity, which, like collectivisation is a form of assimilation
Functionalisation	• Threat group members appear to have assembled for the purpose of performing deviant activities	*Functionalisation* represents social actors as the "doer" of an activity or role, such as an occupation.
Classification by nation (Susi only)	• Reinforces out-group status based on nationality	*Classification* represents social actors according to established, social categories, such as age, gender, or nationality.
Instrumentalisation	• De-humanises the threat group, thus eliminating sympathy • Enhances perceived strength through reference to powerful tools, but avoids direct accusation	*Instrumentalisation* is a form of impersonalisation, and represents social actors by metonymic reference to the non-human instrument that they use to perform an activity (e.g., boats)
Utterance autonomisation by reference to statements	• De-humanises threat group, eliminates sympathy • Mitigates direct accusation, while maintaining association with transgressions	The impersonalising metonymic operation of *utterance autonomisation* represents social actors according to their utterances rather than their human identity (e.g., a statement)

(*Continued*)

Courting controversy 117

Table 6.1 Building block 1: Constructing a pervasive threat group (*Continued*)

Realisation in the strategy	*Function in the strategy*	*Definitions*
Activation in transgressive material and verbal social processes	• Associates the group with transgressive acts • Material processes show concrete impact of their actions • Verbal processes highlight their threatening messages	*Activation* occurs when social actors are represented as the active, dynamic force in an activity. Activation is categorised by social process types, which have different characteristics and outcomes. *Material processes* have a physical, transformative impact on human/non-human objects, involving an actor and a goal or target of the action. Represents the actor or group as the dynamic force in the activity. *Verbal processes* are communicative actions involving a speaker, which are sometimes accompanied by the specification of a listener, or receiver of the information
Nominalisation	• De-humanises, eliminates sympathy by removal of agent • Increases apparent pervasiveness through lack of specificity in terms of agency, modality, and tense • Concealment of information shields newspaper from liability	*Nominalisation* is an impersonalising linguistic operation that transforms a verb into a noun, and suppresses important information such as agency, modality, and tense. E.g., *pembangunan* (development), derived from the transitive verb, *membangun* (to build).
Passive agent deletion	• De-humanises by removal of agent • Avoids direct accusation by not naming human agent responsible • Increases apparent pervasiveness through lack of specificity	*Passive agent deletion* is another linguistic operation that omits the agent responsible for a social action conveyed in the verb. Realised in Indonesian by word order: object + verb, and attaching the *di-* or *ter-* prefix to the verb, while omitting the agent
Use of existential process followed by relative pronoun	• Conceals origins of threat, contributing to its vagueness • Avoids specificity, and enhances pervasiveness	An existential process occurs in clauses headed by "there is/there are" (*ada*), followed by the mention of a vague in a dependent clause headed by the relative pronoun *yang* (who, which, that). E.g., *Ada pihak yang…* (there is a party/group who…)
Use of relational process	• Associates threat with deviant activities	A *relational process* attributes the social actor with a quality or action directly associated with them

118   *Courting controversy*

interference. Members of the threat group were associated with transgressive acts performed against the community and the state. Indetermination invited speculation on the identity of the perpetrators, which likely prompted further reader engagement. The lack of specificity in the portrayal of transgression also shielded the newspaper and the individual journalist from accusations of libel when reporting on transgressions.

Kompas.com used a range of representational choices in the act of indetermination, including the use of *pihak* (third party, person), *orang* (person), and *oknum* (individual, anonymous perpetrator). Commonly used in criminal and legal discourse, pihak and oknum in particular carried the implication of suspicious activity, while alleviating the journalist of the responsibility to identify a clear culprit. These terms often appeared as part of an existential clause, headed by the verb, *ada* (there is) to mystify their origins, followed by a dependent clause, headed by the relative pronoun *yang* (who) to express the deviant actions and purpose of the group. Excerpt (1) demonstrates this pattern of representation, referring to the presence of an anonymous third party, assembled for the purpose of moving homeless people to Surabaya.

(1) *Wali Kota Surabaya Tri Rismaharini mencurigai <u>ada pihak yang</u> sengaja menggerakkan para gelandangan atau penyandang masalah kesejahteraan sosial (PMKS) untuk masuk ke Kota Surabaya.*

Mayor of Surabaya Tri Rismaharini suspects <u>there is a party who</u> deliberately moves the homeless or those with social welfare problems to the City of Surabaya.

Here the existential clause headed by ada (there is) combines with an anonymous pihak (party), and then portrays the anonymous group in the deviant act of "moving homeless or those with social welfare problems" to the city. In this case, the group responsible and their origins remain concealed, and exist in a vacuum of time and space through the use of the empty "ada." Presented through the perspective of Risma, the representation of the threat group establishes her knowledge, and potential to intervene, while the group affected by the actions of the threat group are portrayed as socially vulnerable, and therefore in need of protection.

Excerpt (2) engages a similar method of indetermination followed by the explicit activation of the third-party threat in a deviant social action. The report portrays an anonymous party attempting to bribe Susi in response to her newly implemented anti-IUU fishing policies.

(2) *Menteri Susi Sebut Oknum yang Tawarinya Rp 5 T untuk Mundur adalah Pengusaha "Illegal Fishing"*

Minister Susi Claims <u>the Individual who</u> Offered 5 Trillion to Resign is an "Illegal Fishing" Business Owner

Courting controversy 119

In this example, Kompas.com uses the term, oknum (anonymous perpetrator) to refer to an individual or group. Popularised under the New Order to refer to a vague threat in the community, the use of oknum enhances the impression of deviance through an implicit association with suspicious, unlawful activity, and legitimises Susi's position. The explicit activation of the third party in the practice of bribery supports the representation of their deviance, while by contrast, Susi appears transparent. In this example, functionalisation is employed as an additional way of categorising the threat group, based on their involvement in the deviant act of "illegal fishing," while avoiding direct identification.

Aggregation, or the representation of social actors as a large, quantifiable group (van Leeuwen, 2008, pp. 37–38) was also employed to portray the threat. The representation of a threat group as a large, yet vague quantity enhances their apparent pervasiveness, while avoiding the need for specificity. Excerpt (3) was taken from the lead of a report published following the presidential election, as controversy over Megawati's relationship with Jokowi continued.

(3) *Politisi senior PDI Perjuangan Pramono Anung melihat ada <u>banyak pihak</u> yang berusaha memisahkan Presiden Joko Widodo dengan Ketua Umum PDI-P Megawati Soekarnoputri.*

Senior PDI-P politician Pramono Anung sees <u>many parties</u> who attempt to split up President Joko Widodo and PDI-P Chair Megawati Soekarnoputri.

In this instance, Kompas.com mitigates the controversy surrounding their relationship by turning the readers' attention towards a large, yet unidentified threat group represented as *banyak pihak* (many parties). Following the pattern described in excerpts (1) and (2), the dependent clause that follows defines the deviant purpose of the mysterious pihak (parties), and thus reinforces Megawati's legitimacy.

In conjunction with indetermination, Kompas.com often engaged impersonalisation to obscure markers of the human identity of the threat group. Van Leeuwen (2008, p. 46) defines impersonalisation as the representation of social actors by "abstract nouns or by concrete nouns, whose meanings do not include the semantic feature 'human.'" Krzyzanowski and Wodak (2009), Machin and Suleiman (2006), and van Leeuwen (2008) all emphasise the importance of impersonalisation to the process of othering, which creates a hierarchy of power between the included and the excluded. Impersonalised representations within this strategy involved instrumentalisation, as well as the grammatical operations of passive agent deletion and nominalisation. Impersonalisation contrasted with humanised representations of the vulnerable victims and the powerful individual leaders. The suppression of the identity and agency of the threat group also enabled Kompas.com to publish open-ended allegations without naming anyone

120 *Courting controversy*

responsible, or providing substantiating evidence. Excerpt (4) demonstrates the use of aggregation combined with the impersonalising operations of instrumentalisation and passive agent deletion to construct a sense of a pervasive threat during the Jokowi presidential election campaign.

> (4) *Ketua Umum DPP PDI Perjuangan, Megawati Soekarnoputri tak risau dengan <u>banyaknya kampanye hitam</u> yang <u>dialamatkan</u> pada calon presiden Joko Widodo (Jokowi)*
>
> Chair of the PDI-P, Megawati Soekarnoputri is not concerned with <u>the number of smear campaigns aimed at</u> presidential candidate, Joko Widodo (Jokowi).

Told from the perspective of Megawati as party leader, the report first refers to *banyaknya kampanye hitam* (the number of smear campaigns) used to disrupt the Jokowi presidential campaign. By referring to the smear campaigns rather than the social actors involved, Kompas.com dehumanises them while escalating the threat they pose, in contrast to the clearly identifiable Megawati and Jokowi. Through the agentless passive, "aimed at" (*dialamatkan*) Kompas.com continues to suppress their identity, and facilitates the publication of unsubstantiated claims, while maintaining an impression of objectivity. The representation also functions to alleviate the rumoured tension between Megawati and Jokowi, by diverting attention away from her alleged excessive influence, and directing it towards a mysterious other.

Portraying threat groups and their actions through nominalisation contributed to the construal of negative information without providing substantiating evidence. Nominalisation, or the transformation of social processes into nouns, functions as a form of abstraction or generalisation, which involves the selective filtering of information (Fairclough, 2003, p. 139). It serves to obfuscate human agency, and therefore responsibility, and results in the loss of both tense and modality, making actions appear "timeless" and "doubtless" (Fairclough, 2003, p. 144). Through this process, Kompas.com constructed an impression of concreteness, despite the absence of substantiating detail. Excerpt (5) refers to a special task forced formed by the Surabaya municipal government to eradicate human trafficking, as part of the broader representation of Risma's efforts to protect vulnerable residents of Surabaya.

> (5) *Tim yang dibentuk secara diam-diam itu pun berhasil membongkar <u>praktik perdagangan</u> orang yang menjerumuskan korbannya ke bisnis prostitusi.*
>
> The secretly-formed team has successfully disassembled <u>the practice of human trafficking</u> that forces victims into the prostitution business.

Courting controversy 121

In a dependent clause, rather than an identifiable social actor or group, the nominalised *praktik perdaganangan orang* (the practice of human trafficking) is positioned as the agent responsible for the deviant act of "forcing its victims into prostitution." Through nominalisation, Kompas.com portrays praktik perdagangan orang as a concrete entity. Kompas.com then positions it as the object of the act of being destroyed (*membongkar*) by the Surabayan municipal government, which enhances the power of the government, while reducing the power of the indeterminate threat group.

In the representation of Susi's leadership, the construction of the threat of foreign illegal fishing became a common means of reinforcing her personal political power, and upholding the broader nationalist agenda of the Jokowi presidency. Wodak (2015) identifies nationalism as a common component of right-wing populist discourse that perpetuates fear-mongering and debates about security and protection (p. 71). In this case, Kompas.com discourse tended to follow the patterns of indetermination and impersonalisation outlined above, with the additional practice of classification based on country of origin. Excerpt (6) draws attention to Susi's concerns over a transmigration program as a potential cover for foreign illegal fishing activities.

(6) *Dia menjelaskan, program itu akan menjadi kamuflase bagi <u>masuknya</u> <u>kapal-kapal</u> Thailand atau eks Thailand. <u>Kapal</u> itu kata dia akan <u>dicat</u> ulang dan <u>digunakan</u> untuk menangkap ikan secara besar-besaran di daerah yang ikannya masih melimpah.*

She explains, the program will become camouflage for the <u>entry</u> of <u>Thai or ex-Thai ships</u>. Those <u>ships</u> will be <u>re-painted</u> and <u>used</u> to catch fish on a large scale in areas that still have abundant fish stock.

In this case, the construction of the threat takes place through instrumentalisation, replacing the human actors involved with impersonalised *kapal* (ships). Nominalisation in the form of *masuknya* (the entry of) and passive agent deletion in *dicat ulang* (re-painted) and *digunakan* (used) continue to suppress the identity of the group. With the addition of "Thai" to classify the ships, group Kompas.com identifies the threat group as non-Indonesian, which feeds into the populist nationalist agenda. Through strategic representational choices, Kompas.com manages to publish indirect accusations of the illegal fishing activities of Thai fishing corporations, while justifying Susi's ability to access and wield power for the sake of national security.

Constructing worthy victims

In news reports generally, the representation of a hypothetical threat group tends to occur predominantly in contrast to the representation of passive victims (Reyes, 2011). This practice was evident in Kompas.com reports,

122 *Courting controversy*

Table 6.2 Building block 2: Constructing worthy victims

Realisation in the strategy	Function in the strategy	Definitions
Classification of victims	• Establishes victims of members of vulnerable social group • Humanises victims • Establishes subordinate social status	*Classification* as defined in Table 6.1 above.
Passivation: subjection to deviant actions of the threat groups. The goal in their material processes, or the receiver in a verbal process	• Establishes vulnerability • Justifies need for leaders' protection • Reinforces deviance of the threat group • Shows lack of agency	*Subjection* is a form of passivation that positions social actors as the ones acted upon by an agent in a social process *Goal* is the passive social actor whose position or status is affected by the material process *Receiver* is the addressee, or the listener in a verbal process

where the representation of the threat group also included a group of vulnerable, yet clearly humanised victims. Table 6.2 describes the particular components of this building block. Kompas.com generally represented the victims through the processes of classification and passivation. Classification involved representing the social actors according to a subordinate social category, such as youth. The victims were predominantly subjected to the actions of the threat group, and thus positioned in a passive grammatical role. These modes of representation established both the vulnerability of the local or national population, in contrast to the largely impersonalised, deviant threat group acting upon them. The portrayal of the victims suffering at the hands of a de-humanised threat group triggered an emotional audience response, while reinforcing the legitimacy of the in-group, and the illegitimacy of the out-group. By portraying civil society as weak and vulnerable, this form of representation can enhance the overall power of a political regime (Reyes, 2011, p. 252). For Megawati, Risma, and Susi, such representations boosted their perceived legitimacy, from within the bounds of the regime.

Excerpt (7) comes from a report focusing on Susi's angered response to a Philippine mayor's alleged criticism of Indonesian fishermen. Kompas.com constructs a situation of injustice, in which Indonesians are subjected to abuse by a foreign nation, and establishes a human-non-human, rich-poor dichotomy between the vulnerable Indonesian crew members and the powerful foreign fishing companies.

(7) *Menurut Susi, <u>banyak kapal asal General Santos</u> yang mempekerjakan <u>anak buah kapal</u> asal Indonesia, bahkan ada yang sampai 15 tahun.*

Courting controversy 123

According to Susi, many ships from General Santos employ <u>crew members</u> from Indonesia, even some for up to 15 years.

The Indonesian victims are allocated to a grammatically passive role, and subject to the actions of the General Santos group. While the Indonesians are humanised and functionalised as *anak buah kapal* (crew members), the Philippine group is impersonalised through instrumentalisation, by reference to "ships." As mentioned in Chapters 4 and 5, the term, *anak buah* refers to the socially subordinate category of servants or staff overseen by a leader. The aggregation of the ships further enhances the relative size of the enemy, thus inviting sympathy for the weaker Indonesian crew members who suffer as a result of the large fishing company. Overall, this representation facilitates the positioning of Susi in a protective role and justifies her nationalist stance.

Excerpt (8) also positions Risma in a protective role by intervening in child trafficking, where children are sold into prostitution in the port city of Batam by a deviant, yet unidentified threat group.

(8) <u>*Mereka*</u> *merayu* <u>*para gadis lugu*</u> *dengan iming-iming pekerjaan bergaji besar di Batam. Ujung-ujungnya, di kota perdagangan ini,* <u>*para gadis*</u> <u>*dipaksa*</u> *menjadi pekerja seks*

<u>They</u> lure <u>innocent girls</u> with the offer of high-paying jobs in Batam. Ultimately, these <u>girls</u> are forced to become sex workers in this city of trade.

While Kompas.com anonymises the threat through the use of the indeterminate third person pronoun *mereka* (they), the victims of child trafficking are described more explicitly. Kompas.com classifies them as a collective of *gadis lugu* (innocent girls) and simply *gadis* (girls) through the processes of appraisal and classification. Appraisal through the word, *lugu* (innocent, naïve) establishes their status as worthy victims, while classification establishes both their gender and youth. The term gadis implies virginity and purity (Bennett, 2005), which indicates to the reader that the girls involved were not members of a deviant social category of sex workers. Instead, the innocent girls are subjected to the actions of the deviant other, where they are "forced" (*dipaksa*) into prostitution. In this case, the agentless passive verb, dipaksa establishes their victimhood, while concealing the identity of the agent responsible. The portrayal of these two groups justifies the need for Risma's intervention to prevent further exploitation of the innocent.

Constructing heroic leaders

Alongside the portrayal of the pervasive, largely anonymous threat group and its vulnerable victims, Kompas.com represented the leaders as easily identifiable individuals, activated in mental, material, and verbal processes.

124   *Courting controversy*

Table 6.3 Building block 3: Constructing heroic leaders

Realisation in the strategy	Function in the strategy	Definitions
Individualisation	• Focuses attention on the individual leaders as identifiable social actors in the threat situation • Humanises the leaders in contrast to vague, dehumanised threat group	*Individualisation*, as the name suggests, portrays social actors as individuals as opposed to a member of a collective
Activation in mental processes	• Expresses the leaders' emotion and personal concern • Humanises the leaders as authentic public figures • Encourages an emotional reaction among readers	*Activation* defined in Table 6.1 *Mental processes* relate to thoughts and feelings, and involve a sensor and an optional phenomenon of the thoughts and feelings
Activation in verbal processes	• Positions the leaders in a spokesperson role, "calling out" the deviant threat group	*Activation, verbal processes* defined in Table 6.1
Activation in material processes	• Expresses the leaders' strength • Demonstrates their ability to intervene and gain control over the situation	*Activation, material processes* defined in Table 6.1

Owing to their difference to the norms of the masculine political realm, the women naturally stood out in opposition to the outside threat. Megawati, Risma, and Susi were portrayed standing up to, or speaking out against the threat to uphold the wellbeing and integrity of the community or nation they served. Activation in mental processes foregrounded their humanised response to the dehumanised threat group, while inviting a similar emotional response from readers. Activation in verbal processes positioned the women in the role as spokesperson, or the source of public information on the threat. Activation in material processes established their power to intervene and prevent the threat group from harming the community. The predominant representational choices are listed below.

Excerpts (9) and (10) activate the individualised Risma and Susi in the identical mental process of being *geram* (furious) as a result of the destructive actions of threat groups.

(9) *Risma <u>geram</u> karena <u>pembagian</u> es krim itu tidak beraturan sehingga merusak banyak tanaman di Taman Bungkul.*

Risma was <u>furious</u> because the <u>distribution</u> of ice cream was disorganised and damaged many plants in Bungkul Park.

Courting controversy 125

(10) *Menteri Kelautan dan Perikanan Susi Pudjiastuti <u>geram</u> dengan <u>pernyataan</u> Wali Kota General Santos City, Filipina, Ronnel Rivera, yang merendahkan nelayan Indonesia.*

Minister of Maritime Affairs and Fisheries Susi Pudjiastuti is <u>furious</u> at the <u>statement</u> made by Mayor of General Santos City, Philippines, Ronnel Rivera, who demeaned Indonesian fishermen.

Kompas.com emphasises the leaders' human side by activating them in an intensely emotional social action against a deviant and destructive other. For Risma, while nominalisation, *pembagian* (distribution) conceals the agency and identity of the threat group, Kompas.com establishes her clear-cut social identity. For Susi, utterance autonomisation suppresses the agency of the Philippine Mayor, by referring to his "statement" (*pernyataan*) as the target of her anger. This familiar-unfamiliar dichotomy invites sympathy for the leaders and facilitates the denouncement of the outsiders.

Kompas.com also activated individual leaders in material processes, which emphasised their relative power in comparison to an indeterminate, impersonalised threat group, positioned as the target of their actions. Excerpt (11) exemplifies this representation.

(11) *Selama 100 hari pertama bekerja, Susi telah berhasil <u>menangkap puluhan kapal ilegal fishing</u> di perairan Indonesia.*

Over the first 100 days in office, Susi has succeeded in <u>catching dozens of illegal fishing boats</u> in Indonesian waters.

Susi is activated as the individual involved in the material process of "catching" (*menangkap*) an aggregated and instrumentalised group of "dozens of illegal fishing boats" (*puluhan kapal ilegal fishing*). The portrayal of Susi's individual act of "catching" the large quantity of fishing boats emphasises her personal strength as well as her ability to intervene and dominate the threat.

A similar example can be found in Excerpt (12), where Kompas.com activates Risma in the material process of "breaking up" (*membubarkan*) "a free ice cream giveaway event" (*acara bagi-bagi es krim gratis*).

(12) *Wali Kota Surabaya Tri Rismaharini <u>membubarkan acara bagi-bagi es krim gratis</u> di Taman Bungkul Surabaya, Minggu (11/5/2014).*

Mayor of Surabaya Tri Rismaharini <u>broke up a free ice cream giveaway</u> at Bungkul Park in Surabaya, Sunday (11/5/2014)

Kompas.com obfuscates the identity and agency of the individuals behind the giveaway through instrumentalisation in *acara* (event) and

126　*Courting controversy*

nominalisation in *bagi-bagi es krim* (ice cream giveaway), while foregrounding Risma's identity and personal agency. The report describes Risma's anger at the ice cream company for the damage caused to the park. Given Risma's established reputation for developing the city's green spaces (Sahab, 2017), the personalised portrayal of her intervention in the destructive actions of an impersonalised ice cream company contributes to the perception of her genuine commitment to the city. While Risma's intervention appears small-scale, it remains important in the context of local politics and people-focused, individualised leadership.

Alluding to controversy

The strategy of alluding to controversy fed into the process of contestation in the Kompas.com texts by subtly portraying Megawati, Risma, and Susi at the centre of controversial events that transgressed social, political, and legal constraints. The strategy is relied heavily upon the abstraction of human agency in the portrayal of the controversial or transgressive actions and interactions. Social events can "be represented at different levels of abstraction and generalisation," which serve to constitute a particular ideological vision (Fairclough, 2003, pp. 137–138). The subtle representations did not directly challenge the status quo; however, the strategic construal of information about controversial events prompted reactive reader engagement, and potentially fuelled more rumours, anxiety, and speculation, while shielding the newspaper from responsibility for scandalous reporting. From a sociological perspective, rumours are self-perpetuating, and fit into a pool of information, which grows through the contribution of additional explanations, doubts, arguments, and suggestions (Seymour-Ure, 2003, p. 206). Rumour and speculation also depend on public appetite, while elements of public anxiety fuel their continuation and expansion (Seymour-Ure, 2003, p. 213). Under the New Order, the construction of suspicion and rumour created an excuse for greater control, calling on the government to stabilise the situation (Kroeger, 2003).

Wodak (2002) recognises the use of allusions in politics as a tactical way of "devaluing political opponents, without accepting responsibility for what is implicitly said," which entices audiences to allocate meaning to the events and actors described (p. 501). Indeed, the absence of clear delineations of agency and responsibility in the strategy likely encouraged readers to activate their personal repertoire of knowledge to interpret the story and form an opinion. The vagueness resulting from abstractions also enabled Kompas.com to avoid the need to provide credible evidence to substantiate claims. The inclusion of both elite and public opinion also became way of legitimising conjecture (van Leeuwen, 2007, van Leeuwen, 2008). Reference to these authoritative sources supported the construal of vague rumours and subjective opinion in Kompas.com texts without an impression of bias.

The strategy drew attention to the conspicuousness of the female leaders in the political realm. As outsiders, the women attracted public attention; however, the strategic construal of information did little to challenge the status quo, and instead, fuelled reactive engagement, and potentially laid the grounds for greater authoritarian leadership and governance to control the situation. Although both the strategies of alluding to controversy and constructing threat bear some similarities through the cautious construal of information and promotion of public anxiety, alluding to controversy is not based on the construction of a particular out-group, nor does it always benefit the women, particularly Megawati and her claim to power.

Reference to thoughts and feelings

The use of affectual autonomisation, or reference to thoughts and feelings in place of the social actor became a key way of representing controversial events while abstracting the agency and identity of the actors involved. Affectual autonomisation served to highlight rumours or evaluative opinion, while imbuing the report with a sense of objectivity, and the subjective ideas with a sense of concreteness. Affectual autonomisation often combined with an existential clause starting with ada (there is/there are) to construe subjective information without providing significant detail. A description of this building block can be found in Table 6.4.

Excerpt (13) engages affectual autonomisation within an existential clause to construe tenuous information as a tangible fact regarding Megawati's influence on Jokowi.

(13) *Pengamat komunikasi politik dari Universitas Indonesia, Agung Suprio, mengatakan, <u>ada kekhawatiran</u> bakal calon presiden Partai Demokrasi Indonesia Perjuangan (PDI-P) Joko Widodo alias Jokowi akan menjadi "boneka" Megawati Soekarnoputri jika terpilih menjadi presiden.*

Political communication observer from the University of Indonesia, Agung Suprio, has stated that there is concern would-be presidential candidate of the Indonesian Democratic Party of Struggle (PDI-P) Joko Widodo alias Jokowi will become a "puppet" of Megawati Soekarnoputri if elected as president.

Through affectual autonomisation in "concern" (*kekhawatiran*), Kompas. com obscures the agent responsible for the speculation that Jokowi will become Megawati's puppet. By abstracting agency, Kompas.com is able to present highly subjective and controversial information with the potential to undermine Megawati's legitimate exercise of power, while upholding a perception of journalistic objectivity. The origins of the concern are further obscured through the use of the existential clause headed by ada.

128　*Courting controversy*

Table 6.4 Building block 1: Reference to thoughts and feelings

Realisation in the strategy	Function in the strategy	Definitions
Affectual autonomisation	• Conceals agency and responsibility for potentially transgressive thoughts and feelings that upset the status quo • Protects the newspaper from responsibility for publishing transgressive acts associated with the political elite • Imbues the conjecture with a sense of tangibility, making the thoughts and feelings appear like a real "thing"	*Affectual autonomisation* is a novel category based on van Leeuwen's taxonomy of social actor analysis. It is a form of metonymical objectivation that involves the representation of social actors by reference to their thoughts or feelings, rather than the humans behind the process. While this category does not appear on van Leeuwen's (2008) original list of impersonalisation types, it demonstrates similar characteristics to the other objectivations listed, by representing social actors by reference to a product of their actions, rather than as humans
Use of existential process	• Conceals the origins of the thoughts and feelings • Supports the repression of the identity of the agent responsible for the thoughts and feelings • Enables the specification of allegations of wrong-doing, but mystifies origins of the perpetrator	*Existential process* defined in Table 6.1

The absence of the agents or origins imbues the rumours with a sense of tangibility or incontestable truth, while inviting readers to speculate further. The inclusion of a "political communication observer" endorses the legitimacy of concerns regarding Megawati's influence.

Excerpt (14) demonstrates the use of affectual autonomisation in combination with an existential process headed by "ada" to construct an impression of contestation over Susi's appointment, without identifying the social actors responsible.

> (14) *Yang paling menjadi <u>pro dan kontra</u> adalah soal pendidikan terakhirnya. Susi tak menyelesaikan pendidikan menengah atas. <u>Ada yang</u> tak mempermasalahkan, tetapi <u>ada pula yang</u> mempertanyakan <u>kapabilitas</u> Susi karena <u>dianggap</u> hanya lulusan SMP.*
>
> What has become a <u>pro and con</u> is the matter of her highest level of schooling. Susi did not complete secondary school. <u>There are</u>

Courting controversy 129

<u>some</u> who don't problematise, but <u>there are those</u> who question Susi's capability because [she is] considered to have only completed middle school.

Through affectual autonomisation, in *pro dan kontra* (pro and con, for and against), Kompas.com refers to conjecture about Susi's educational background. Affectual autonomisation imbues the subjective opinions and feelings with a sense of tangibility, while concealing the agents behind them. As in the case of Megawati, the obscurement of agency functions to avoid the "contextually inappropriate" (van Dijk, 2006, p 174) portrayal of direct criticism of an elite figure and her suitability for her role. The removal of the identity of social actors responsible for the conjecture also expands the scope for participatory public speculation about Susi and her educational background. The use of the uniquely Indonesian pronoun and conjunction, *yang* (those who) acts as a subject within the existential clause headed by ada (there are). Both ada and yang maintain the anonymity of the social actors behind the belief that Susi only completed middle school and protect Kompas.com from any impression of libel.

Indirect conflict and criticism

The second major representational choice in the strategy of alluding to controversy involved the prudent use of instrumentalisation, or the impersonalised portrayal of social actors "by reference to the instrument with which they carry out an action" (van Leeuwen, 2008, p. 46). When used in reports covering conflict between, or criticism of elite figures, the impersonalised representation was placed as the target of the attack rather than the social actor, which mitigated its direct impact. For example, a policy was positioned in the grammatical role of the object, as the target of the criticism. Through possessivation, however, Kompas.com maintained a topical link between the target of criticism and the social actor to which it was attached. As possessivation is realised in Indonesian by placing the owner after the noun, the direct impact of the attack was minimised. The elements of this building block are outlined in table 6.5.

Possessivised instrumentalisation gained greater efficacy in the construal of controversy when combined with other modes of discursive ambiguity, such as grammatical operations concealing human agency. In Excerpt (15), possessivised instrumentalisation combines with passive agent deletion to portray indirect conflict between Susi and members of the business community regarding a new ban on transhipment introduced under her ministry.

(15) <u>*Kebijakan*</u> *Menteri Kelautan dan Perikanan Susi Pudjiastuti melarang bongkar muat di tengah laut atau transhipment sempat <u>ditentang</u> pengusaha. Pasalnya, <u>aturan</u> itu <u>dinilai</u> akan membuat biaya*

130   *Courting controversy*

Table 6.5 Building block 2: Indirect conflict

Realisation in the strategy	Function in the strategy	Definitions
Instrumentalisation	• Mitigates the impact of conflict and transgression when placed between the agent and the target of their critical actions	*Instrumentalisation* defined in Table 6.1
Possessivation	• Turning the instrumentalised representation of the social actor into a possession maintains a "human connection" to the act of conflict or criticism, • Mitigates the direct impact upon the social actor	*Possessivation* portrays a social actor as the "owner" of an object, while the object, whether human or non-human, is transformed into a possession or "thing." This process generally semi-activates the owner as the participant in the social action, while the possessivised object is passive. Possession is indicated by word order in Indonesia, where the possessor follows the object.

operasional kapal naik karena harus melakukan bongkar muat di pelabuhan.

Minister of Maritime Affairs and Fisheries, Susi Pudjiastuti's <u>pol-icy</u> of banning transhipment has been opposed by business owners. This is because that <u>regulation</u> is <u>believed</u> to increase the operational costs for ships because of having to offload at the port.

In the first sentence, Kompas.com positions *kebikjakan Menteri Kelautan dan Perikanan Susi Pudjiastuti* (Minister of Maritime Affairs and Fishery Susi Pudjiastuti's policy), rather than Susi herself as the phenomenon in the process of being "opposed" (*ditentang*) by a collective group of "business owners." In the sentence that follows, again through instrumentalisation, Kompas.com refers to a "regulation" (*aturan*) rather than Susi as the target of criticism. To express the negative evaluation, Kompas.com engages passive agent deletion in the verb, *dinilai* (evaluated, believed), which conceals the agency and identity of the critics responsible.

While instrumentalisation worked to protect the female leaders from direct acts of conflict or criticism, it also worked in the opposite direction to remove other social actors from becoming the direct targets of the leaders' criticism. In the process, Kompas.com mitigated the force of the criticism and the intensity of the conflict, while still managing to construe controversial information. In Excerpt (16), through instrumentalisation, Kompas.

Courting controversy 131

com impersonalises the target of Megawati's criticism in the lead up to the presidential election.

(16) *Dalam wawancara ini, Megawati mempertanyakan metode yang digunakan sejumlah partai politik untuk memilih calon presiden mereka.*

In the interview, Megawati questioned the method used by a number of political parties when choosing their presidential candidate.

Through this impersonalising operation, Kompas.com places a "barrier" between Megawati and the parties involved, in which *metode* (method) is positioned as the target of her "questioning" (*mempertanyakan*). Combined with aggregation in *sejumlah partai politik* (a number of political parties), Kompas.com generalises the target of her criticism rather than singling out a particular group. Through generalisation, Kompas.com invites speculation, while avoiding the identification of social actors involved. In the immediate context, given the intense rivalry between Jokowi and Prabowo as the final two presidential candidates, readers are likely to activate their repertoire of knowledge to interpret Megawati's criticism as an implicit attack upon Prabowo and his supporters.

Concealing agency and construing rumours

Within the strategy of alluding to controversy, the concealment of agency through grammatical operations requires special attention. In particular, nominalisation and passive agent deletion facilitated the construal of rumours and speculation on controversial issues, while bypassing the need to identify specific agents. It thus enabled Kompas.com to present controversial information involving members of the elite in a factual news report. Through nominalisation, "a difficult situation can be glossed over rather than attended to in any detail" (Hart, 2014, p. 130), and therefore works effectively in news journalism. This process of nominalisation transformed rumours into general knowledge, while concealing responsibility for controversial actions. Similarly, Fowler (1991) argues that the grammatical process of passivation functions to conceal writers' attitudes in a news text. Both operations were frequently combined with other strategic acts of impersonalisation to convey rumours as fact and minimise the expression of direct responsibility. Table 6.6 lists the elements that combine to form this building block.

Excerpt (17) combines nominalisation with utterance autonomisation to cover rumours of Megawati's intervention in the appointment of the potential corruption suspect, Budi Gunawan to chief of police.

(17) *Polemik pencalonan Komjen Budi Gunawan sebagai Kepala Polri memunculkan rumor adanya intervensi Ketua Umum PDI Perjuangan Megawati Soekarnoputri kepada Presiden Joko Widodo*

132   *Courting controversy*

Table 6.6 Building block 3: Concealing agency and construing rumours

Realisation in the strategy	Function in the strategy	Definitions
Representing social action and social actors through nominalisation	• Obfuscates responsibility behind potentially sensitive rumours • Gives actions a sense of tangibility, lending a sense of authority to rumours • Enables newspaper to publish rumours without directly accusing an agent responsible	*Nominalisation* is an impersonalising linguistic operation that transforms a verb into a noun, and suppresses important information such as agency, modality, and tense. E.g., *pembangunan* (development), derived from the transitive verb, *membangun* (to build).
Removal of agent responsible through passive agent deletion	• Navigates need to substantiate the identity of the agent responsible • Absence of human agent invites speculation • Protects newspaper from impression of direct accusation	*Passive agent deletion* is another operation that excludes the participant(s) in the portrayal of a social action. Realised in Indonesian by word order: object + verb, and attaching the *di-* or *ter-* affix to the verb, without including the agent

The issue of the nomination of Commissioner General Budi Gunawan as Chief of Police has given rise to rumours of the presence of the intervention of Chair of the PDI-P Megawati Soekarnoputri on President Joko Widodo.

Through nominalisation in the noun, *pencalonan* (nomination), the process rather than the agent behind it becomes responsible for the act of "giving rise to rumours" (*memunculkan rumor*). The use of utterance autonomisation to refer to "rumours," further compounds speculation while avoiding blame, without identifying a specific social actor responsible. The absence of the specific agents responsible for both the nomination and the criticism avoids direct public criticism of the current government, while hinting at its very existence. In the second sentence, Kompas.com engages nominalisation again in *adanya intervensi* (the presence of intervention) to construe Megawati in a. meddling role, while avoiding the direct representation of her agency in the process. In contrast to the suppression of the role of the government through nominalisation, however, the use of possessivation to associate Megawati with the intervention maintains an impression of her involvement.

Like nominalisation, passive agent deletion also removed social actors from the action, which constructed an impression of generalised consensus, while mitigating responsibility for negative opinions. Excerpt (18) was published following the closure of Gang Dolly and Risma's rising popularity.

Courting controversy   133

(18) *PDI-P <u>dinilai akan</u> merugi jika tidak mengusung lagi Tri Rismaharini sebagai calon wali kota Surabaya 2015-2020. PDI-P juga <u>diprediksi</u> akan kalah jika mereka tidak mengusung Risma sebagai calon wali kota dalam pemilu wali kota (pilwali) nanti*

The PDI-P is <u>considered</u> to lose out if [they] do not nominate Tri Rismaharini as Surabaya mayoral candidate for 2015-2020. The PDI-P is also <u>predicted</u> to lose in the next mayoral election if they do not put Risma forward as a mayoral candidate.

In this excerpt, published as her popularity rose, Kompas.com construes a controversial rumour that the PDI-P will not back Risma in the next mayoral election. Through passive agent deletion in *dinilai* (considered, believed), and *diprediksi* (predicted), Kompas.com represents these evaluative mental processes about Risma's importance to the PDI-P as a generalised, and therefore shared opinion. Passive agent deletion enables Kompas.com to publish this subjective opinion covertly, while upholding journalistic standards of objectivity, which helps avoid the impression of direct criticism of the powerful PDI-P.

Legitimising conjecture by reference to expert and public opinion

In conjunction with impersonalising and deagentalising operations, Kompas.com incorporated both expert and public opinion as a means of legitimising conjecture in the strategy of alluding to controversy. Van Leeuwen (2007) identifies the role of both "personal" and "expert" authority as key sources of the legitimation of social practices in public communication. Reference to these sources can help avoid the impression of bias in reporting, despite portraying extremely negative evaluations. In Kompas.com reports, while both experts and members of the public provided a source of legitimacy to the coverage of controversial, speculative topics, the elite experts and non-elite public were portrayed differently; reflective of the importance of social status in regulating the public expression of political opinion.

Kompas.com portrayed expert figures in the strategy of alluding to controversy as agentalised individuals, which foregrounded their authority and their direct participation in the news event. Kompas.com also employed representational choices such as utterance autonomation and nominalisation within an existential clause, to convey critique of members of the political elite from a "safe" distance. This is evident in Excerpt (19) below, which concerns rumours of Megawati's alleged influence upon Jokowi.

(19) <u>*Pengamat Politik LIPI Ikrar Nusa Bakti menyoroti komunikasi*</u> *Ketua Umum DPP PDI Perjuangan Megawati Soekarnoputri yang kerap menyebut 'petugas partai.' <u>Kalimat</u> itu kerap <u>dikaitkan</u> dengan Presiden Joko Widodo.*

134   *Courting controversy*

Table 6.7 Building block 1: Legitimising conjecture by reference to expert and public opinion

Realisation in the strategy	Function in the strategy	Definitions
Experts: Formal nomination Functionalised in accordance with prestigious role Activation in authoritative verbal processes Activation in authoritative mental processes	• Formal nomination establishes their identity, authority and status • Functionalisation associates the experts with a prestigious role • Activation in verbal processes imbues the experts with authority and direct agency behind their message • Activation in mental processes creates a direct link between the expert and their opinions	*Formal nomination* represents social actors by their full name and official title *Functionalisation* defined in Table 6.1 *Activation* and *verbal processes* defined in Table 6.1 *Mental processes* defined in Table 6.3
Ordinary people: Objectivation through instrumentalisation: reference to the public via surveys Aggregation of survey results through quantity Functionalisation	• Instrumentalisation via reference to surveys legitimises the public voice in politics, and constructs a sense of consensus • Aggregation validates rumours and constructs consensus by reference to significant numbers • Functionalisation regulates the role of the ordinary people as a viable source of opinion by portraying them according to their participation in legitimate social actions	*Instrumentalisation* defined in Table 6.1 *Aggregation* defined in Table 6.1 *Functionalisation* defined in Table 6.1

LIPI Political Observer, Ikrar Nusa Bakti has highlighted the communication of Chair of the PDI-P, Megawati Soekarnoputri that frequently uses the term 'party staffer.' That line is frequently associated with President Joko Widodo.

Kompas.com first activates a political expert from a prestigious national research organisation in the verbal process, which "highlights" (*menyoroti*) Megawati's communication. The initial activation of the authoritative expert imbues the negative assessment to follow with a sense of legitimacy, while clearly positioning the expert rather than Kompas.com as the source. Through possessivised utterance autonomisation, *komunikasi Ketua Umum DPP PDI Perjuangan* (the communication of the Chair of the

Courting controversy 135

PDI-P) rather than Megawati herself becomes the focus of the expert's criticism. Possessivised utterance autonomisation creates a "barrier" between Megawati and the expert's criticism, thus mitigating its direct impact. Next in sequence, again through utterance autonomisation, the "communication" rather than Megawati herself becomes the subject of the subordinate clause responsible for "frequently using the term, 'party staffer.'"

In the sentence that follows, Kompas.com again uses utterance autonomisation, referring to *kalimat itu* (that line) rather than Megawati as the cause of the problem. Through passive agent deletion in the verb, *dikaitkan* (associated with), Kompas.com links Megawati's utterance specifically to Jokowi, while concealing the agent responsible for drawing the link. Ultimately, Kompas.com provides no evidence on which to base these assertions about Megawati; however, through the combination of expert authorisation and the strategic concealment of agency, Kompas.com manages to construct an impression of a genuine power imbalance between Megawati and Jokowi.

Van Leeuwen observes that the concreteness of expert opinion has nevertheless come increasingly under doubt (2007, p. 95). In a democratic political system, reference to public opinion surveys also functions as a means of expressing a legitimate opinion, while manufacturing consensus (van Leeuwen, 2008, p. 37). In the construal of contestation, the role of public opinion provided an additional source of legitimation. In contrast to the personalised representations of experts, however, Kompas.com represented the public mainly through impersonalised instrumentalisation in the form of surveys, thus maintaining a hierarchical differentiation between the identifiable elite and the anonymous public. In addition to instrumentalisation, Kompas.com also collectivised and aggregated the public when referring to survey results. Aggregation of survey results contributed to a sense of the consensus of the majority (van Leeuwen, 2008, p. 37).

Excerpt (20) first draws upon the authoritative voice of an expert, followed by survey results to contest Megawati's suitability for political leadership on the basis of her age. As an older woman in the political realm, Megawati transgressed unwritten rules determining political participation. Without reference to the authority of the expert and survey results, however, the report would appear completely subjective and biased against Megawati.

(20) *Direktur Eksekutif Cyrus Network Hasan Nasbi mengatakan, hasil survei ini menunjukkan bahwa Megawati harus segera menyerahkan tampuk kepemimpinannya kepada tokoh PDI-P yang lebih muda. Dukungan publik terhadap Megawati, menurut dia, sangat minim.*

Executive Director of the Cyrus Network, Hasan Nasbi has stated, survey results indicate that Megawati must quickly hand over the reins of her leadership to a younger member of the PDI-P. Public support for Megawati, according to him, is very low.

136 Courting controversy

Kompas.com filters the subjective opinion that Megawati is "too old" to lead the PDI-P through an individual expert, backed up by survey results. The expert, Hasan Nasbi is clearly identified according to his full name and position, while the public are impersonalised through instrumentalisation in *hasil survey* (survey results), indicative of their differentiated status. While differentiating the two, both are activated in a similar verbal process, where the expert performs the process of "stating" (*mengatakan*), and the survey results, "indicating" (*menunjukkan*). Through these two legitimate channels, Kompas.com then presents the explicit recommendation that Megawati should "hand over her leadership to a younger PDI-P figure."

While instrumentalisation through surveys provided a legitimate, yet impersonal source to express public opinion in a news report, functionalisation allocated the public to a slightly more agentalised role. Through initial reference to the authority of survey results, in Excerpt (21) Kompas.com aggregates and functionalises the public according to their role as survey "respondents."

> (21) *Menurut hasil survei tersebut, sebanyak 33,8 persen responden menilai Megawati lebih layak "nyapres". Sedangkan Jokowi, mendapatkan suara sekitar 24,6 persen. Posisi ketiga ditempati putri Megawati, Puan Maharani dengan 6,5 persen.*
>
> According to these survey results, 33.8 per cent of respondents consider Megawati to be more likely to run for the presidency. While Jokowi received 24.6 per cent of the vote. Megawati's daughter, Puan Maharani sat in third place with 6.5 per cent.

Published prior to the announcement of the PDI-P presidential candidate, the report foregrounds speculative opinion on the candidate's identity, naming Megawati as the one most likely to run. Having defined the role of the public according to their participation in a survey, Kompas.com activates them in the mental process of directly *menilai* (considering, evaluating) Megawati. Whereas on other occasions, a barrier was placed between social actors in critical mental processes, Megawati is positioned as the direct phenomenon of this public evaluation. By functionalising and aggregating members of the public through the survey mechanism, Kompas.com grants the public the ability to critically evaluate those in positions of higher authority.

Managed responses

Managed responses emerged as a minor strategy in Kompas.com reports, which maintained the topical relevance of contestation by representing the leaders' and their allies' responses to critique or accusations of wrongdoing.

Courting controversy 137

Orientation to difference is central in the operation of relations of power, and the production of interaction involves active and constant negotiation of differences of meaning (Fairclough, 2003, p. 41). In this case, the three women became a source through which the negotiation of differences took place. Two major patterns were identified in the representation of responses, which resulted in the allocation of different power roles to the women. These two patterns were labelled *defensive elite response* and *proactive elite response.*

The first mode of representation was primarily evident in the portrayal of Megawati and involved the activation of elite social actors responding to negative accusations and speaking on her behalf. They were activated chiefly in verbal processes of denial. In so doing, Kompas.com abstracted Megawati's role in the response, while maintaining a focus her as a source of contestation. In contrast to Megawati, Kompas.com portrayed Risma and Susi in a more active role in confronting criticism. Kompas.com also demonstrated greater variation in the types of responses they gave and constructed them in a proactive, rather than defensive role. Response to criticism thus became a means of representing Risma and Susi prevailing in attempts at public criticism, placing them in a position of power and control. In both cases, social actors responsible for criticism and rumours were both personalised, through nomination and activation, and impersonalised through utterance autonomisation, passive agent deletion, or nominalisation.

Defensive elite response

In the first manifestation of managed responses, Kompas.com activated and individualised members of the elite acting on behalf of the leader who was under attack. In most cases, Megawati became the target of critique, while high-ranking party officials responded on her behalf. Activation of the elite predominantly occurred in the verbal processes of denial, constructing the party allies in a defensive role. Defensive verbal responses were frequently followed by a clause specifying the initial accusations in detail. By specifying this information in addition to the denials, Kompas. com fuelled the practice of contestation rather than extinguishing it. In contrast to the individual members of the elite, the sources of the accusations were often impersonalised through utterance autonomisation, nominalisation, and passive agent deletion. Abstracting human agency when conveying the criticism avoided an impression of direct confrontation, while protecting the sources and Kompas.com from direct responsibility. For Megawati, while some Kompas.com reports normalised her relationship with power, reports highlighting a defensive elite response functioned to undermine her legitimate claim to power and in particular, her professional relationship with Jokowi. The components of this building block are listed below.

138   *Courting controversy*

Table 6.8 Building block 1: Defensive elite response

Realisation in the strategy	Function in the strategy	Definitions
Formal nomination of individual elites including full name and title	• Establishes authoritative position • Establishes right to speak on behalf of the leader • Establishes relation to the leader	*Formal nomination* represents social actors by their full name and official title *Individualisation*, as the name suggests, portrays social actors as individuals as opposed to a member of a collective
• Activation of elites in reactive verbal or emotional mental process • Detailed specification of allegations following acts of denial	• Both processes position the denier in a defensive role • Does not empower the denier by taking charge or offering a tangible solution • Verbal and mental processes do little to impact directly on other social groups, or the broader social-political order • The initial denial justifies inclusion of original accusation of wrongdoing • Despite denial, the iteration of the transgression maintains its topical salience	*Activation, verbal processes* defined in Table 6.1 *Mental processes* defined in Table 6.3
Concealment of identity and agency behind rumours and criticisms through forms of impersonalisation and passive agent deletion	• Enables the publication of rumours or accusations of wrongdoing without providing substantiating evidence • Protects the identity of those responsible • Impersonalisation suggests existence of rumours and criticism without providing evidence of true origins • The absence of an agent creates a sense of universality behind the rumours—it is possible for anyone and everyone to believe it	*Impersonalisation* removes the human identity of the social actor involved in the event. Impersonalising operations already discussed in this chapter include instrumentalisation, utterance autonomisation and nominalisation. *Passive agent deletion* defined in Table 6.1

Excerpt (22) was published as rumours circulated in the media and general public of newly-elected President Jokowi's plans to appoint a rumoured corruption suspect, Budi Gunawan to the role of chief of national police. Megawati was alleged to be behind Gunawan's planned appointment despite a pending investigation by the Corruption Eradication

Commission (KPK). Here, a PDI-P party official, Hasto Kristyanto denies the rumours.

(22) *Pelaksana tugas Sekretaris Jenderal DPP PDI Perjuangan Hasto Kristyanto membantah kabar Presiden Joko Widodo bertemu dengan Ketua Umum DPP PDI Perjuangan Megawati Soekarnoputri di kediaman Megawati, Jalan Teuku Umar Nomor 27A, Menteng, Jakarta Pusat, Kamis (29/1/2015).*

Task Executor of the Secretary General of the PDI-P Hasto Kristyanto has denied the news that President Joko Widodo met with Chair of the PDI-P Megawati Soekarnoputri in her home, Number 27A Teuku Umar Street, Menteng, Central Jakarta, on Thursday (29/1/2015).

While using *membantah* (to deny) to activate the party official in a verbal process, the subsequent detailed specification of Jokowi's alleged private engagement with Megawati reduces the effect of this denial, while maintaining the integrity of the original allegations. Furthermore, the impersonal reference to "news" (*kabar*) through utterance autonomisation enables Kompas.com to allege that their meetings took place without identifying a social actor or group as the source of this information. Obscuring the agent contributes simultaneously to upholding an impression of objectivity, while facilitating the circulation of rumours without providing evidence. Despite the initial denial, the strategic construal of information functions to insinuate Megawati's influence on Jokowi and undermine her relationship with power.

Excerpt (23) portrays another act of denial from the PDI-P elite while reiterating Megawati's transgressive actions in the political realm. In this report, Kompas.com once again engages the voice of Hasto Kristyanto to deny Megawati's apparent intervention in the Jokowi-Jusuf Kalla government.

(23) *Pelaksana Tugas (Plt) Sekjen DPP PDI Perjuangan Hasto Kristyanto membantah jika Ketua Umum PDI Perjuangan Megawati Soekarnoputri disebut selalu mengintervensi kebijakan yang diambil pemerintahan Joko Widodo-Jusuf Kalla. Menurutnya, isu intervensi Megawati itu sengaja dibuat untuk menjatuhkan Jokowi pada saat pemilu lalu.*

Task Executor of the Secretary General of the PDI-P Hasto Kristyanto has denied that the Chair of the PDI-P Megawati Soekarnoputri is said to always intervene in the policies undertaken by the Joko Widodo-Jusuf Kalla government. According to him, the issue of Megawati's intervention was created purposefully in order to bring down Jokowi in the last election.

140   *Courting controversy*

Following a similar pattern to Excerpt (22), Kompas.com iterates allegations of Megawati's influence after the initial denial. Kompas.com obscures the agent responsible for the allegation through passive agent deletion in the verb, *disebut* (is said to). The absence of the agent imbues the claims with a general sense of agreement without providing the identity of the agent responsible. The absence of details enables Kompas.com to report rumours, while maintaining an impression of objectivity. Despite containing Hasto's denial, the sentence that follows invites negative speculation through the use of passive agent deletion in the verb, *dibuat* (created). The absence of the agent here enables Hasto, and by extension, Kompas.com to make an accusation of attempts to undermine Jokowi without naming a guilty party. Overall, the publication of the act of denial does little to quash rumours of Megawati's undue influence and instead fuels speculation.

Proactive elite response

In the coverage of Megawati, the representation of response to criticism and rumours followed a common pattern of denial from a third party, and indirect allegations of the wrongdoing. By contrast, Kompas.com portrayed Risma and Susi in a more proactive role, as undeserving of criticism while taking direct action against it.

Excerpt (24) is an example of the representation of Susi's active response to criticism of her suitability for the role of minister, published shortly after her appointment.

> (24) *Menteri Kelautan dan Perikanan Susi Pudjiastuti kembali <u>mendapat komentar dari</u> kalangan akademisi. Setelah sebelumnya <u>mendapat komentar</u> keras <u>dari</u> ahli kelautan Institut Teknologi Bandung (ITB) ihwal kepakarannya di kelautan dan perikanan, kini giliran seorang ahli oseanografi Institut Pertanian Bogor (IPB) yang menyoroti kebijakan perikanan tangkap.*
>
> Minister of Maritime Affairs and Fisheries Susi Pudjiastuti has again <u>received comments from</u> the academic field. After previously <u>receiving</u> harsh <u>comments</u> from maritime expert at the Bandung Institute of Technology (ITB) on the matter of her maritime and fisheries expertise, now it is the turn for an oceanographer from the Bogor Institute of Agriculture (IPB) to draw attention to the policy on wild-caught fish.

Rather than positioning Susi as the target of criticism, Kompas.com activates her in the process of "receiving" (*mendapat*) criticism. In contrast to Susi's active stance, Kompas.com downplays the agency of those responsible for the criticism, and conceals their identity through utterance autonomisation in *komentar* (comments). While subsequently identifying her

Table 6.9 Building block 2: Proactive elite response

Realisation in the strategy	Function in the strategy	Definitions
Formal nomination and individualisation for individual leaders	• Establishes authoritative position	*Formal nomination* defined in Table 6.7. *Individualisation* defined in Table 6.3
Activation of leaders in verbal and mental processes	• The activation of the leaders themselves rather than a spokesperson indicates their ability to manage criticism directly • Verbal processes indicate their ability to speak out • Mental processes show their thoughts and feelings regarding the allegations • Specification of their positive deeds delegitimises criticism	*Activation, verbal processes* defined in Table 6.1. *Mental Processes* defined in Table 6.3
Concealment of the agency and identity of critics through impersonalisation and use of passive voice	• Impersonalisation relative to an active leader indicates their lack of agency, while concealing their full social identity • Representing their actions in passive voice in contrast to the active leaders reinforces the power of the leader, and the weakness of the critics	*Impersonalisation* defined in Table 6.8 *Passive voice* places the object affected by the action in subject position, followed by the verb, while placing the agent responsible after the verb, thus concealing the presence of the agent in the discourse.

critics by reference to their title, Kompas.com does not name them directly, which has the effect of depersonalising them in contrast to a personalised and proactive Susi.

Excerpt (25) portrays criticism of Risma's apparent lack of concern for non-Surabayan families during the AirAsia air disaster. As discussed in Chapter 4, Risma's direct involvement in responding to the air disaster received widespread praise across the country, and contributed to her rising status as a household name. In the excerpt below, Kompas.com constructs Risma in a proactive role, while placing her critics in a position of limited agency.

(25) *Aksi Wali Kota Surabaya Tri Rismaharini yang "menjemput bola" mencari data warganya yang ikut hilang bersama pesawat AirAsia QZ8501 diprotes keluarga penumpang yang bukan berasal dari Surabaya. Mereka cemburu mengapa hanya warga Surabaya yang diperhatikan wali kotanya. Protes dari warga non-Surabaya diterima Risma sendiri, Senin (29/12/2014) sore.*

142 *Courting controversy*

> The actions of Mayor of Surabaya Tri Rismaharini in "picking up the ball" and searching for data on her residents who went missing with AirAsia QZ8501 have been criticised by families of passengers from outside of Surabaya. They are jealous that only residents of Surabaya are receiving attention from the mayor. The complaints from non-Surabayan residents were received by Risma personally, Monday evening (29/12/2014).

Kompas.com first portrays Risma as the target of criticism indirectly, through the impersonalised representational choice of possessivised instrumentalisation. In this case, Risma's actions (*aksi Wali Kota Surabaya Tri Rismaharini*) rather than Risma herself become the target of criticism. Moreover, Kompas.com specifies Risma's good deeds of "picking up the ball and searching for data on her residents..." as the target of what appears to be illegitimate criticism. Kompas.com represents the criticism from families of non-Surabayan residents in passive form, *diprotes* (criticised, protested), which weakens the force of the critique, while allowing Risma's positive actions to shine through. The families are further undermined by attributing them to the negative mental process of being jealous (*cemburu*). Next, through utterance autonomisation in *protes* (complaints), Kompas.com lowers their agency. Similar to the portrayal of Susi in Excerpt (24), Kompas.com activates Risma in the process of actively "receiving" these complaints, and highlights her willingness to confront criticism, rather than portraying her as the passive target.

Excerpt (26) also serves to empower Risma in the midst of criticism. The extract was taken from a report on conflict between Risma and the chair of the Surabaya Zoo Association, and his intention to sue Risma for defamation[1]. Risma had allegedly mentioned his name when reporting a case of suspected corruption at the zoo to the Corruption Eradication Commission.

> (26) *Sebelumnya, Risma memang melaporkan dugaan korupsi dalam aksi pertukaran satwa oleh pengurus KBS dengan pihak lain. Risma menilai, pertukaran itu menyalahi aturan dan berpotensi korupsi. Risma juga melaporkan dugaan itu ke Mapolrestabes Surabaya.*

> Beforehand, Risma had indeed reported suspected corruption in the act of exchanging animals performed by the management of the Surabaya Zoo and other parties. Risma believes that this exchange violates regulations and has potential for corruption. Risma also reported these suspicions to Surabaya Police Headquarters.

Rather than focusing on Risma's denial of wrongdoing, Kompas.com activates her in the verbal process of "reporting" (*melaporkan*) suspected corruption, and in the evaluative mental process of "evaluating, considering" (menilai) the exchange of animals to be a potential source of corruption.

The reaffirmation of Risma's act of reporting corruption and her evaluation of the negative actions of zoo management functions as an act of resistance against her critics and undermines their legitimacy. Risma's defiant stance against corruption aligns with the popular anti-corruption movement (Kramer, 2013), thus negating the necessity of her denial. Moreover, the use of nominalisation in *korupsi* (corruption) and *pertukaran* (exchanging) reduces the level of agency of zoo management in comparison to Risma. Suppressing agency also navigates the journalistic constraints governing reporting on a legally sensitive matter, by avoiding the identification of a guilty party and the specificity of their actions before trial.

A similar example can be found in Excerpt (27), which was taken from a report covering Susi's response to a defamation case launched against her by a fishing company she had previously accused of illegal fishing.

(27) *Menteri Kelautan dan Perikanan Susi Pudjiastuti dilaporkan ke Badan Reserse Kriminal (Bareskrim) oleh pemilik kapal MV Hai Fa, Chandkid, dengan dugaan pencemaran nama baik. Susi pun* <u>*mengatakan siap meladeni pemilik kapal yang menangkap hiu-hiu asal Indonesia tersebut di meja hijau*</u>.

Minister of Maritime Affairs and Fisheries Susi Pudjiastuti has been <u>reported</u> to the Criminal Investigation Unit by the owner of MV Hai Fa, Chandkid, on the grounds of suspected defamation. Susi then <u>stated</u> that <u>she is prepared to face up to the owner of the ship that caught sharks from Indonesia</u> in court.

While initially positioning Susi as the target of the act of "being reported" (*dilaporkan*) by the ship's owner, Kompas.com activates her immediately thereafter in the verbal process of "stating" (mengatakan). Susi then directly expresses her preparedness to "face up to" (*meladeni*) the owner of the ship in court. The specification of the owner's deviant actions such as "catching Indonesian sharks," throughout the report delegitimises their legal challenge while legitimising Susi's accusations of illegal fishing. Overall, the Kompas.com representations of Susi and Risma's responses are far more proactive and justifiable than the portrayal of Megawati's. The challenges directed at Risma and Susi become an opportunity to reinforce their power, while undermining those who attempt to undermine them.

Conspicuous women and contested politics

This chapter described three strategies involved in the contestation of power involving Megawati, Risma, Susi in Kompas.com discourse. It critically evaluated the function of these strategies as part of the reporting practices of Kompas.com, the individual circumstances of the leaders, and their position within broader relations of power and discursive patterns in Indonesian

144 *Courting controversy*

politics. Overall, the three different strategies positioned the women as key figures in the portrayal of contestation, while generally reinforcing existing relations of power and highlighting their conspicuousness at the centre of controversial events. The representational choices in the Kompas.com texts created excitement around potential transgressions, but did not provide readers with detailed information on the events and social actors involved or sufficient evidence to pose a genuine challenge the status quo.

In particular, this chapter highlighted the effects of the strategic personalisation and impersonalisation of social actors as a means of surreptitiously contesting power relations. Through these representations, Kompas.com regulated the perception of the agency and responsibility of social actors involved, and their degree of inclusion in potentially controversial acts transgressing social, moral, or legal boundaries. Furthermore, by providing partial information, Kompas.com created vagueness in the construal of factually tenuous or contentious storylines based largely on subjective opinions and speculation. The absence of substantiating information fuelled further speculation, while strategically avoiding the impression of bias. The intermittent personalisation and activation of certain figures added legitimacy to the events portrayed in the texts. Overall, the subtle strategies used to construe contestation provided Kompas.com a "warrant" to produce highly subjective, controversial, and thereby newsworthy news reports in the mainstream online media.

In the construction of threat, through the differentiation of three major groups of social actors, Kompas.com alluded to transgression and potential harm to the vulnerable public, while fortifying the power of the three individual leaders. The construction of an impersonal, indeterminate threat group united only for the purpose of conducting deviant activities encouraged an unsympathetic response from readers. In contrast, the construction of a subordinate group of worthy victims was likely to arouse sympathy, while reproducing a unidirectional flow of power emanating downwards from the leader towards dependent citizens. Activation of the individual leaders against the deviant threats also illustrated their power relative to the threat as well as their protective role.

In the strategy of alluding to controversy, Kompas.com mystified both the human source of the conjecture as well as the details of the actual issue at hand. Components of the strategy included the use of affectual autonomisation to represent generalised public opinion and transform speculation and rumours into "common knowledge." The use of grammatical operations, such as the existential clause headed by ada along with nominalisation and passive agent deletion, contributed to a sense of general consensus while obfuscating direct responsibility. Instrumentalisation separated human actors involved in direct conflict and criticism by placing an impersonal "shield" between the agent and the human target. While reporting on problematic interactions, the absence of the direct human participants enabled Kompas.com to publish controversial information without allocating blame to a particular social actor or group. The analysis also uncovered the importance of both members of the elite and the general public as legitimate sources behind the construal of conjecture. Nevertheless, the differing portrayals indicated a hierarchical regulation of participation in political discourse. The consistent activation and identification of members of the elite in verbal and mental processes constructed an authoritative framework through which to filter rumours and speculation. In the case of the public, reference to opinion polls also contributed to constructing conjecture, by aggregating and legitimising opinion through instrumentalised surveys. While a means of measuring public opinion, these surveys provided a narrow scope for public participation in political contestation. Instead, they functioned primarily to legitimise rumours and facilitate speculation.

The strategy of managed responses contributed to the reproduction, rather than the mitigation of contestation, while the strategic representation of responses resulted in different outcomes for the three leaders. A noticeable difference was evident in the representation of Megawati. Aside from the higher frequency of the occurrence of the strategy in coverage of Megawati, the portrayal of responses to accusations largely undermined her personal agency. Instead, Kompas.com activated other elite figures who spoke on her behalf, in the defensive verbal processes. The specific reiteration of allegations that accompanied the verbal process of denial maintained the discursive relevance of the allegations. In the case of Risma and Susi, Kompas.com activated them more frequently as the agents in responding to conflict, criticism, and conjecture directly. Furthermore, rather than simply portraying them in acts of denial, Kompas.com activated Risma and Susi in a range of proactive social processes, while undermining their critics. The consistent activation of Risma and Susi in positive social actions in contrast to others suggests that they remained in a position of greater advantage.

Note

1 In 2008, the Indonesian government tightened defamation laws, which critics argue impinges on the ability of whistle-blowers to speak out on corruption (Weiss, 2014, p. 102).

References

Ahlstrand, J. (2020). Strategies of ideological polarisation in the online news media: A social actor analysis of Megawati Soekarnoputri. *Discourse & Society, October 2020*.

Bennett, L. (2005). *Women, Islam and modernity. Single women, sexuality and reproductive health in contemporary Indonesia*. Routledge.

Duile, T., & Bens, J. (2017). Indonesia and the "conflictual consensus": A discursive perspective on Indonesian democracy. *Critical Asian Studies, 49*(2), 139–162.

Fairclough, N. (2003). *Analysing discourse: Textual analysis for social research*. Routledge.

146 *Courting controversy*

Foucault, M. (1991). Governmentality. In G. Burchell, C. Gordon, & P. Miller (Eds.), *The Foucault effect: Studies in governmentality* (pp. 87–104). University of Chicago Press.

Fowler, R. (1991). *Language in the news: Discourse and ideology in the press.* Routledge.

Hart, C. (2014). *Discourse, grammar and ideology: Functional and cognitive perspectives.* Bloomsbury.

Haryanto, I. (2011). Media ownership and its implications for journalists and journalism in Indonesia. In K. Sen & D. Hill (Eds.), *Politics and the media in twenty-first century Indonesia: Decade of democracy* (pp. 104–118). Routledge.

Hasell, A., & Weeks, B. E. (2016). Partisan provocation: The role of partisan news use and emotional responses in political information sharing in social media. *Human Communication Research, 42*(4), 641–661.

Kramer, E. (2013). When news becomes entertainment: Representations of corruption in Indonesia's media and the implication of scandal. *Media Asia, 40*(1), 60–72.

Kroeger, K. (2003). AIDS rumors, imaginary enemies, and the body politic in Indonesia. *American Ethnologist, 30*(2), 243–257.

Krzyzanowski, M., & Wodak, R. (2009). *The politics of exclusion: Debating migration in Austria.* Transaction Publishers.

Lim, M. (2017). Freedom to hate: Social media, algorithmic enclaves, and the rise of tribal nationalism in Indonesia. *Critical Asian Studies, 49*(3), 411–427.

Machin, D., & Suleiman, U. (2006). Arab and American computer war games: The influence of a global technology on discourse. *Critical Discourse Studies, 3*(1), 1–22.

Masaki, K. (2007). *Politics, participation and policy: The "emancipatory" evolution of the "elite-controlled" policy process.* Lexington Books.

Melissa, E. (2019). *The internet, social media, and political outsiders in post-Suharto Indonesia: A case study of Basuki Tjahaja Purnama.* [Doctoral dissertation, University of Western Australia], University of Western Australia Research Repository.

Reyes, A. (2011). *Voice in political discourse: Castro, Chavez, Bush and their strategic use of language.* Continuum International Publishing Group.

Sahab, A. (2017). Realitas citra politik Tri Rismaharini. *Masyarakat, Kebudayaan dan Politik, 30*(1), 20–34.

Seymour-Ure, C. (2003). Grapevine politics: Political rumours. In C. Seymour-Ure (Ed.), *Prime Ministers and the media: Issues of power and control* (pp. 203–229). Blackwell Publishing.

Shin, J., Jian, L., Driscoll, K., & Bar, F. (2016). Political rumoring on Twitter during the 2012 US presidential election: Rumor diffusion and correction. *New Media & Society, 19*(8), 1214–1235.

Tan, L. (2012). Indonesian national security during the Suharto New Order (1965–1998): The role of narratives of peoplehood and the construction of danger. *New Zealand Journal of Asian Studies, 14*(1), 49–70.

Tapsell, R. (2012). Old tricks in a new era: Self-censorship in Indonesian journalism. *Asian Studies Review, 36,* 227–245.

Turner, G. (2018). The media and democracy in the digital era: Is this what we had in mind? *Media International Australia, 168*(1), 3–14.

van Dijk, T. A. (1996). Discourse, power and access. In C. R. Caldas-Coulthard & M. Coulthard (Eds.), *Texts and practices: Readings in critical discourse analysis* (pp. 84–104). Routledge.

van Dijk, T. A. (2006). Discourse, context and cognition. *Discourse Studies, 8*(1), 159–177.

van Leeuwen, T. (2007). Legitimation in discourse and communication. *Discourse & Communication, 1*(1), 91–112.

van Leeuwen, T. (2008). *Discourse and practice: New tools for critical discourse analysis.* Oxford University Press.

Weiss, M. (2014). New media, new activism: Trends and trajectories in Malaysia, Singapore and Indonesia. *International Development Planning Review, 36*(1), 91–109.

Wijayanto (2015). Old practice in a new era: Rasa as the basis of self-censorship in Kompas daily newspaper. *GSTF Journal on Media & Communications (JMC), 2*(2), 66–74.

Wodak, R. (2002). Friend or foe: The defamation or legitimate and necessary criticism? Reflections on recent political discourse in Austria. *Language and Communication, 22*(4), 495–517.

Wodak, R. (2008). 'Us' and 'them': Inclusion and exclusion – discrimination via discourse. In G. Delanty, R. Wodak, & P. Jones (Eds.), *Identity, belonging and migration* (pp. 54–77). Liverpool University Press.

Wodak, R. (2015). *The politics of fear: What right-wing populist discourses mean.* Sage.

7 Gender and news media discourse: Populism, authoritarianism, and democratic transition

Chapters 4, 5, and 6 revealed the multiple facets and dynamic nature of Megawati, Risma, and Susi's relationship with power expressed in Kompas.com discourse over the course of the 2014 presidential election. This chapter synergises the major findings uncovered, and draws explanatory links between the discourse strategies and the compelling social-political factors which imbue the strategies with efficacy and meaning. The interpretation of findings incorporates an understanding of Indonesia's social-political context of democratic transition, emergent populism, alongside its legacy of authoritarianism and gendered structures of power. In so doing, this chapter brings to the surface the implications for women's political participation, Indonesian politics, and online news media practices. This chapter acknowledges the relationship between the individual leaders' political circumstances and the patterns of representation in the discourse, and integrates knowledge of the commercial interests and journalistic practices of the online news media.

Departing from the conventional use of social actor analysis to examine dichotomous practices of social inclusion and exclusion (van Leeuwen, 2008; van Leeuwen & Wodak, 1999), this book set out to capture the fluidity of power relations in Indonesia through the study of discursive representations of women in the political realm. Examining the Kompas.com representations of Megawati, Risma and Susi in an interactive network provided insight into the distribution of power among the social actors and social groups in a fluid, yet essentially vertical hierarchy—a legacy of New Order power arrangements. The in-depth examination of the practices of mitigating, augmenting and contesting power revealed how Kompas.com discursively defined the social roles and agentive potential of the social actors in this fluid, yet hierarchical network of power. As the concept of power relates to the ability to exercise control over others (van Dijk, 1996), the study of the representations of social actors included the study of their social actions in interaction served to identify the exercise of control, and thereby power, of certain social groups or individual actors over others. The inclusion of knowledge of the social political context, the legacy of gendered structures of power, and Indonesian journalistic

DOI: 10.4324/9781003083252-7

Gender and news media discourse 149

practices supports a more profound understanding of the discourse and its social-political impact.

Overall, the heterogeneity of representations uncovered reflects a context of "intense sociocultural and discoursal change" as described by Fairclough (1992, p. 269), characterised by inconsistencies, dilemmas, and a diversity of subject positions expressed in the discourse. While discourse produced in contexts of democratic change may appear heterogenous, it does not automatically result in more democratic outcomes; in fact, it may contain more subtle means of obfuscating asymmetrical relations of power (Wodak, 1996). Women gaining recognition in the political realm as unique outsiders or powerful individuals with institutional backing may herald a new era in political discourse; however, the extent to which their discursive representations reflect or influence change to underlying structures of power remains to be seen. Moreover, as Chapter 6 has shown, supposedly oppositional discourses produced in this context of intense discursive change are not always anti-hegemonic (Blommaert, 2005). In accordance with the critical aims of CDA, the interpretation of findings that follows uncovers the explicit and implicit tensions, contradictions, and opportunities contained within the representation of Megawati, Risma, and Susi in Kompas.com discourse.

Forging a political niche for women

One of the most compelling features to emerge in the Kompas.com discourse was the construction of the individual leader as a novel, accessible and at times, vulnerable character. Such representations simultaneously highlighted their unique status in the political realm, while imbuing their leadership with a sense of legitimacy, motivated by duty rather than self-interest. Emerging at the crossroads of residual gendered notions of duty-bound womanhood, contemporary democratic ideals of limited power, and populist values of breakthrough, pro-people leadership, the discursive pattern of mitigation positioned the women in a niche role, which produced short-term enabling, but long-term constraining effects. While enabling their political participation, a closer reading of the Kompas.com texts reveals a trade-off between the leaders' political legitimacy and their ability to accumulate and exercise power freely.

Across a variety of contexts across Asia, abiding by the norms of apolitical, duty-bound leadership has been shown to increase a woman's perceived moral capital and political appeal, while validating her presence in the male dominated political realm (Derichs & Thompson, 2013; Derichs et al., 2006; Thompson, 2013). The discursive mitigation of the women's power in Kompas.com also corresponded to the residual values of *ibuism*, promoting duty or obligation to others over personal gain in the performance of their role (Bennett, 2005; Djajadiningrat-Nieuwenhuis, 1987; Gerlach, 2013; Rhoads, 2012; Suryakusuma, 2011). Portraying the women in conformance with latent gender norms created a niche for all three to operate in the

150   *Gender and news media discourse*

political realm, often quite conspicuously, without posing a serious threat to the status quo. The representations, however, ultimately upheld gender norms defining access to power, which constrained the women's ability to participate in politics on equal terms with men.

In the immediate context of the 2014 democratic presidential election marked by a rising desire for pro-people leadership, strategies of mitigation produced different outcomes for the individual leaders. For Susi and Risma, as political newcomers, downplaying their perceived relationship with power, while emphasising their accessibility and visibility constructed them as norm-breaking, yet non-threatening female changemakers. For Megawati, the mitigation of her power helped navigate her fraught relationship with Jokowi, assuage fears of her ambitions for greater power, and normalise her continued presence in the political realm in an era of anti-elite sentiment. Informal nomination imbued all three women with an approachable, non-threatening political persona. Grammatical passivation and impersonalisation also separated the individual leader from the direct act of accumulating or perpetuating personal power, which contributed to their perceived moral standing. In the coverage of Risma's struggles with political pressure as mayor of Surabaya, for example, her grammatical passivation in contrast to the activation of the PDI-P illustrated her dependence on others for support, indicating the underlying limits of her power despite her skyrocketing popularity. Susi's passivation and the portrayal of her vulnerability when engaging with the public also illustrated the limits of her power, despite her important status as a minister. In the portrayal of Megawati's relationship with Jokowi, belittling nomination along with her passivation relative to the activation of Jokowi resolved the dilemma of who was in charge of whom.

The strategy of constructing spectacle highlighted the women's incongruity, with political life by drawing attention to their unusual behaviour and physical appearance. While marking their difference to the political norm, the portrayals of their physical appearance or candid behaviour against a serious political backdrop signified a potential challenge to the status quo. When examined through the lens of transitivity, however, the portrayal of the leaders' norm-breaking behaviour limited them to predominantly self-oriented social actions that garnered public attention, yet did not directly impact on others or the social-political order. Through somatisation, the women were also subject to a degree of control through their visibility, which implicated a pervasive public gaze in the process. In this regard, while the focus on their behaviour and appearance at odds with the political realm enhanced their visibility, it reinforced their subordinate status, much in line with Hatley (1990) and Keeler's (1990) recognition of the trade-off between women's social manoeuvrability and status in Java.

While the representations of the women in the practice of mitigation reflected both underlying gendered notions of power as well as emergent political values, the explicit role of Islam was noticeably absent. Scholars of gender and politics in Indonesia have recognised the role of Islam in both

Gender and news media discourse 151

facilitating and constraining women's political agency (Dewi, 2015; Rinaldo, 2010; van Wichelen, 2006), and deliberated on the influence of political Islam in the democratic era (Aspinall, 2012; Elson, 2010; McCoy, 2013). In the Kompas.com discourse, however, only the minor, indirect reference to the value of female modesty commonly associated with Islam was evident. The largely secular agenda of Kompas.com arguably played a role in its absence. It is also important to recognise the overlap between popular Islamic values and traditional gender norms in Indonesia. While commonly associated with Islam, modesty in terms of dress and behaviour is often claimed as a national cultural value, blurring the lines between the secular and Islamic. The conservative values of duty and self-sacrifice above self-interest also correspond to certain Islamic interpretations of ideal womanhood.

The personalisation of female leadership

While mitigation played a key part in negotiating a viable, albeit constrained space for Megawati, Risma, and Susi to operate in the political realm, certain aspects of the Kompas.com discourse also portrayed them in a more dominant role, augmenting their perceived relationship with power. The strategy of personification portrayed the women in top down, agentive roles, as representatives of an institution with the power to act over others in the social-political hierarchy. Formal nomination techniques and prominent positioning in the headline and lead demonstrated their high public status, while pseudo-titles established their legitimate place in politics. Activation in both "soft" and "hard" power roles in relation to subordinate social groups also indicated the scope of their authoritative leadership. Considering the historical political marginalisation of women in Indonesia (Dwyer, 2004; Robinson, 2009; Wieringa, 2002), this representation provides some evidence of new opportunities for women to adopt a stronger, politically dominant stance in the democratic era, and move away from the New Order model of subordinate womanhood, towards active public leadership. While personification positioned the women in a dominant role, however, such portrayals were still sanctioned by an adherence to duty, and only in relation to sanctioned subordinate social groups.

Alongside personification, Kompas.com also portrayed the leaders and their actions interchangeably in cooperation with an institution, city, or nation. Through impersonalising operations, institutionalisation concealed human identity and responsibility, and gave their leadership a sense of impersonal authority (van Leeuwen, 2008, p. 47). The representation of an institution or location in place of the women as the primary social actor, however, resulted in the obfuscation of agency, responsibility, modality, and temporality in the portrayal of events (Fairclough, 2003, p. 143). Their role as a prominent, individual agent became assimilated within the broader structures of the state or institution to which they belonged. Institutionalisation carried the message that behind the leaders' iconic public facade, the

152 *Gender and news media discourse*

pervasive impersonal authority of the institution remained. While arguably reinforcing the power of the individual women, this allegiance constructed in the discourse impinged on their ability to act and influence political outcomes directly, while eliminating space for alternative opinions on the political action.

Women, precarity, and the perpetuation of the status quo

As reiterated throughout this book, as gendered structures of political power shift, women in politics can become highly visible figures. Discourse produced in contexts of social change tends to "accentuate difference, conflict, polemic, a struggle over meaning, norms, [and thereby] power" (Fairclough, 2003, p. 42). Where multiple social groups attempt to redefine or defend existing relations of power based on their interests, women in politics can become key figures in struggles over societal visions and value systems undergoing transformation (Brenner, 2011; Fleschenberg & Derichs, 2011, p. 5; Hatley, 2008). The study of women in the practice of contestation revealed that some facets of the Kompas.com discourse exploited their symbolic difference, implicating them in a conflict-based agenda to create contestation and destabilise rival groups, yet, ultimately legitimise the interests of those already in power. Conversely, particularly in the case of Megawati, other aspects of the discourse highlighted her incongruity with politics and her apparent threat to masculine structures of power. In both cases, the women became icons in an apparent power struggle that ultimately reinforced a political hierarchy, fuelled by commercial media interests.

The strategy of constructing threat took advantage of the women's prominent identity, placing them in a pivotal role between a deviant, yet vague threat group and innocent victims worthy of sympathy. While the construction of a threat group is not new to either the Indonesian political scene or populist agendas worldwide, this book has highlighted the role of women in the process. In this case, their gender not only created heightened levels of attention, but also mobilised traditional ideas of protective, nurturing motherhood when portraying their stance against the supposed threat. The representation of their involvement in emotional acts responding to threat also emphasised their humanness and their personal investment in attending to the problem, which contrasted against the largely non-human portrayal of the threat group. Positioning an elite male politician in a similar act would presumably result in a different outcome. Highlighting the role of women in this discursive process adds a further dimension of understanding to the interplay of residual gender values and emergent political values in this well-known strategy.

The strategy of alluding to controversy also positioned the women as prominent figures operating in the midst of instability and uncertainty. Presenting vague rumours about alleged transgressions and interpersonal conflict highlighted the women's precarity and vulnerability in politics, albeit without directly accusing them of wrongdoing. Instead, the Kompas. com discourse created intrigue by hinting at the possibility of transgression through the strategic obfuscation of the identity and agency of the social actors responsible. Kompas.com also often relied on expert opinion or surveys as a mechanism to legitimise the construal of controversial information in the discourse. These vague rumours carried the potential to unhinge their political career if pressed further, but the strategic presentation of information prevented a direct attack upon the women's integrity. Moreover, the extent to which the allusions of wrongdoing affected the women's status and reputation in the political realm depended largely on the ongoing representation of their political agenda, as a proactive change-maker or a member of the incumbent elite.

For the individual women, while Kompas.com featured all three in the contestation of power, the discourse posed the greatest obstacle to Megawati and her ability to participate freely in the political realm. Kompas.com discourse problematised her relationship with other members of the elite, and precluded her from accessing a legitimate path of recourse. Megawati's difference to Risma and Susi was particularly evident in the strategy of managed responses, which positioned her in both a passive and defensive role when responding to allegations of wrongdoing, while Risma and Susi appeared in a proactive role. Attempts at challenging Risma and Susi's power ultimately resulted in the delegitimation of those responsible for the attack. While others spoke on Megawati's behalf, simultaneously denying and reiterating her alleged transgressions, Risma and Susi responded directly to the criticism and offered an alternative perspective. Kompas.com emphasised Risma and Susi's innocence, and the illegitimacy of their detractors. Such representations granted newcomers, Risma and Susi permission to participate in the contested political space, albeit on shaky grounds. For Megawati, her disempowered response undermined her continued presence in the political realm. Overall, through the construal of conflict and struggle, Kompas.com placed all three women within a contested space of power, which reinforced the precarity of their role in politics.

Women at the crossroads of political change

Within Indonesia's broader political framework, the representation of Megawati, Risa, and Susi in Kompas.com discourse indicates both change and continuity in political discourse and structures of power in the democratic era, 16 years since the fall of the New Order government. The 2014 presidential campaign ignited anti-status quo discourse, whereby the public viewed individual changemakers as a panacea to the perceived political stagnation of the SBY government (Aspinall, 2015; Hatherell & Welsh, 2017). Globally, scholars have recognised the role of personalised representations of politicians, rather than faceless institutions as a way of constructing greater public appeal, while simultaneously obscuring asymmetrical relations of power

154 *Gender and news media discourse*

(Campus, 2010; Fairclough, 2013; Garzia, 2011; McAllister, 2007; Mulderrig, 2011). The charismatic changemaker is not a foreign concept to Indonesians. A focus on the individual, such as Soekarno and Suharto has been a long-standing model of political leadership in Indonesia. The familiarity of the individual leader to the Indonesian political scene arguably contributed to the successful emergence and acceptance of populist tactics in the 2014 election. Adhering to a model of Arche-politics, Indonesian political discourse remains preoccupied with a leaders' traits and personality, whose status and credibility are defined against an enemy out-group.

The strategy of institutionalisation, with its linguistic properties obfuscating agency, responsibility, modality, and temporality, was also identified alongside the strategy of personification as a way of augmenting the power of the individual leaders and the institutions they represented. The hegemonic impact of the linguistic obfuscation such as nominalisation and a reliance on reference to institutional power upon structures of power has been observed by CDA practitioners worldwide. Such examples include Fairclough's (2000) study of New Labour discourse in the UK, and Harrison and Young's (2005) study of new capitalist management in Canada. Heryanto's (1995) study of the ubiquitous key word, *pembangunan* (development) in Indonesia also demonstrated the power of linguistic obfuscation as a regulatory force in the New Order. In democratic Indonesia, the widely popular concept of *perubahan* (change), in itself another nominalisation, formed the vision and mission of the Jokowi-Jusuf Kalla presidential campaign (Widodo & Kalla, 2014). Uniquely, the analysis of Kompas.com discourse revealed the interconnection between the strategy of institutionalisation and personification. Recognising the mutually constitutive nature of the individual and the institution provides a clearer understanding of the reproduction of hierarchical relations of power as well as the ability of the individual leader to gain traction in the political realm.

Both nationalist and localist discourse also emerged in the co-occurring strategy of institutionalisation, whereby the leader came to embody the city or nation they represented through the impersonalising representational choice of spatialisation. Through reference to the identical desires of "Indonesia" and the individual leader, spatialisation created a sense of consensus. Disagreement with the shared vision would thus indirectly render the critic "un-Indonesian." Indicative of the increasing power of localist discourses of belonging since decentralisation began in 1998 (Robinson, 2014), spatialisation was also evident at the local level in the coverage of Risma and the campaign to close Gang Dolly red light district. Risma's campaign to close Gang Dolly took on both a moralist and localist stance, by the portrayal of her efforts to eradicate deviance and protect the city. Reference to the city of Surabaya in demanding the closure manufactured consent and excluded alternative voices, while assimilating Risma's vision with that of the entire city. The representation of human actors by means of reference to the place in which they resided also had the coercive effect of diminishing

Gender and news media discourse 155

the individual agency of its inhabitants, while eliminating dissenting voices. Such a representational choice has also been recognised in the "one-nation politics" of the UK New Labour government as a means of manufacturing consent (Fairclough, 2000, pp. 34–35).

The role of nationalism was also evident in the strategy of constructing threat, which ultimately reinforced hierarchical relations of power between the included and excluded; the aggressor and worthy victim; and the strong, protective leader and the weak citizens. The orientation towards an external source was predominantly evident in the representation of Susi and her agenda to tackle illegal fishing, and became a means of asserting national identity, while reinforcing power through the need to protect the vulnerable. This representation connected to the revival of Indonesia's national identity as a maritime nation, and the emergent discourse of sovereignty (*kedaulatan*), which sat within the broader discourse of change. The representation of the threat as an external force constructed Indonesia's maritime agenda within a simplified dichotomy of "good" (Indonesia) and "evil" (neighbouring countries), while providing limited details on the complexity of the situation.

The broader interpretation of the strategy of constructing threat and its discursive characteristics contributes to a significant body of research examining the political causes and consequences of the practice of othering taking place within a populist agenda. In a European context, Wodak and Boukala (2015, p. 89) argue that in-group members create "imagined communities" while excluding the "others," which has contributed to the revival of European nationalism. In the context of modern Indonesian history, the construction of threat has functioned as a source of nation- and people-building (Tan, 2012). The ideal of an organically closed and uniform political body or the hegemonic paradigm of Arche-politics remains a fundamental ideal of Indonesia's democracy (Duile & Bens, 2017). While contestation, conflict, and antagonisms can symptomise, or become a catalyst for social-political change, the construction of threat in Kompas. com discourse directs dissent towards an external source. Portraying the transgressive actions of the threat group undermined their position on the periphery, while reinforcing the power of the leaders, and the vulnerability of civil society.

The constrained role of civil society:
Opportunities and limitations

The representation of civil society in Kompas.com discourse revealed their precarious position, and their ambiguous influence upon the political order. Good governance is not merely the responsibility of government, but is dependent upon a variety of actors, including the ordinary people (Morrell, 2005, p. 130). Under the New Order, members of the general population were portrayed as a floating mass without grassroots political ties

156   *Gender and news media discourse*

(Jackson, 2005; van Langenberg, 1986). The *rakyat* (ordinary people) were positioned at the bottom of a political hierarchy and denied a clear social identity (Anderson, 1990). The duties of the population were to the state and the interests of national development (Heryanto, 1995). In the early years following the onset of *Reformasi,* scholars such as Aspinall (2004) articulated an ambitious view of the transformation of civil society as a politically engaged social group. Other scholars, however, quickly dismissed the significance of civil society, and adopted the cynical view of Indonesia as an illiberal democracy hijacked by elite oligarchic forces (Robison & Hadiz, 2004). In the time period of the 2014 presidential election, researchers highlighted the revitalised role of civil society in influencing political outcomes as a partial result of newfound online activism and online media engagement (Mietzner, 2015; Suwana, 2018; Tapsell, 2015).

The analysis of the corpus of Kompas.com texts reveals an inconsistent representation of civil society. This inconsistency is indicative of change hampered by uncertainty regarding the role of both citizens and political leaders in shaping political life. Kompas.com consistently indexed the female leaders' relationship with power relative to subordinate social actors, such as the ordinary people or low-ranking staff. In contrast to the female leaders, these social actors were allocated to passivised grammatical roles, and were often represented according to their subordinate social category. In the strategy of regulating access, the greater levels of agency allocated to the public in interaction with the leaders pointed to a tentative erosion of the hierarchical distance between the elite and the non-elite. The strategy demonstrated greater diversity in the discursive allocation of grammatical roles to participants in social interaction. Indeed, Van Leeuwen (2008, p. 53) asserts that in the representation of social actors, boundaries can be blurred deliberately for the purpose of achieving specific ideological effects. The intersection of grammatical role allocation, personalisation, impersonalisation, and categorisation of social actors revealed both moments of empowerment and disempowerment for these social groups. Nevertheless, while portraying members of the public in a more active role, aggregation combined with activation to construe their mass compliance, thus limiting their scope for political expression. Moreover, the activation of the ordinary people occurred predominantly in expressions of support for the leaders, creating a narrow scope for their political participation.

In the contestation of power, the ordinary people appeared in the strategy of constructing threat, and were portrayed as vulnerable victims in need of protection. Bazzi (2009), Kroeger (2003), and Reyes (2009) all identified the construction of binary oppositions between an aggressor and a worthy victim as a key element of the discursive representation of threat. Members of the public were largely portrayed in a grammatically passive role, while both members of the threat group and the individual leaders were activated. Kompas.com also highlighted social class and personal disadvantage. This

Gender and news media discourse 157

not only worked to establish the human vulnerability of the ordinary people and intensify the perceived deviance of the threat group, but also perpetuated a hierarchy of power based on dependency on the political leaders.

When portraying the public in a more active role in the practice of contestation, Kompas.com limited their level of direct participation through impersonalised representations in the form of opinion polls. The survey mechanism, primarily conducted online, legitimised public opinion of the leaders, and created a niche mode of political participation. The survey mechanism, often conducted online, concealed the identity of respondents and arguably facilitated freedom of expression in the context of both historical and ongoing legal restrictions on freedom of speech in Indonesia (Weiss, 2014). While oppositional discourse can fracture unities and rearrange groupings in a network of power relations (Blommaert, 2005), limiting public participation to survey results carried less counter-hegemonic potential.

In contrast to the public, individual members of the elite were consistently identified and activated as a legitimate means of disrupting the female leaders' relationship with power. To establish their clear identity, Kompas.com used the formal name and title of members of the elite and functionalised them according to their role. The individual figures were activated in critical verbal and mental processes in relation to the leaders. Given that the omission of the human agency and identity of a social actor can foreground the salience of others (Langacker, 2008, p. 384), the contrasting representation of the elite and the general public provides evidence of the perpetuation of a hierarchy of opinion in Indonesia, much like elsewhere around the world. Overall, the differing representations of social actors in a social power network reflected a political landscape undergoing tentative change, yet underpinned by a latent vertical hierarchy of power.

Provocation, censorship, and cursory reporting in the online news media

Scholars have recognised the growing importance of the online news media to political discourse worldwide, and its resulting democratic and undemocratic outcomes. Patterns in Kompas.com texts shared similar characteristics to news discourse identified elsewhere around the world. The personalisation of politics (Campus, 2010; Garzia, 2011; McAllister, 2007; Wodak, 2011), and the superficial focus on rumour, sensation, and provocation to boost online interaction and revenue (Hasell & Weeks, 2016; Miller, 2015; Turner, 2016) were two major features to appear in Kompas. com discourse. Indeed, the increasingly rapid production and consumption of news content online emerging around the world has led to news sites offering simplified, bite-sized news stories focusing on individuals and their immediate actions. Readers, on the other hand, engage with the texts at a superficial level before sharing, commenting, or liking, and then moving on

158   *Gender and news media discourse*

(Gazali, 2014; Lim, 2013). In the era of digital media, journalists work to strict deadlines with limited resources, and are expected to produce stories as part of a 24-hour news cycle. Under these circumstances, Kompas.com took advantage of the three female leaders' difference, and positioned them in a conspicuous role—as icons of difference, with the potential to trigger a reader response.

The free media in a democracy should function "to build awareness of social and political issues," and contribute to shaping "the informed environment required for developing social capital and a strong civil society" (Morrell, 2005, p. 129). The portrayal of the women as provocative, yet approachable and clearly gendered political leaders fulfilled the media's values of novelty, and firmly established their difference to the average politician. Establishing their incongruity with the political realm had both beneficial and detrimental effects upon democratic relations of power. Headlines focusing on their norm-breaking behaviour or candid interactions with the public prompted a response from the readers, and invited them to identify with the politicians. Such discourse, however, played into the increasingly dominant trend of politics-as-entertainment evident in Indonesia and the rest of the world. As Kramer (2013) explains, this trend encourages a cosmetic interest and a superficial understanding of politics, in turn, leading to a diminished quality of political discourse. Combining with the rapid online news production and consumption habits in resource-poor newsrooms (Lim, 2013), this reporting style had limited benefits for meaningful and effective public engagement. While generating public interest in symbolic politics, and stimulating clicks, comments, and shares, the portrayal of iconic women promoted superficial knowledge of social actors and events.

While the demands of the commercial media undoubtedly influenced the content and reporting styles of Kompas.com journalists, the professional constraints of objectivity, the presence of the defamation law, and the residual practice of self-censorship also played a role in shaping news discourse in Kompas.com reports. Hanitzsch (2006), Kramer (2013), Tapsell (2015), and Wijayanto (2015) point to a strong desire among Indonesian journalists in the democratic era to produce news reports that not only appeal to popular interests, but also cover issues at an in-depth level. The portrayal of the media *by* the media in the strategy of regulating access provided insight into journalists' implicit self-perceptions. Members of the media were represented as part of a large, active, and professional collective, with a degree of audacity when interacting with the perceivably accessible leaders. The constraints in which journalists must operate, however, continue to stifle their ability to take risks that challenge the status quo.

Reporting on conflict, criticism, rumours, and speculation involving the political elite in Indonesia represents a particularly newsworthy, and potentially controversial event. The media, civil society, foreign governments and individuals, and dissident members of the elite were all present in the

Gender and news media discourse   159

portrayal of contestation in Kompas.com reports. Flowerdew (2008) refers to "hidden transcripts" employed by the powerless to resist the powerful, and in the case of Kompas.com, the various means of impersonalisation functioned as a way of contesting power covertly. The absence of the explicit agent through impersonalisation enabled Kompas.com to represent potential challenges to relations of power indirectly, while "shielding" the news organisation from an impression of bias, the perpetuation of falsehoods or anti-elite sentiment, all while avoiding potential retribution. Furthermore, impersonalisation generalised the situation, often on the basis of limited or speculative information, eliminating opportunities for closer scrutiny. Among practices of impersonalisation, the category of affectual autonomisation in this strategy of alluding to controversy illustrated the importance of thoughts and ideas to portraying public conjecture. This novel category is a worthy addition to van Leeuwen's (2008) list of impersonalising objectivation types, and is of particular salience to the current media context where an interest in controversial opinions influence reporting styles, in the midst of commercial, legal and ethical constraints.

The portrayal of conflict in the practice of contestation also employed impersonalising representational choices, which managed social actors' level of involvement, and functioned to create distance between the social actor and a certain undesired social practice. In particular, instrumentalisation functioned as a barrier between the agent responsible and the target of conflict and criticism. It also abstracted the social actors' level of involvement in the potentially negative act. This pattern of representation worked in accordance with the grammatical structures of the Indonesian language governing word order, but has potential for further exploration in other languages, particularly in news media discourse given the opportunity it creates for construing controversial information.

Reflecting on the salience of women, media, and power

In this book, gender, media, and politics intertwined, while online news discourse became the site for capturing the interplay between these three fields. The analysis took into account the immediate political context characterised by intense contestation, rising populist values, and hopes for political renewal. It also incorporated knowledge of Indonesia's authoritarian past, where a model of Arche-politics defined the nation as a closed political body within a strict vertical hierarchy, and directed citizens into socially-sanctioned roles. The historical depoliticisation of women and the masculine domination of the political realm enhanced the social-political salience of Megawati, Risma, and Susi's presence as political leaders over the course of the 2014 presidential election. The Kompas.com representations contributed to the creation of a unique space for their political participation, albeit on restricted terms determined by gender norms, political values, and media interests.

160   *Gender and news media discourse*

The three leaders' political careers after the 2014 election followed a trajectory that upheld the patterns of representation identified in the Kompas.com discourse, whereby all three remained public icons in the media spotlight. Backed by the PDI-P, in 2015, Risma was re-elected to her mayoral position, achieving 86% of the vote—a 48% increase on her previous 2010 election results. While speculation about the continuity of her relationship with the PDI-P preceded the election, Risma maintained her alliance with the party, and remained a much-loved public figure. In December 2020, after years of speculation about her potential ascension to a ministerial role, Risma was appointed to the role of minister of Social Affairs in the second term of the Jokowi presidency in a cabinet reshuffle. Occurring on the back of several corruption scandals that rocked the Jokowi cabinet, her apparent uninterest in power along with her perceived commitment to social welfare made her an ideal, morally upright ministerial appointment. Her current standing as a minister in the Jokowi government has become increasingly precarious, and her former widely popular local-level leadership strategies have not transferred seamlessly to the national level.

Throughout her time as minister of Maritime Affairs and Fisheries, Susi maintained a high public profile, regularly appearing in news headlines, and even becoming a popular internet meme as a result of her quirky behaviour and defiant, nationalistic stance against illegal fishing. Her appointment ended somewhat controversially in October 2019 when the newly re-elected Jokowi announced his second-term cabinet line-up. Contrary to public expectations, Susi was not reinstated, and was instead replaced by the politician Edhy Prabowo.[1] True to form, Susi did not voice any complaints when departing from office and readily embraced her life outside of politics. She continues to make media appearances, advocate for the protection of Indonesian fisheries, and has amassed an enormous social media following.

Megawati remains a durable fixture on the Indonesian political scene. In her capacity as leader of the PDI-P, Megawati was heavily involved in Jokowi's second run for the presidency. Her portrayal in the news media continued to focus on her relationship with Jokowi and speculate on her own electability in comparison to Jokowi. Despite the speculation, Megawati continues to lead her party, and actively participates in negotiations among powerful political actors. Her daughter, Puan Maharani, served her full term as a cabinet minister, and following the 2019 presidential election, was appointed to the role of speaker of the house. The political dynasty appears to continue from Megawati to her daughter.

For gender scholars, this book has shed new light on how women operate and are perceived in historically-gendered contexts of transition. The findings presented in the book have potential application to studies of women in non-political leadership positions, plagued by historically masculine structures of power. Further international studies of the discursive representation of prominent women in positions of power, particularly in contexts of change, can uncover constant and variable factors influencing women's relationship with power and the way they participate in the political realm. The findings can also contribute to a framework for investigating shifting dimensions of power through the lens of political women, mediated through the news media.

For scholars of political science, the research presented demonstrates a novel approach to examining political transition through the intersection of gender, discourse, and media. The analysis of social actors in an interactive, yet ultimately hierarchical social power network demonstrated how relations of power are negotiated and contested in a context of change. Social actor analysis proved highly effective to uncovering relations of power in a context where individual leaders capture the public imagination and media attention, standing in for a largely populist political agenda. The discourse strategies identified contained emergent and residual values, and have potential applicability to the study of discourse produced in contexts of transition, where historical constraints interact with emergent freedoms.

The in-depth analysis of contemporary online news discourse through social actor analysis paves the way for future research on the online news media. It challenges the superficial and ultimately undemocratic reporting habits of a supposedly free media operating in a highly competitive, yet constrained online environment. Where news media organisations become increasingly online practices of news production and consumption, journalists turn their focus towards prompting reader engagement in the form of clicks, likes, shares, and comments. Self-censorship resulting from historical constraints as well as contemporary commercial interests also influences reporting habits. The strategies uncovered in the examination of contestation, for example, demonstrate how the online news media engaged implicit discourse strategies to position social actors in a way that tells a story that appeals to reader interest, while navigating commercial goals and limitations on press freedom.

While this book focused on the news texts, critical analysis bridging online news discourse and reader engagement represents a fruitful direction for future research. A study of reader engagement would add an important new dimension to understanding the impact of news discourse on the reader. Moreover, the changing practices of online media institutions warrant further scrutiny of the production side of the newsroom to support the interpretation of the discourse strategies. Finally, given readers' reactive, bite-sized consumption of online news media, images rather than words used in a news report become highly significant communicative features of the text. A focus on the visual-semiotic features of the online news media texts can complement the analysis of discourse produced and consumed in an online environment.

Above all, this book highlights the salience of the study of political women in media discourse to capturing and critically analysing shifting relations of power. The novel study of language, and the identification of discourse strategies tied to structures of power also contribute new knowledge of how the

162 *Gender and news media discourse*

news media regulates women's political participation and broader relations of power. These findings have potential future applications to the study of other political contexts in transition, not only in the regional limits of Asia. While Kompas.com represents a middle-class, largely male, urban secular ideological orientation, the Indonesian news media, broader civil society is characterised by a diversity of ideological orientations. Comparative analysis of the discursive representation of power relations across a number of range of perspectives could contribute new knowledge to the field of CDA. In particular, a comparative analysis of discourse produced by secular and non-secular (Islamic), or national and local news sources in Indonesia, could provide a broader view of relations of power and how they are played out discursively in the democratic era.

Note

1 Edhy Prabowo was later arrested on corruption charges in November 2020 for allegedly receiving bribes from private companies to secure the export of lobster hatchlings. Susi banned this form of export during her time as minister due to its negative impact on lobster populations, and the subsequent viability of the industry.

References

Anderson, B. (1990). *Language and power. Exploring political cultures in Indonesia.* Cornell University Press.

Aspinall, E. (2004). Indonesia: Transformation of civil society and democratic breakthrough. In M. Alagappa (Ed.), *Civil society and political change in Asia: Expanding and contracting democratic space* (pp. 61–96). Stanford University Press.

Aspinall, E. (2012). Indonesia: Moral force politics and the struggle against authoritarianism. In M. Weiss, E. Aspinall, N. Patricio, & S. Abinales (Eds.), *Student activism in Asia* (pp. 153–179). University of Minnesota Press.

Aspinall, E. (2015). Oligarchic populism: Prabowo Subianto's challenge to Indonesian democracy. *Indonesia, 99*, 1–28.

Bazzi, S. (2009). *Arab news and conflict: A multidisciplinary discourse study.* John Benjamins Publishing Company.

Bennett, L. (2005). *Women, Islam and modernity. Single women, sexuality and reproductive health in contemporary Indonesia.* Routledge.

Blommaert, J. (2005). *Discourse: A critical introduction.* Cambridge University Press.

Brenner, S. (2011). Private moralities in the public sphere: Democratization, Islam, and gender in Indonesia. *American Anthropologist, 113*(3), 478–490.

Campus, D. (2010). Mediatization and personalization of politics in Italy and France: The cases of Berlusconi and Sarkozy. *The International Journal of Press/Politics, 15*(2), 219–235.

Derichs, C., Fleschenberg, A., & Hüstebeck, M. (2006). Gendering moral capital: Morality as a political asset and strategy of top female politicians in Asia. *Critical Asian Studies, 38*(3), 245–270.

Derichs, C., & Thompson, M. R. (2013). Introduction. In C. Derichs & M. R. Thompson (Eds.), *Dynasties and female political leaders in Asia: Gender, power and pedigree* (pp. 11–26). Lit Verlag.

Dewi, K. H. (2015). *Indonesian women and local politics*. NUS Press.

Djajadiningrat-Nieuwenhuis, M. (1987). Ibuism and priyayization: Path to power? In E. Locher-Scholten & A. Niehof (Eds.), *Indonesian women in focus: Past and present notions* (pp. 43–51). Foris Publications.

Duile, T., & Bens, J. (2017). Indonesia and the "conflictual consensus": A discursive perspective on Indonesian democracy. *Critical Asian Studies, 49*(2), 139–162.

Dwyer, L. (2004). Intimacy of terror: Gender and the violence of 1965–1966 in Bali. *Intersections: Gender and Sexuality in Asia and the Pacific* (10).

Elson, R. (2010). Nationalism, Islam, 'secularism' and the state in contemporary Indonesia. *Australian Journal of International Affairs, 64*(3), 328–343.

Fairclough, N. (1992). Intertextuality in critical discourse analysis. *Linguistics and Education, 4*(3–4), 269–293.

Fairclough, N. (2000). *New Labour, new language?* Routledge.

Fairclough, N. (2003). *Analysing discourse: Textual analysis for social research*. Routledge.

Fairclough, N. (2013). *Language and power* (2nd ed.). Routledge.

Fleschenberg, A., & Derichs, C. (2011). Women and politics in Asia: A springboard for democracy? A tentative introduction and reflection. In A. Fleschenberg & C. Derichs (Eds.), *Women and politics in Asia: A springboard for democracy?* (pp. 1–19). Lit Verlag.

Flowerdew, J. (2008). Critical discourse analysis and strategies of resistance. In V. Bhatia, J. Flowerdew, & R. Jones (Eds.), *Advances in discourse studies* (pp. 195–211). Routledge.

Garzia, D. (2011). The personalization of politics in Western democracies: Causes and consequences on leader–follower relationships. *The Leadership Quarterly, 22*(4), 697–709.

Gazali, E. (2014). Learning by clicking: An experiment with social media democracy in Indonesia. *The International Communication Gazette, 76*(4–5), 425–439.

Gerlach, R. (2013). 'Mega' expectations: Indonesia's democratic transition and first female president. In C. Derichs & M. Thompson (Eds.), *Dynasties and female political leaders in Asia: Gender, power and pedigree* (pp. 247–290). Lit Verlag.

Hanitzsch, T. (2006). Journalists in Indonesia: Educated but timid watchdogs. *Journalism Studies, 6*(4), 493–508.

Harrison, C., & Young, L. (2005). Leadership discourse in action: A textual study of organizational change in a government of Canada department. *Journal of Business and Technical Communication, 19*(1), 42–77.

Hasell, A., & Weeks, B. E. (2016). Partisan provocation: The role of partisan news use and emotional responses in political information sharing in social media. *Human Communication Research, 42*(4), 641–661.

Hatherell, M., & Welsh, A. (2017). Rebel with a cause: Ahok and charismatic leadership in Indonesia. *Asian Studies Review, 41*(2), 174–190.

Hatley, B. (1990). Theatrical imagery and gender ideology in Java. In J. Monnig Atkinson & S. Errington (Eds.), *Power and difference: Gender in island Southeast Asia* (pp. 177–208). Stanford University Press.

Hatley, B. (2008). Hearing women's voices, contesting women's bodies in post-New Order Indonesia. *Intersections: Gender and sexuality in Asia and the Pacific, March*(16), 1–14.

164 *Gender and news media discourse*

Heryanto, A. (1995). *Language of development and development of language: The case of Indonesia.* (Pacific linguistics. Series D–86). Research School of Pacific and Asian Studies, Australian National University.

Jackson, E. (2005). *'Warring Words': Students and the state in New Order Indonesia, 1966–1998* [Doctoral dissertation, Australian National University], Australian National University Open Research Library.

Keeler, W. (1990). Speaking of gender in Java. In J. Monnig Atkinson & S. Errington (Eds.), *Power and difference: Gender in island Southeast Asia* (pp. 127–152). Stanford University Press.

Kramer, E. (2013). When news becomes entertainment: Representations of corruption in Indonesia's media and the implication of scandal. *Media Asia, 40*(1), 60–72.

Kroeger, K. (2003). AIDS rumors, imaginary enemies, and the body politic in Indonesia. *American Ethnologist, 30*(2), 243–257.

Langacker, R. (2008). *Cognitive grammar: A basic introduction.* Oxford University Press.

Lim, M. (2013). Many clicks but little sticks: Social media activism in Indonesia. *Journal of Contemporary Asia, 43*(4), 636–657.

McAllister, I. (2007). The personalization of politics. In R. Dalton & H. Klingemann (Eds.), *The Oxford handbook of political behaviour* (pp. 571–588). Oxford University Press.

McCoy, M. (2013). Purifying Islam in post-authoritarian Indonesia: Corporatist metaphors and the rise of religious intolerance. *Rhetoric and Public Affairs, 16*(12), 275–315.

Mietzner, M. (2015). *Reinventing Asian populism: Jokowi's rise, democracy, and political contestation in Indonesia.* East-West Center.

Miller, T. (2015). Unsustainable journalism. *Digital Journalism, 3*(5), 653–663.

Morrell, E. (2005). What is the news? Criticism, debate and community in Indonesia's local press. *Asian Journal of Social Science, 33*(1), 129–144.

Mulderrig, J. (2011). Manufacturing consent: A corpus-based critical discourse analysis of New Labour's educational governance. *Educational Philosophy and Theory, 43*(6), 562–578.

Reyes, A. (2009). *Shifts, voices and positionings in political discourse: A comparative analysis of creating allies and enemies through linguistic choices.* [Doctoral dissertation, University of Illinois], ProQuest Dissertations Publishing.

Rhoads, E. (2012). Women's political participation in Indonesia: Decentralisation, money politics and collective memory in Bali. *Journal of Current Southeast Asian Affairs, 31*(2), 35–56.

Rinaldo, R. (2010). Women and piety movements. In B. Turner (Ed.), *The new Blackwell companion to the sociology of religion* (pp. 584–605). Blackwell Publishing.

Robinson, K. (2009). *Gender, Islam and democracy in Indonesia.* Routledge.

Robinson, K. (2014). Citizenship, identity and difference in Indonesia. *RIMA Review of Indonesian and Malaysian Affairs, 48*(1), 5–34.

Robison, R., & Hadiz, V. (2004). *Reorganising power in Indonesia: The politics of oligarchy in an age of markets.* Routledge.

Suryakusuma, J. (2011). *State ibuism: The social construction of womanhood in New Order Indonesia.* Komunitas Bambu.

Suwana, F. (2018). *Digital media and Indonesian young people: Building sustainable democratic institutions and practices* [Doctoral dissertation, Queensland University of Technology], QUT ePrints.

Tan, L. (2012). Indonesian national security during the Suharto New Order (1965–1998): The role of narratives of peoplehood and the construction of danger. *New Zealand Journal of Asian Studies, 14*(1), 49–70.

Tapsell, R. (2015). Indonesia's media oligarchy and the "Jokowi phenomenon". *Indonesia, Apr 2015*(99), 29–50.

Thompson, M. (2013). Presidents and 'people power' in the Philippines: Corazon C. Aquino and Gloria Macapagal Arroyo. In C. Derichs & M. Thompson (Eds.), *Dynasties and female political leaders in Asia: Gender, power and pedigree* (pp. 151–190). Lit Verlag.

Turner, G. (2016). *Re-inventing the media.* Routledge.

van Dijk, T. A. (1996). Discourse, power and access. In C. R. Caldas-Coulthard & M. Coulthard (Eds.), *Texts and practices: Readings in critical discourse analysis* (pp. 84–104). Routledge.

van Langenberg, M. (1986). Analysing Indonesia's New Order state: A keywords approach. *RIMA Review of Indonesian and Malaysian Affairs, 20*(2), 1–47.

van Leeuwen, T. (2008). *Discourse and practice: New tools for critical discourse analysis.* Oxford University Press.

van Leeuwen, T., & Wodak, R. (1999). Legitimising immigration control: A discourse-historical analysis. *Discourse Studies, 1*(1), 83–118.

van Wichelen, S. (2006). Contesting Megawati: The mediation of Islam and nation in times of political transition. *Westminster Papers in Communication and Culture, 3*(2), 41–59.

Weiss, M. (2014). New media, new activism: Trends and trajectories in Malaysia, Singapore and Indonesia. *International Development Planning Review, 36*(1), 91–109.

Widodo, J., & Kalla, J. (2014). *Jalan perubahan untuk Indonesia yang berdaulat, mandiri dan berkepribadian: Visi misi, dan program aksi.* Jakarta: Sekretariat Nasional Joko Widodo.

Wieringa, S. (2002). *Sexual politics in Indonesia.* Palgrave Macmillan.

Wijayanto (2015). Old practice in a new era: Rasa as the basis of self-censorship in Kompas daily newspaper. *GSTF Journal on Media & Communications (JMC), 2*(2), 66–74.

Wodak, R. (1996). *Disorders of discourse.* Addison Wesley Longman.

Wodak, R. (2011). *The discourse of politics in action: Politics as usual.* Palgrave Macmillan.

Wodak, R., & Boukala, S. (2015). European identities and the revival of nationalism in the European Union. A discourse historical approach. *Journal of Language and Politics, 14*(1), 87–109.

Index

activation 9, 63, 88, 91
abstraction 59–62, 80
affectual autonomisation 127–129
agentless passive 107, 108, 120, 123
aggregation 68–70, 96, 98–100, 116,
    119–120, 123, 131, 134–135, 156
Ahok *see* Basuki Tjahaja Purnama
algorithmic enclaves 6, 43
allusions 39, 126
anak buah 97, 122–123
Arche-politics 1, 20, 21, 115, 154,
    155, 159
Arroyo, Gloria Macapagal 3, 72
Aung San Suu Kyi 3, 25, 27, 72
authoritarianism in Indonesia 1, 6,
    19–20, 38–39, 109, 110, 154, 159
azas kekeluargaan 19

bapak 20
Basuki Tjahaja Purnama 29, 45,
    55–56, 82

Calonarang 22
CDA (critical discourse analysis) 3, 4,
    7–10
class: middle class 2, 7, 20, 42, 43, 44;
    working class 20, 23, 58, 69, 71–72,
    99, 107–108
consensus 61, 69–70, 104–106, 110,
    132–135, 144, 154
consent 70–71, 96, 99, 104, 105, 110,
    154–155
corruption 1, 4, 24, 29, 41, 46, 92, 97,
    103–104

Dharma Wanita 21
digital media *see* online news media
discourse: and context 7; definition of 7;
    and social-political change 10, 149

discourse strategy: alluding to con-
    troversy 114, 126–136; constructing
    spectacle 53, 72–80; constructing
    threat 114–126, 152, 155, 156; defini-
    tion of 10–12; institutionalisation 86,
    101–108, 151, 154; managed responses
    136–143; personification 86–101, 151;
    regulating access 53–72, 156, 158

elites: and female political figures 6,
    27, 28, 30–31, 53, 95–98, 153; and the
    media 39, 40, 41, 43, 65–68, 113, 131,
    136–143, 158–159; in the New Order
    19, 20, 21, 22, 23; opinion 126,
    128–129, 133–135; and the ordinary
    people 62, 68–72, 98–101, 115, 156–157;
    and populism 2–3, 4, 54, 94

galak 29, 56
Galuh Candra Kirana 23, 78
Gandhi, Indira 22
Gerwani (Indonesian Women's
    Movement) 21–22

halus 73, 76
honorifics in Indonesian 54–57

ibu 20
ibuism;
    20, 23, 29, 149; state ibuism 21
impersonalisation 58–62, 69, 77, 81,
    104–108, 119–121, 131, 138, 141, 144,
    150, 159
indetermination 115–116, 118–119, 121
individualisation 63, 66, 68–72, 88,
    95–101, 103, 108, 124–125, 138, 141
Indonesian media: and defamation
    laws 40–41; in the democratic era
    40–41; digital transformation of 6,

Index 167

14, 41–42; in the New Order 38–39; in Reformasi 39; and the representation of women 39–40; and the 2014 presidential election 2, 38
Indonesian military: and anti-communist massacres on 1965–66 21–22; in the democratic era 1, 26, 40, 78, 90; in the New Order 19, 24, 38
Indonesian presidential election of 2014 4–6, 8, 18, 38, 43, 52, 85, 113–115, 150, 154, 156
Indonesian women in politics 22–25, 149–155; and dynastic pathways to power 5, 25; and grassroots pathways to power 28, 30; and Islam 29, 150–151; and social-political change 1, 3, 9, 18, 27, 53, 80, 81, 159
instrumentalisation 59–60, 80, 104–107, 116, 119–121, 123, 125, 129–131, 134–137, 142, 159
Inul Daratista 39–40
ITE (Electronic Information and Transactions) law 40–41

Jokowi *see* Joko Widodo
Joko Widodo: election as president 55, 58; presidential agenda 31, 73, 103–104, 121; presidential cabinet 5, 30, 59, 160; presidential campaign 3, 4, 45, 120, 106, 131, 154; relationship with Megawati 5, 27–28, 45, 54, 56–57, 64, 75–76, 82, 89–90, 106, 119–120, 127, 131–135, 137–140, 150

Kartini 23
Kodrat wanita 20
Kompas: censorship 43; ownership 43; readership 2; reporting style 43; reputation 2, 43
Kompas.com: business model 6; history 44; journalists 158; popularity 44; production schedule 6, 44, 157; readership 2, 44; reporting practices 6, 44, 157–159
Kompas Gramedia Group: business and political interests 6, 43; history 43
KPK (Corruption Eradication Commission) 46, 103–104

legitimation 133; through expert opinion 133–135; through opinion surveys 135–136
localism 28, 104, 106, 110

malu 20–21
Megawati *see* Megawati Soekarnoputri
Megawati Soekarnoputri: ambition 56, 98, 150; appearance 76; leadership of PDI-P 26, 27, 45, 64; and New Order political activism 26; and political Islam 27; in the presidency 28; reference to father's legacy 5, 6, 25, 26, 89; relationship with Jokowi 5, 27–28, 45, 54, 56–57, 64, 75–76, 82, 89–90, 106, 119–120, 127, 131–135, 137–140, 150; in the vice presidency 26

nationalism 31, 104, 115–116, 121, 155, 160
New Order: power arrangements 1, 4, 6, 20, 21, 115, 155, 159; collapse of 24; and gendered structures of power 19–23, 109; and media regulation 38–39; and rumours 126
nominalisation 104–108, 117, 120–121, 131–137, 154
nomination 54–58, 63, 71, 88–91, 96, 98–101, 134, 138, 141

oknum 118–119
online news media in Indonesia: access 42; and political discourse 2, 4, 6, 9, 43, 48, 158; production and consumption 6–7, 41–43, 157–158; and social media 42
ordinary people: in the New Order 19; and participation in politics 68–72, 98–100, 134, 135–136, 155–157; and relationship to political leaders 4, 55, 58, 62, 68, 106, 115

Pancasila 19, 91–92
Park Geun-hye 3, 25, 72
passivation 9, 63, 66, 68, 69, 71, 74, 81, 96, 98, 99, 100, 122, 131, 150, 156
passive agent deletion 61, 79, 104, 105, 107, 108, 117, 119, 120, 121, 129, 130, 131, 132–133, 135, 137, 138, 140, 144
PDI-P (Indonesian Democratic Party of Struggle) 1, 25–27, 45, 46, 57, 62, 64, 79, 89, 91–92, 97–98, 133–136, 150, 160
pembangunan 19, 154
personalised leadership 9, 86, 109, 126, 153
perubahan 4, 154,
PKI (Indonesian Communist Party) 21
PKK (Family Welfare Movement) 21

168 Index

populism: and accessibility 4, 54, 80; and the charismatic outsider 2, 5, 8–9, 29, 30, 53, 85, 91, 149, 161; and the construction of threat 114–115, 121, 152, 155; and the online media 2, 9, 42, 113; in the 2014 presidential election campaign 4, 52
possessivation 58–62, 77, 80, 95–101, 129–133
power: and agency 8; augmentation of 10, 85–86, 109–110; contestation of 10, 113–114, 143–145, 152–153; definition of 8; and discourse 7, 8; and gender 1, 2, 4, 10, 18, 19–21, 109; hierarchy 1, 6, 8; mitigation of 10, 52–53, 80, 150; and social-political change 2, 3, 9–10, 11–12, 109, 110, 113, 114, 155
Prabowo Subianto 4, 27, 131
pseudo-title 54, 55, 58, 86–87, 88, 89–90, 151
Puan Maharani 45, 160

rakyat 58, 95, 156
Rangda 22
Reformasi 1–2, 18, 26, 27, 28, 29, 39, 156
Risma *see* Tri Rismaharini

SBY *see* Susilo Bambang Yudhoyono
SIP (Voice of Concerned Mothers) 24
social actor analysis 4, 9–10, 11, 53, 115, 148, 161
social actors in Indonesian politics 3, 8–9
social process 9, 63, 73, 87, 88, 102, 117; behavioural process 63, 64, 65, 66, 71, 73, 74, 75, 76, 79; material process 63, 64, 68, 70, 71, 73, 74, 75, 76, 80, 87, 88, 93, 98, 99, 101, 103, 108, 109, 117, 123, 124, 125; mental process 61, 63, 65, 66, 67–68, 69, 71, 72, 87, 88, 91, 94, 97, 106, 109, 123, 124–125, 133, 134, 135, 136, 138, 141, 142, 145; self-oriented process 64, 68, 74, 75, 79, 150; verbal process 63, 64, 65, 66, 67, 69, 81, 88, 91–92, 95, 96, 97, 98, 99, 101, 109, 117, 123, 124, 134, 136, 137, 138, 139, 141, 142, 143, 145, 157

Soekarno 25, 26, 89–90, 92, 154
Somatisation 77–80
Spatialisation 104–107, 110, 154
Suharto 1, 19–20, 21, 24
Susilo Bambang Yudhoyono 4, 27, 153
Susi Pudjiastuti: appearance 31, 78, 81; appointment to ministerial role 5, 30, 47; background 5, 30,47; criticism 47–48, 128–129, 129–130, 140, 143, 153; media interest 5, 30–31, 67, 89, 90; policies 31, 47, 62, 87, 93, 107–108 125, 129, 155; as a political newcomer 54, 56, 102, 150; smoking habit 5, 31, 73, 75; Susi Air ownership 30, 90; tattoo 5, 31
systemic functional grammar 9

Tanaka Makiko 30, 72
Tjut Meutia 23
Tri Rismaharini: agenda to improve Surabaya 29, 46, 91, 94, 107, 118, 124, 125, 142; AirAsia aviation disaster response 47, 79–80, 95, 97, 141–142; background 5, 6, 28; closure of Gang Dolly 46, 76–77, 91, 93, 100, 103, 106, 154–155; and Islam 5, 29–30, 78; Mata Najwa appearance 28–29, 46, 68; personality 29, 56; popularity 46–47, 59–61, 62, 133, 160; as a political newcomer 6, 54, 102, 150, 153; relationship with PDI-P 28, 46, 133; rumours of resignation 28–29, 46, 62, 64, 65, 68

utterance autonomisation 116, 125, 131– 132, 133–135, 137, 138, 139, 140, 142

victims 39, 114, 115, 119, 120–121, 121–123, 144, 155, 156–157
visibility of women 9, 18, 32, 72, 75–80

women in politics: ambition 19, 20, 25, 53, 60, 80; in contexts of social-political change 1, 3, 18, 32, 52, 53, 72, 152, 161; duty 25, 27, 28, 29, 53, 58–59, 86, 149; in dynastic politics 25; and moral capital 3, 19, 24, 26, 72, 149; in opposition 24, 26, 72

Printed in the United States
by Baker & Taylor Publisher Services